D0214186

Confronting Tennessee Williams's
A Streetcar Named Desire

Jessica Tandy, Kim Hunter, and Marlon Brando in the Broadway (1947) premiere of *A Streetcar Named Desire*. Photo courtesy of the Ransom Humanities Research Center, University of Texas at Austin.

Confronting Tennessee Williams's
A Streetcar Named Desire

ESSAYS IN CRITICAL PLURALISM

Edited by
PHILIP C. KOLIN

Contributions in Drama and Theatre Studies, Number 50

GREENWOOD PRESS
Westport, Connecticut • London

Library of Congress Cataloging-in-Publication Data

Confronting Tennessee Williams's A streetcar named Desire : essays in
   critical pluralism / edited by Philip C. Kolin.
      p.   cm.—(Contributions in drama and theatre studies, ISSN
   0163–3821 ; no. 50)
      Includes bibliographical references and index.
      ISBN 0–313–26681–6 (alk. paper)
      1. Williams, Tennessee, 1911–1983.   Streetcar named Desire.
   I. Kolin, Philip C.   II. Series.
   PS3545.I5365S8   1993
   812'.54—dc20   92–19843

British Library Cataloguing in Publication Data is available.

Library of Congress Catalog Card Number: 92–19843
ISBN: 0–313–26681–6
ISSN: 0163–3821

First published in 1993

Greenwood Press, 88 Post Road West, Westport, CT 06881
An imprint of Greenwood Publishing Group, Inc.

Printed in the United States of America

The paper used in this book complies with the
Permanent Paper Standard issued by the National
Information Standards Organization (Z39.48–1984).

10 9 8 7 6 5 4 3 2

FOR SHARRON
THE SOURCE AND FULFILLMENT OF MY DESIRE

Contents

Preface

This is the first and only collection of original essays devoted exclusively to *A Streetcar Named Desire*, Tennessee Williams's most famous play and one of the two or three most significant American plays on the world stage. *Confronting Tennessee Williams's* A Streetcar Named Desire: *Essays on Critical Pluralism* radically departs from the two earlier anthologies of criticism on the play—Jordan Y. Miller's *Twentieth-Century Interpretations of* A Streetcar Named Desire (G. K. Hall, 1971) and Harold Bloom's *Tennessee Williams's* A Streetcar Named Desire (Chelsea House, 1988). Although these anthologies are useful, they offer readers only previously published and (now) dated material on the play. In Miller's anthology, the essays, sometimes abridged, and theatre reviews focus on the criticism of the 1940s and 1950s; in Bloom's volume the gaze, too, is more backward than forward. Of the eleven essays Bloom includes, nine were written before 1976, and three of these come from Jac Tharpe's *Tennessee Williams: A Tribute* (UP of Mississippi, 1977). The fifteen essays in *Confronting Tennessee Williams's* A Streetcar Named Desire, on the other hand, represent the most current and (I believe) provocative thinking about the play; they advance our understanding of *Streetcar* in particular, Williams's canon in general, and the ever-present paradoxes in both the work and the man in innovative, challenging ways.

Unlike previous anthologies, each of the essays in this collection looks at *Streetcar* from a different critical/theoretical perspective. The subtitle of the volume, *Essays in Critical Pluralism*, insistently specifies that the most profitable way to approach, read, understand and/or deconstruct a work as multifaceted, culturally and artistically, as *Streetcar* is through a plurality of discourses. While the fifteen essays written expressly for this collection do not typify every critical discourse, they do nonetheless represent most major critical approaches in vogue today. Among the different schools/

camps/theories represented in this collection are feminism, Marxism, reader response theory, mythology, cultural/regional studies, chaos and antichaos theory, perception theory, film aesthetics, translation theory and practice, and formalism. The voices of Foucault, Kristeva, Lacan, Jameson, and so forth penetrate and elucidate *Streetcar* in this volume. Equally noteworthy, each of the essays in this collection serves as a model of the type of critical investigation being done by researchers in these respective theoretical/methodological camps. Thus, in addition to shedding light on Williams's play, the essays offer an introduction, via application, to these various critical/cultural/linguistic theories/methods. Each contributor has used the text of *Streetcar* found in volume 1 of *Theatre of Tennessee Williams* (New Directions, 1971), though in several instances contributors have also read the play through the acting edition published by Dramatists Play Service (1947).

Each essay begins with a clear articulation of the principles and methods of the school/critical approach the author is following. Using those principles and methods, the authors then apply these insights to reading(s) of *Streetcar*—the script and/or film/teleplay. Each essay is carefully documented with references to major work done in a given area (e.g., feminism, Marxism). The result is a collection of essays that is critically/theoretically grounded and that provides substantive and fresh readings of *Streetcar*. Yet in many instances these essays do more than read and respond to the play. They supply cultural critiques of the society that *Streetcar* characterizes and has been characterized by.

What emerges from this collection, then, is not uniformity or homogeneity. Quite to the contrary: The essays should be read as polyphonic voices, quarreling with, advancing, complementing, subverting, extending, modifying each other. If the ghost of Tennessee Williams could be lured back from the Elysian Fields neighborhood of heaven, he might say, I believe, that *Streetcar* criticism has come a long way, baby, since the 1960s and 1970s. I hope that this collection points the way forward, not backward. For too long, criticism of *Streetcar* (and of Williams in general) has recycled, relooped, and stultified because it has relied on the unquestioned commonplaces of the previous generation without injecting skeptical inquiry. I proposed and edited the present volume to challenge where necessary, and affirm where warranted, received opinion in *Streetcar* criticism.

I am deeply indebted to the contributors for their hard work and splendid cooperation. I am honored to include original work written by some of the most important critics/Williams scholars writing today. (The "About the Contributors" section announces their credentials.) I am also grateful to many people at the University of Southern Mississippi who have assisted me and given generously of their encouragement. They include two of my doctoral students, Anne Stascavage and LaNelle Daniel; David Wheeler, Chair of the English Department; Glenn T. Harper, Dean of the College of Liberal Arts, and my patron; Vice Presidents Karen Yarbrough and G. David

Huffman; and President Aubrey K. Lucas. I am also grateful to the Phil Hardin Foundation for their support given to me as the Charles W. Moorman Distinguished Professor in the Humanities. Finally, I thank Sharron Lee King, R.N., for her inspiration and her love, and Mary for watching over me. May God bless us all.

Confronting Tennessee Williams's
A Streetcar Named Desire

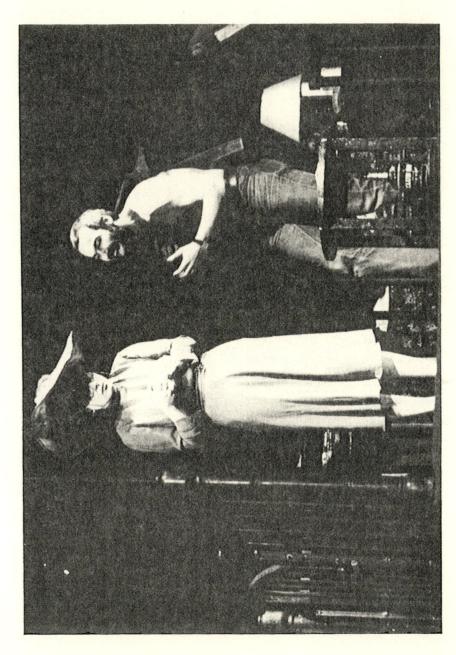

Photo courtesy of Dimiter Hadjirachev, Literary Manager, The Adrianna Budevska Drama Theatre, 36 Tsar Assen St., 8000 Bourgas, Bulgaria.

Reflections on/of *A Streetcar Named Desire*

Philip C. Kolin

A Streetcar Named Desire is a polysemous production of American culture. As Thomas P. Adler observes, *Streetcar* "has become an ingredient in our popular culture" (7). Similarly, playwright Arthur Sanier remarks that "Williams wrote a play that has taken up permanent residence in our culture" (quoted in Kolin, "Playwrights' Forum" 202). As both "ingredient" and "residence"—food and home—*Streetcar* has given us sustenance for the imagination and a mandatory locus of desire over the last forty-five years. The play is characteristically American—vicarious and self-reflexive simultaneously. It cancelstamps our cultural vices and virtues, pains and pleasures. *Streetcar* tells tales about us and is one of the most haunting tales we tell about ourselves, often revealing what we want concealed and concealing what we want revealed. Like Blanche's slip in the famous Thomas Hart Benton painting about the play, *Streetcar* both teasingly strips and hides.

Embedded in *Streetcar* are many American icons, sacred and profane— Poe, Hawthorne, and Whitman along with Mae West and Barnum and Bailey; Jax beer on sultry poker nights and cherry sodas sipped on endlessly long, rainy afternoons; blunt-speaking Huey P. Long keeps company with the silent, romantic Shep Huntleigh; neon-lit corner bars with names like a gambler's wish coexist with Moon Lake Casino where love invites self-immolation. *Streetcar* is a bible of American passion, evocatively, richly unfolding. The play oozes with distinctively American sexuality; sweaty-chested Marlon Brando's cries of "Stella" are pure American primitive. Connected with desire and sexuality in *Streetcar* are heavy doses of violence, mostly the domestic variety, for which America has been vilified. The *Streetcar* setting, too, is irreproducibly American, taking place in that most intriguing of American cities, New Orleans, which has long since passed from geography to mythography. "New Orleans isn't like other cities," explains Stella to her sister from Laurel, Mississippi. Like American society itself, the *Streetcar* gumbo tantalizes the palate with its dark roux, its blend of cultures. *Streetcar* potboils black, Mexican, Creole, WASP, and southern aristocrat with plebeian Pole. Because of all this—and reflecting all this—*Streetcar* is one of our most representative works of art. For Dennis Reardon, another playwright, it is our best: "The search for the Great American Play can stop with *A Streetcar Named Desire*" (quoted in Kolin, "Playwrights' Forum" 192). *Streetcar* is the *Huck Finn* of our theatre.

Moving through time and space—emotional and political—*Streetcar* is protean. Productions change *Streetcar* as the play casts its spell over those who produce and those who watch it. Like the America of which it is a vital part, *Streetcar* abhors the static, the single-track view of itself. *Streetcar* redefines desire with each new decade, no, each new year. The stage history of *Streetcar*, written only in parts, clearly limns the diverse properties of the script, showing how multifaceted it is. The many so-called traditional productions of *Streetcar* (imitating Vivien Leigh and Marlon Brando in the 1951 film of the play) are undeniably fruitful, but fraught with constricting stereotypes.

Some seemingly mainstream productions of *Streetcar* have shown, not always successfully, that not all Stanleys have to be Brando. Jon Voight's sensitive portrayal of Stanley in 1973 was attacked. Stephen Faber complained that "Voight's studious attempt to underplay the role is...disastrous. His relatively quiet, halting, ineffectual Stanley makes little sense on any level. He even throws dishes politely. Voight simply has no menace; he never believes that he has the power to destroy Blanche" (1). Similarly, Aiden Quinn playing Stanley in 1988 was said to be miscast. "Watching him, you find yourself wondering what it would have been like to see Montgomery Clift in the role. Like Clift, Quinn seems to specialize in playing Clean-Cut Young Everyman. His sexual magnetism tends, like Clift's, to his being cast as a figure who is in some sense sexually off-limits...He's too much a man of the eighties to make sex seem menacing..." (Oliver 82). These two Stanleys reveal how precarious the balance must be between Blanche and Stanley, yet how disarming Brando's macho image has been for reviewers and all those who judge sex roles by this actor's behavior.

Perhaps even more revealing are the productions of the play by black, alternative, and foreign theatre companies. It is at the margins of theatre history that the script of *Streetcar* opens up most clearly to chart the necessary waywardness of seduction and desire. Productions of *Streetcar* by black theatre companies, for example, over the last forty years or so—neglected until recently (see Kolin, "Williams in Ebony")—bring up themes and interpretations never allowed to surface in white productions. Miscegenation, race relations, colorism, and so on, not privileged on Broadway or in regional theatres, assume an unexpected urgency in performances of *Streetcar* by black actors and actresses. Not all Blanches have to have blond hair and be southern belles à la Vivien Scarlett O'Hara Leigh. Desire, like tragedy, is not confined to a single race or socioeconomic group.

Equally productive and provocative, alternative (gay and lesbian) theatres have used *Streetcar* to challenge gender/sex roles that have been culturally imposed. A February–March 1991 "gender-bent deconstruction" (Leonard 386) of *Streetcar*, christened *Belle Reprieve*, was done at The Club at LaMama E.T.C. Gay and lesbian theatre companies Bloolips and Split Britches reversed benign expectations of social and sexual roles. "Excerpting only a handful of Williams's lines, *Belle Reprieve* exposes *Streetcar*'s underlying tensions, attractions, and sexual politics" (Leonard 386). Blanche was played by the famous drag queen Bette Bourne and Stanley by lesbian actress Peggy Shaw. Reminiscent of Shakespeare's androgynous heroines, Shaw was a woman playing a man and Bourne a man playing a woman. A reviewer for *Theater Week* observed that this production "showed that cross-dressed roles in the 1990's America can attain the artistic heights of cross-dressed Kabuki or Peking opera." Moreover, the reviewer continued, *Belle Reprieve*'s "successful treatment of gendered role-playing ranks up there with the 'new historicist' theories of Foucault . . . " ("Bloolips and Split Britches"). Even this very loose adaptation of *Streetcar* validates the play's powerful contribution to culture and sexuality.

A fringe theatre production of *Streetcar* by Seattle's General Company in July 1991 also demonstrates how elastic Williams's script is. Here is a description of this carnivalesque production, courtesy of Calvin Bedient:

Blanche was played by a male in drag (the evening began with the actor putting on his make-up and slip and dress at a table in front of the audience). At moments he was brilliant, far and away the best thing in the show. The director turned darkly creative with the closing lines: he had the entire cast, minus Blanche, chant "I have always depended on the kindness of strangers," in harsh, disbelieving mockery. The man and woman from the mental home were dressed (in the man's case, mostly undressed) for Mardi Gras. Blanche, distraught, ran to the end of the stage/floor (was it a volley-ball court? I don't know) where a great sheet of milky plastic was hung from a balcony (her hallucinations had been acted out behind it), pulled it all down on top of her, somehow rolled under it, and disappeared entirely. Whereupon the actress playing Stella ran shrieking to the same end of the stage and missed catching her baby, which Eunice flung down (God knows why) from the balcony. Stella picks up doll-baby and holds it up like a sacrifice. It goes "maa-maa" at an astonishingly loud volume for so tiny a (dead) body. And that would have brought down the curtain had there been one. (Letter to author)

Although some purists may shriek with horror at the transformation (travesty) of *Streetcar* at the hands of General Company's director/producer Robert Lawson, there can be little doubt that *Streetcar*'s place in America's cultural pantheon is so well established that it can risk and enjoy such inversions. In fact, through these outlandish permutations *Streetcar* speaks a strong, social (contemporary) message. In the words of Michael Oaks, the actor who played Blanche:

Try to personalize Blanche for yourself. Own her experience. For she is anyone who has ever suffered unjustly from a world gone suddenly wrong. She is the bag lady you scurry past on your way to work. She is every AIDS patient abandoned by a misunderstanding society. Blanche is you. Leave here tonight elated, enraged and informed.

(General Company playbill)

Who could have imagined Jessica Tandy, the first Blanche or Ann-Margret, the Blanche of the 1980s, as bag ladies? But then, as this 1991 production proves, *Streetcar* has evolved with an American culture that is both the cause and the product of Williams's play.

One of our most significant cultural exports, *Streetcar* staged overseas also stunningly tests our ideologies, our mythologies. A Belgian production of the play (*De Elysese Velden*) in March of 1989, for example, is remarkable for the director's use of "cultural reminiscences, specifically cinemato- graphic." The Belgian Stanley "models himself, muscles, underwear and grunts, after Marlon Brando's original" and to emphasize the relationship, the director "quotes even further from the Hollywood actor's career; ... Stanley got all greasy not from helping the mechanics fix his car but rather from his black motorcycle, a reminder of Brando's role in *The Wild One*, a totally rapt prototype for a character in a play in which 'One-Eyed Jacks are wild' " (Debusscher 88). Brando and Stanley have been fused into the same charioteer of desire. As these and other productions abundantly prove, it is in experimenting with *Streetcar* that the play continues to experiment with us, testing who and what we are on the (worldwide) stage.

If *Streetcar* has been diversely represented, it has been even more diversely read. Criticism of *Streetcar* reflects the shifts in our perceptions, assump- tions, our awareness of awareness itself. *Streetcar* sails through cultural/ critical drifts. A multitude of critical voices speaks the different discourses of *Streetcar*: love, hate, women, men, law, politics, reason, insanity, music, family, sports, and art (from expressionism to *arte povera*). *Streetcar* crit- icism has evolved light years since 1974 when S. Alan Chesler published his "*A Streetcar Named Desire:* Twenty-Five Years of Criticism." It is in- structive to compare the critical conclusions Chesler surveyed with what is being read and thought about *Streetcar* today, some twenty years after Chesler and forty-five years after *Streetcar*'s stellar debut on Broadway. Since the publication of Chesler's article, of course, criticism in general has undergone cataclysmic changes, moving from formalistic to theoretical econ- omies. The flourescence of feminism, reader response theory, Foucault-Kris- teva-Lacan-inspired -*isms* are leaving their imprint on Williams's play. The explosion of these discourses into the world of *Streetcar* shows that the play hospitably accommodates the critical inquiries exploring it.

As unassailable today as in 1974 is Chesler's conclusion that "scholarly evaluation of *Streetcar* has, for the most part, concentrated on its two leading characters, Blanche DuBois and Stanley Kowalski, and the relationship between them" (44). As long as *Streetcar* is read and performed, that will always be the case; for Blanche and Stanley are the Ying and Yang, the Alpha and Omega, the left and right hemispheres of *Streetcar*. But saying that is hardly new. What is far more problematic today than when Chesler wrote are the merits and demerits of the relative "cases," "agendas" of these dual protagonists. As Chesler admitted, critics "still vary considerably in their interpretation of Stanley" (47). As a number of the essays in this collection suggest, Stanley's sympathizers have been growing since the 1970s, increasing their tenacity in putting forth his case. Does that mean that Blanche's stock has fallen in the last two decades or since Chesler reviewed the work of critics who "discern[ed] the universality and symbolic ramifications of Blanche's desperate struggle" (47)? Perhaps yes and perhaps no. The desire Blanche represents is and always will be enigmatic, ambiguous—wonderfully refreshing and despondently dangerous. I do not believe a more suitable poetic corollary for Blanche's sweetly tainted desire can be found than William Carlos Williams's enchanting "Queen-Anne's-Lace." This 1921 poem on the white flower with a dark spot in its center could very well have inspired Tennessee in creating Blanche. Like the flower, Blanche is "white as can be," yet with a purple stain. In the end, the flower, like Dame Blanche, fills the field with "white desire, empty, a single stem." Too often Blanche's complexity is leveled by a critical rage for order that is uncomfortable with contradictions.

For many critics since Chesler's survey, the sites of the conflict between Blanche and Stanley have changed, the ground rules have been modified, and prototypical responses toward the two have been subverted. It is no longer indispensable, or even fashionable, to allow a single issue to divide the two characters into warring camps of "sensualist" and "puritan," "artist" and "brute," "culture" and "chaos." The dichotomies that have frozen Blanche and Stanley in critical inquiries for years are being dislocated. As Thomas Adler again perceptively cautions: though Williams offers dualities, he "makes his thematic point that to fragment or dissociate human experience by seeing it as mutually exclusive, either/or series of options, rather than to regard it from an integrative, both/and perspective is one of our greatest sins, debilitating both to the individual and to society" (33).

Some contemporary criticism of *Streetcar* concerns itself more with Blanche and Stanley's similarities than their differences. Or, reversing the hierarchies of the 1950s and 1960s, a good number of critics see Stanley as the more sensitive and honest of the two and Blanche as the one who deceives. It might be premature to predict, but Stanley has in certain critical quarters gained ground on Blanche in love, honesty, and respectability. C.W.E. Bigsby was ahead of many readers in noting that "despite [Stanley's] inhumanity, there are moments of tenderness between Stella and Stanley which clearly offer some slight hope for the future" (258). That is not to say, of course, that Stanley does not (nor should not) attract his equitable share of detractors. He is still suitably apish for critics, including many in this volume, regardless of their theoretical leanings.

Perhaps the most imposing change in direction of *Streetcar* criticism since the 1970s is signaled in the quotation from Martin Gottfried that closes Chesler's survey: *Streetcar* "does not aim for philosophical grandiose, it is *art* and its art will endure. For it is an exquisite play—perhaps the most romantic, poetic sensitive play ever written for the American theatre" (51). It is easy to fall under *Streetcar*'s lyrical spell with its Circe-like invitations. But the view expressed by Gottfried, a commonly held view wrongly adjudged complimentary to both play and playwright, contains the seeds of divisiveness. Gottfried's dichotomies of "philosophical grandiose" and "sensitive play" actually work to the detriment of *Streetcar* and to Williams as a thinker. Williams is as much a word magician as a thought magus; his roots lie "in the social theatre of the 1930s" (Bigsby, 252). Williams himself proudly acknowledged his keen social awareness. Recalling the "ugly rows of apartment buildings the color of dried blood and mustard" that surrounded him in St. Louis, he observed in *Where I Live* (60):

If I had been born to this situation I might not have resented it deeply. But it was forced upon my consciousness at the most sensitive age of childhood. It produced a shock and a rebellion that has grown into an inherent part of my work. It was the beginning of the social consciousness which I think has marked most of my writing. I am glad that I received this bitter education for I don't think any writer has much purpose back of him unless he feels bitterly the inequities of the society he lives in. I have no acquaintance with political and social dialectics. If you ask what my politics are, I am a Humanitarian.

Contemporary criticism of *Streetcar*, as many of the essays in this collection prove, explores the theoretical underpinnings of the play, revealing it to be a work that does not shrink from the philosophical interventions/ social commitments of a Kristeva, Foucault, Lacan, or Jameson. The ideas of these and other theorists can be persuasively illustrated and validated by and through *Streetcar*, which, contrary to Gottfried's opinion, radiates with the "philosophical grandiose."

Streetcar follows no party line, nor should it. Because of its expansive presence, the play accommodates many modalities, either individually or in combination. As the following summaries of the essays that I have included in this collection prove, *Streetcar* is a highly contentious yet enchanting script that invites, yet defies, any one reading. What the creator of *Streetcar*,

Tennessee Williams, said of himself might easily be said by his greatest creation: "I *am* contradictory, baby" (Devlin 228).

Herbert Blau's provocative essay on "Readymade Desire" opens this collection. Blau gives us something of a tour de force, discussing in short space many of the larger issues that occupy subsequent essays. Starting in 1947, with the opening of *Streetcar*, Blau moves from Williams's own anxieties about success to the sublimation of his earlier politics to a rethinking of the play as a "cultural production" or "social text" within the ideological context of "the postmodern condition." Having become in that context an "icon of popular culture," *Streetcar* was constructed to begin with, Blau points out, from "already charged and precoded materials...." If certain elements of the play are in their familiarity "dangerously on the edge of kitsch," it is as if Williams had realized long before Andy Warhol (picking up on Duchamp) that it is "only as readymades that they can function mythologically." So far as behavior is concerned, however, it is also possible to reassess certain aspects of the play, as Blau does at the end of his essay, in view of changing social awareness, from the opening of a discourse on the battered-wife syndrome to the mixed feelings aroused by the Clarence Thomas hearings.

William Kleb next reads *Streetcar* "by way of Foucault," finding that Williams's plays "construct and animate the same shifting ontological landscape" mapped out by the French historian-philosopher. Produced at a time in American history when the sexual limits of culture came sharply into focus through the publication of Alfred Kinsey's *Sex Behavior in the Human Male*, *Streetcar*, Kleb argues, demonstrates the dynamics of Foucault's "repressive hypothesis" at work. In *Histoire de la folie*, *Discipline and Punish*, and *The History of Sexuality, Volume 1*, Foucault identified the strategies of control that Western society used to restrain the sexually aberrant, the criminal, and the insane. Kleb calls attention to the correspondences between these control strategies and Stanley's treatment of Blanche. As Foucault does through most of his texts, *Streetcar* concentrates on the struggle to control by the power of knowledge (confessional and interrogatory) and the manipulation of truth.

In Kleb's view of *Streetcar*, the definition of the "Same" and the "Other" are central to both Foucault and Williams. Blanche is the Unreason, the feminine "Other," attempting to control and redefine the "Same"—Stanley, Stella, New Orleans. Kleb's view of New Orleans as the "idealized tableau of working class life" contrasts vigorously with others' view of the city (see the essays by Kolin and Holditch, for example). Reconstituting "her otherness (her difference) as sameness," Blanche is a threat to Stella's marriage by reminding her sister of her psychological inheritance and to Mitch by exacerbating his "unmanly sensitivity" and "sexual confusion." Through the rape—reminiscent of the 18th century *supplice*, or punishment, that Foucault discusses—Stanley tries to contain Blanche's promiscuity, her sexual lunacy. Rather than dismissing Stanley as the brute, Kleb sees him Foucault-fashion as the "absolute monarch" who interrogates and then punishes physically. Sending her sister to the asylum, Stella is one with Stanley—both of them "guardians of the Same" commissioned to act against the "forces of discontinuity and rupture." However, Kleb concludes, Stanley is "not in control at the end" of *Streetcar*. Though sent off, Blanche "implants her otherness" in Stanley by branding the "male prerogatives" of his rape as "domestic tyranny," by locating "infantilism" in Stella's love, and by publicizing the "moral cowardice" betraying Mitch's actions. Thanks to Foucault's vision, Tennessee Williams and his *Streetcar* can be freed from the asylum and returned to the liminal world—"dangerous and disruptive."

If Kleb is guided through *Streetcar* by Foucault, Calvin Bedient is instructed by Julia Kristeva as he looks at the play. According to Bedient, Julia Kristeva's *Powers of Horror: An Essay in Abjection* and *Black Sun* "help us to view the coherence and etiology of the ills in *Streetcar*" and to understand "the play's jangly, if truthful, failed catharsis." In addition, Kristeva's "analysis of the 'theological sacrifice of the body in *Revolution in Poetic Language* points one to the cultural centrality of Williams's tragic intention.'" Characterizing *Streetcar* as a "powerful work of mourning," Bedient claims that the play represents the need to escape the "archaic engulfing mother." Fixated on the past (perhaps, unconsciously, even on the encrypted fantasy of the all-empowering mother), Blanche comes to symbolize the Phallic Mother. Incorporating the insights of Jean Baudrillard (on seduction and desire) into his Kristeva-inspired reading of *Streetcar*, Bedient shows that a fidelity to the mother is the sign of "inability to feel desire." As a seducer, one who deceives and destroys meaning, Blanche does not offer desire, or "the getting outside herself."

Painting Blanche in light of Kristeva's psychology of feminine depression, Bedient portrays Blanche as the "Mona Lisa of dread" (a "whited sepulcher"), the figure of death who does not want to be called away from the mother. *A Streetcar Named Desire* thus enacts the purgation of abjection ("the fear of the mother as murky, suffocating materiality," identity-threatening corporeality) from the community. To Stanley, her antagonist, Blanche represents the abjection he must destroy in order to free himself from being feminized. Blanche's seduction opposes Stanley's poker. Blanche is the victim of hysteria, melancholy, and guilt; Stanley stands for "phallic definiteness," radical democracy, desire, and "socio-symbolic order." As the "bullying Phallus," Stanley supplies the masculine appropriation of the archaic mother's strength. With a sickened ambivalence, the play underwrites the sacrifice that occurs when Stanley quashes Blanche. While the poetry of *Streetcar* utters incest (in Kristeva's terms), the plot crucifies it. "When the cards are down, the playwright prefers identity-sustaining law to the engulfing archaic mother. He thus injures and humiliates part of himself—the unspoken part of every speaking being."

Laura Morrow and Edward Morrow study *Streetcar* in light of one of the most recent and elusive current theoretical constructs—Chaos Theory and its corollary, Antichaos Theory. This interdisciplinary, scientific approach concentrates on discontinuous, erratic, and disorderly systems of behavior. In sum, Chaos and Antichaos focus on turbulence, of which *Streetcar* has an abundance. The Morrows argue that there are immense theoretical advantages to applying the principles of Chaos and Antichaos to Williams's masterpiece, chief of which is that although other methodologies consider Williams's text fragmentarily, this approach offers a holistic reading. According to that reading, the Chaos paradigm offers us a means of resolving a number of central critical questions in *Streetcar*—whether the play is Blanche's or Stanley's; the extent to which the behavior of Stanley, Stella, and especially Blanche is deterministic or freely chosen. Stanley follows the patterns of the Chaotic system, or the most freely formatted. Blanche, on the other hand, follows the Antichaotic, or the most deterministic. Through focusing on the orderly/disorderly systems of language embodied in the playtext, the Morrows demonstrate that Blanche is indeed the protagonist of *Streetcar*; and from a study of Blanche's characterization grounded in the concepts of the "strange attractor" and the "basin of attraction," they argue for the determinacy of her behavior. The reader's recognition of this determinacy is reinforced by Blanche's own actions, which can be elucidated from the perspective of Boolean $N = K$ networks, or the ways in which patterns of turbulence, or even disruptions of patterns, are formed. Of the behavior of *Streetcar*'s characters, Blanche is the most "frozen" or "canalized"—in psychological terms, the most deterministic. The mathematical-based/physics-oriented Chaos/Antichaos models provide a provocative way to talk about such humanistic topics as character, plot, and artistic creation.

Approaching *Streetcar* from reader response theory as articulated by Wolfgang Iser and Hans Robert Jauss, June Schlueter argues for, and recreates, a dual reading of the play. In a first or prospective reading, Schlueter claims that the reader must weigh and anticipate the contradictory histories of a Blanche who memorializes and a Stanley who deconstructs and decontextualizes. In this reading, which is "insistently prospective," the reader searches for more information, makes "periodic readjustments" as he or she responds to Blanche, perceived as sympathetic, and to Stanley. The reader looks for the "narrative showdown." That occurs, maintains Schlueter, with the rape, where the "narrative line of Blanche's story of self fails at the same time that the narrative line of Stanley's story reaches its frightening conclusion." In a second or retrospective reading, "Stanley's story of Blanche has priority" and is "legitimized through completion." By granting Stanley's story authority, the reader becomes implicated in the "public endorsement of Stanley's achievement" and is thereby coerced to accept Stanley's stereotypical "taxonomy of female sexuality" and to "agree to

Blanche's future." In thus seeking closure, the reader shows little kindness in his or her reading.

But Schlueter wisely cautions that while Stanley's narrative ends with scene 10, Williams's play continues into scene 11. A sympathetic and careful reading of that last scene of *Streetcar* presents a far different picture of Blanche than projected in Stanley's tainted closure in scene 10. Schlueter accordingly shows how the 1951 film of *Streetcar* and the 1984 teleplay bring *Streetcar* to closure at Stanley's expense and for Blanche's benefit. While the Kazan film ends with moral censure of Stanley, the John Erman teleplay concludes with a "sacramental context for Blanche's wish for purification." Schlueter alerts us to the seductions that readers of *Streetcar* need to be aware of lest they fall into a Stanley trap.

Blanche fares far differently in the following essay by Laurilyn Harris, who views *Streetcar* as "a tragedy of misperception, thwarted creativity, and misplaced priorities." Viewing the play in light of perception theory, Harris challenges a number of critical stereotypes about Blanche. For one thing, Harris claims the "fundamental struggle in *Streetcar* is not between fantasy and reality but between two radically different perceptions of reality." Blind to each other's virtues, Blanche and Stanley vie for whose perception will dominate in the struggle for the prizes of Mitch and Stella. Harris provocatively argues that neither illusion nor narcissism motivates Blanche, but, on a much deeper level, her perception is flawed by an unstable ego. Nor is Blanche the artist/martyr since her value system prevents her from fulfilling her artistic potential. Unable to break away from the beauty myth imposed on her by others' perceptions, Blanche becomes an accomplice in her own destruction. Because she is "trapped within the contradictions of her stereotypic role and forever at the perceptions of others, [Blanche] injudiciously clings to her protective camouflage and the sterile, frozen misguided creation that eventually contributes to the destruction of her last chance for happiness." Because of such sexual stereotyping, Blanche is denied a "real vocation" and "legitimate channel for creativity" and trivializes herself by playing artificial roles. She becomes a "cartoon Scarlett O'Hara."

Harris also refutes those critics who label Blanche a nymphomaniac; each of her lovers is a youthful replica of Allan Grey as Blanche attempts to restore and relive that failed relationship. Searching to "validate the ideal Fantasy Self," Blanche looks for responding mirrors but instead finds only fragmented selves. Perhaps one of the most intriguing points in Harris's essay is that the rape might have been avoided. Harris links Blanche's madness not to Stanley's brutality but to Blanche's flawed perception that Stanley's view of her could be true and that her only escape lies through madness and death. Blanche's distorted tragic perceptions link her with Cassandra and in such a context, Harris asserts, Blanche's red satin wrapper has greater "sacrificial overtones" than lustful ones. Harris's work contributes significantly to both feminist and psychoanalytic readings of *Streetcar*.

My own essay on Eunice Hubbell explores the importance of this character in *Streetcar* from the perspective of feminist thematics. Because she has been dismissed as comic and "insistently feminine," Eunice has been marginalized by both the male characters and the male critics of *Streetcar*. In fact, even feminist readers have misjudged the Kowalskis' upstairs neighbor. Eunice's "authenticity as a character" and her function as foil/analogue "help define the masculine/feminine dynamics of *Streetcar*." Like so many of Williams's characters, Eunice elicits multiple responses. She suggests provocative parallels with Stella as a wife and with Blanche as a woman who seeks love. Almost always overlooked in discussions of scene 6, the famous newspaperboy scene of *Streetcar*, Eunice's presence alerts us to a major structural pattern—the love chase—that ends comedically for Eunice but tragically for Blanche. Eunice also underscores the problems Stella confronts with Stanley's infidelity, since Eunice herself believes her husband Steve has cheated on her.

But Eunice's function in *Streetcar* extends further than foil or analogue. Independently, she symbolizes the virtues of female friendships—which Williams frequently contrasts with their more violent and less trustworthy male counterparts—and feminine community. A vital part of Eunice's character is occupied with caregiving; she represents the maternal side of the French Quarter, which has been overshadowed by Stanley's patriarchal aggressions and clouded by masculine critical imperatives. Equally important, and in fact flowing from Eunice's maternal presence, is her function as a feminine protector. Eunice's apartment symbolizes feminine place by supplying a refuge for Stella and Blanche when none else exists. Moreover, her feminine cordiality and solicitude are graphically conveyed through stage directions that empower her as a doorkeeper, a protector of portals. In light of these virtues, it is unfair to attack Eunice for moral cowardice because she advises Stella to accept the status quo (Stanley's story of what happened to Blanche). In no way a Stanley supporter, Eunice offers Blanche respect and comfort, and Stella survivor's advice and future sanctuary should she ever need it.

The next two essays read *Streetcar* in terms of history and myth, but in radically different ways. Lionel Kelly studies the "ethnicity of the play's setting" and the "mythological encoding" of the names and situations in *Streetcar* to explore Williams's use of "realism as a strategy of dramatic expression." Focusing on the opening scene with the unnamed Negro woman, Kelly accuses Williams of "ethnic typecasting" by undermining this woman's role. Williams's oft-quoted stage direction about the *"easy intermingling of the races in the old part of town"* is contradicted by his marginalizing the Negro woman. Though "undermined," the Negro woman is still a significant figure as the "prolepsis of Blanche." Challenging history, the "Polack" Kowalski is "markedly extraneous to the [New Orleans] ethnic mix," argues Kelly, but through his territorial possessiveness and the "strained formalism" of his legalistic thrusts, Stanley ensures that he is "made room for." As the parvenu intruder, Stanley with his immigrant ambitions for an American identity clashes with Blanche's sense of history and place.

Though the characters in *Streetcar* "are controlled by their ethnic roles," a larger sense of time prevails in the play for Kelly through its mythic associations. Blanche's history goes much further back than to the romanticized antebellum South. Studying her in the light of British poet Robert Graves's *The White Goddess* (published one year after *Streetcar*), Kelly links Blanche to the "primal energies" of this female deity. The White Goddess is, in Graves's words, "the Muse, the Mother of All Living, the ancient power of fright and lust—the female spider or the queen-bee whose embrace is death." Like that goddess, Blanche is associated with the astral, especially the moon, whose different phases mark the stages in the goddess's life and display "demonological manifestations." Kelly points out, however, that Blanche is a "secularized version" of the White Goddess because Blanche's "nymphomania is a thwarted mimesis of the goddess's predatory sexuality." Kelly concludes that in terms of realism and the politics of desire, Stanley's conflict with Blanche should be read as a latter-day version of the failures of Unionist accommodation, pictured as an opposition between a brutally masculine legalism and a feminine recourse to performance aware of its own performative functions.

The approach taken by Mark Royden Winchell might best be termed subversively mythic. Inspired by the work of Leslie Fiedler, Winchell accounts for why and how *A Streetcar Named Desire* has effectively transcended "the distinction between elite and popular culture." In his Fiedlerian analysis, Winchell concentrates on the "mythopoeic power" of *Streetcar* as it "raises disturbing questions about hearth and home, sex roles, family loyalty, and the power of eros." A loyal disciple of the shockingly brilliant Leslie, Winchell places *Streetcar* within the two traditions of American literature—the "misogynist" and the "domestic" and finds that the Kowalski household indeed portrays a "vision of home as Heaven," a heaven, of course, that is undilutedly patriarchal. In fact, according to Winchell, "Stanley's motives—if not his methods—are superior to Blanche's"; Stanley is no victim of "petticoat government." Clearly no feminist critic, Winchell accuses Blanche of having "too many flaws, too little stature, and almost no self-knowledge." For Winchell, she is promiscuous, a "pathological liar," and home wrecker, and if Mitch had married her, she would probably have cheated with the paperboy. Blanche is undone not by a vibrant, sexual masculinity but by a "failed patriarchy," the type that unglued the South of Margaret Mitchell's *Gone With the Wind*. The paternity to which Blanche was exposed, claims Winchell, was neither assertive nor protective enough.

Though Stanley's rape is "inexcusable," there are for Winchell mitigating circumstances that may diminish Stanley morally but still encourage males in the audiences to bond with him. "As males, we have secretly cheered the

bad boy on as he proves something we have always wanted to believe—
that the sententious schoolmarm is really a secret nympho." Although the
rape may promote male gratification at Blanche's expense, women also
receive gratification from watching the ever-popular *Streetcar*. They identify
with Stella, the "real heroine of the play," as she enjoys the way that Stanley
can satisfy her lusts by getting the colored lights going. Winchell concludes
that because Williams's sympathies, and those of his elite critics, lie with
Blanche, *Streetcar* has escaped being labeled a sexist fantasy. Mass audiences, however, respond more readily to Stanley's sexual charisma and to
the patriarchal myth it embodies. "For men it is a fantasy of complete
domination; for women, one of complete submission."

W. Kenneth Holditch next interprets *Streetcar* against the background of
two famous Southern novels—Kate Chopin's *The Awakening* and William
Faulkner's *The Wild Palms*—and believes that these novels "help elucidate
the dilemma Blanche faces in *Streetcar* and the one truth about the human
condition with which Williams's greatest drama is concerned." Each of these
works, maintains Holditch, is built around the "inevitable battle between
Romance and the 'broken world' of Naturalism." In *"The Awakening, The
Wild Palms*, and *A Streetcar Named Desire*, Romance is frustrated by the
harsh reality of economics, social convention, religion, and the biological
reality of birth and death, all those hereditary and environmental forces
with which the Naturalistic writers from Zola to Dreiser were concerned,
even obsessed." Edna Pontellier in *The Awakening*, Charlotte Rittenmeyer
in *Wild Palms*, and Blanche DuBois share the "plight of any Romantic in
the real world." Trying to navigate in a Platonic world of transcendence,
each of these women searches for an ideal, ethereal lover but instead is
forced to embrace the physical and ultimately becomes "trapped in a naturalistic environment." That environment is the same in all three works:
New Orleans, an ambivalent, paradoxical world of decadence and romance,
materialism, and charm.

Holditch relates Blanche's troubles to Chopin's and Faulkner's heroines
as all three are caught unto death in the "tragic paradox" of the spirit and
the flesh. Casting Stanley as "the Naturalistic breeder," Holditch persuasively describes him in light of Arthur Schopenhauer's philosophy of the
"primacy of the will." Accordingly, Stanley fulfills the two strongest human
urges: "to mate and to recreate." The brutish Kowalski is the indisputed
king in the "sensual, broken world" to which Blanche flees for help but
that inevitably destroys her and her dreams. In Holditch's view, Blanche
enters that broken world out of guilt, to escape Allan Grey's death, but as
the "romantic idealist and passionate female," she has to confront reality
and consequently is swept away by its strong sexuality. Yet, Holditch concludes, Williams does not believe that we are left helplessly alone in the vile,
naturalistic world. Williams wants us, like Blanche, to "cling to some vestige
of hope in something beyond Naturalism." That message spoke forcefully

to the young Thomas Lanier Williams whose own experiences in New Orleans in the 1930s paralleled and gave birth to Blanche's.

Professing that he has "no ideological axe to grind," Bert Cardullo takes issue with sociopolitical and feminist interpretations of *Streetcar* for their "superficial reading" of the script and for their attempts to turn the play into a "political tract." Describing his own approach as a close reading informed (or prejudiced) only by humanism, Cardullo claims that Blanche and Stanley are less villain and prey, as Marxists and feminists contend, than "mutual victims of desire" whose pasts and futures were not and will not be different. Rather than dichotomizing Blanche and Stanley, Cardullo identifies parallels between the two as "human beings," not symbols, though, of course, he stresses the moral difference between the two. The major thrust of Cardullo's essay, however, is on exploring representations— verbal and physical—of birth and death, rebirth and death-in-life, especially in scenes 5, 7, 9, 10, and 11, whose juxtaposition reveals meaning that less formal considerations of the play overlook. In so doing, Cardullo has provocative things to say about the Mexican woman ("the cumulative symbol of death and desire" at Belle Reve and in *Streetcar*); the Kowalski baby, who ironically frees Stella from the domination of Stanley's lust; and the paperboy, who allows Blanche to recall her lost innocence. In his interpretation, Cardullo judiciously incorporates lines from both the reading and the acting editions of the play.

The following two essays primarily concern the political questions/implications that *Streetcar* raises: the ideological structures in the play's subtext. Reading *Streetcar* in light of contemporary Marxist theory, Robert Bray believes that "Williams does seem conscious of at least an abstract notion of Marxist dialectic in first choosing such obvious class opposites as Blanche and Stanley and then determining who would prevail in the struggle." After a brief but useful survey of *Streetcar*'s reception on Soviet and other Communist stages, Bray explores such key Marxist concepts as history, property, and class struggles that energize the play. He believes it is wrong to limit Blanche's desire for sex; rather, it embraces something much larger, her "sense of belonging to and merely surviving in a society to which she's temperamentally unsuited." Bray maintains that at the heart of her and Stanley's existence is property. Although Blanche is diminished by a "reduction of property values" to being reduced to an intruder in New Orleans, Stanley, by acquiring Belle Reve (or what might be left of it), gains "leverage" over Blanche in "the power-property equation." This transition from "rural-agrarian to urban-mechanistic" illustrates the downfall of the "landed aristocracy" and the victory of the common working folk. Bray contends that in showing this transition, *Streetcar* "perhaps more than any other single piece of literature . . . [demonstrates] the futility of romanticizing and clinging to the days of cavaliers and cotton fields."

Studying other characters in *Streetcar* from a Marxist perspective, Bray maintains that the poker players actually help Stanley to preserve order and "ensure his dominance" but that Mitch symbolizes the "ultimate dependency of the working class existence." The proletarian Stanley "becomes the ruling class." Most significant of all for Bray is that the Hegelian dialectic of thesis, antithesis, and synthesis, which embodies the core of Marxism, is exemplified and worked out through the three leading characters in *Streetcar*—Blanche, Stanley, and Stella—as they articulate their struggles. Representing opposing "cultural levels," Blanche and Stanley are engaged in a deadly historical/political battle. The "synthetic Stella," however, through her choice at the end of *Streetcar* is "guaranteed relative economic and familial security" in the future with Stanley. Stella has successfully "adapted to his world." Thus, Bray reaches the same conclusion about Stella that Mark Royden Winchell does, though from a vastly different perspective.

In his essay on *Streetcar* in Germany, Jürgen Wolter contends that the play in its German context exemplifies the problems created by every cultural transfer. Wolter asserts that translators and directors, in addition to tackling questions of idiom and style, have to take into account that the political, economic, and ideological background of the target audience is not only different but also constantly changing. Theatre history reflects this perpetual transformation in the cultural context, as Wolter demonstrates through his perspective survey of the German reception of *Streetcar* from the 1950s to the 1980s. After chronicling the sensation *Streetcar* created in an intellectually starved postwar Germany, Wolter turns to why and how *Streetcar* became part of the German repertoire in the 1960s but concludes that, given the political crises of those years, the play was frequently believed to have lost its relevance. Consequently, in the following decades, some directors attempted to heighten the play's attractiveness, first, in the 1970s, by spectacular casting and then, in the 1980s, by emphasizing its universality and dehistoricizing the stage setting. Wolter concludes with a discussion of *Streetcar*'s reception in the communist German Democratic Republic where the play was not produced until 1974 because it was considered retrospective and did not agitate for a change in American society. Wolter's history and assessment of *Streetcar* in Germany sheds light on the confluence of two cultures with Williams's play being the chief vehicle of such transference.

Using information from an important Tennessee Williams letter and from interviews with Williams and Elia Kazan, Father Gene Phillips traces the history of *Streetcar* from stage to film. Guiding Phillips's discussion is his belief that Tennessee Williams's plays do not need much rearranging in order to be transferred to the screen and that those film adaptations of his works that stick closest to the original play are most artistically successful. In the case of *Streetcar*, however, Kazan and Williams were "aware that care would have to be exercised if a film version of the play was to steer successfully through the narrow straights of the film industry's production code and reach the screen with its artistic integrity intact." Phillips describes the cinematic techniques inherent in Williams's dramaturgy and the ways in which Kazan's opening the play up for the film extended the action of Williams's script "from the train depot to the bowling alley to the dance casino and the factory." Because of film's elasticity, Kazan was able to take advantage of lighting, close-up shots, and a shrinking Kowalski apartment to capture the claustrophobic feeling that overcomes Blanche. Adapting the play for the screen to appease the censor, Kazan and Williams had to address the sensitive issues of Allan Grey's homosexuality. Yet even though the film could not be as direct as the play, Williams's rewriting for the censor none-theless "telegraphs to a mature moviegoer that Allan is homosexual, even without the play's explicit reference to his having a male lover." Kazan and Williams successfully fought the censor's demand to cut the rape scene, but bowed to the request to include an ending in which Stanley is clearly pun-ished for his misdeeds by his estranged wife. Phillips emphasizes that "Wil-liams was never satisfied with this compromise ending" of the film. Studying the "complex motivational forces at work in the rape scene," Phillips points out that the censor wanted "a clearer distinction between the villainous and admirable characters in [keeping with] the Hollywood tradition of family films." However, as Kazan told Phillips, "You're not in there rooting for someone.... There is no hero, no heroine; the people are people, some dross, some gold...."

Regardless of their theoretical/methodological allegiances, each of these fifteen essays expands our understanding of *Streetcar* and its place in Amer-ican (world) culture. If these essays prove anything, it is that no one critical approach owns the rights to *A Streetcar Named Desire*.

WORKS CITED

Adler, Thomas P. *A Streetcar Named Desire: The Moth and the Lantern*. Twayne Masterwork Studies No. 47. Boston: Twayne, 1990.

Bedient, Calvin. Letter to the author. 30 July 1991.

"Bloolips and Split Britches." *Theater Week* 4 Mar. 1991: 38.

Bigsby, C.W.E. "Tennessee Williams: Streetcar to Glory." In *The Forties: Fiction, Prose, Drama*. Ed. Warren French. DeLand, Fla.: Everett/Edwards, 1969. 251–58.

Chesler, S. Alan. "*A Streetcar Named Desire*: Twenty-Five Years of Criticism." *Notes on Mississippi Writers* 7 (1974): 44–53.

Desbusscher, Gilbert. "*De Elysese Velden*." *Studies in American Drama, 1945-Present* 5 (1990): 88–91.

Devlin, Albert J. *Conversations with Tennessee Williams*. Jackson: UP of Mississippi, 1986.

Faber, Stephen. "Blanche Wins the Battle." *New York Times* 1 Apr. 1973, sec 3:1, 15.

Kolin, Philip C. "*A Streetcar Named Desire*: A Playwrights' Forum." *Michigan Quarterly Review* 39 (Spring 1990): 173–203.

————. "Williams in Ebony: Black and Multi-Racial Productions of *A Streetcar Named Desire*." *Black American Literature Forum* 25 (Spring 1991): 147–81.

Leonard, Gail. "Belle Reprieve." *Theatre Journal* 43 (Oct. 1991): 386–88.

Oliver, Edith. "Blanche and the Boys." *New Yorker* 28 (Mar. 1988): 81–82.

Williams, Tennessee. *Where I Live: Selected Essays.* Ed. Christine R. Day and Bob Woods. New York: New Directions, 1978.

2

Readymade Desire

Herbert Blau

Out of his frightened heart, Tennessee Williams once wrote "that the only somebody worth being is the solitary and unseen you that existed from your first breath and which is the sum of your actions and so is constantly in a state of becoming under your own violation..." ("Catastrophe" 140).[1] This was three years after the opening of *The Glass Menagerie* in Chicago and four days before the New York opening of *A Streetcar Named Desire*. By that time, the solitary in Williams had been violated by the little vanities and deceits and equivocal pleasures of dubious reputation, which caused him to say as well: "Many people are not willing to believe that a playwright is interested in anything but popular success" ("Catastrophe"). One of the more scathing unbelievers about this particular playwright was Mary McCarthy, who wrote in her notorious putdown, entitled "A Streetcar Called Success," that "Mr. Williams's lies, like Blanche's are so old and shopworn that the very truth upon which he rests them becomes garish and ugly, just as the Kowalskis' apartment becomes the more squalid for Blanche's attempts at decoration" (134). I want to come back to these charges in a moment, but at the time she made them, it was not very likely that McCarthy had seen very much of Williams's drama, except perhaps for *The Glass Menagerie*, which even among his detractors usually escapes disdain. It was not very probable, in any event, that she knew anything of his earliest work.

That work is still unknown and unpublished. One doesn't normally think of a little theater in St. Louis with a name like the Mummers as being political, but the plays by Williams that were produced there in the thirties were specifically so—to which, if scholars can't, the FBI can apparently attest. Williams was later to study with Brecht's friend, Erwin Piscator, at the New School in New York, but there were Brechtian inclinations from the beginning. They persisted, we know, into his "memory play" about the

Wingfield family, where legends and titles were to be back-projected in order to give "structural value" to scenes that might seem "fragmentary rather than architectural" (*Glass Menagerie* 132). It's still hard to know what was being signaled, what incipient violation or subsequent depth of capitulation, when the alienating "screen device" disappeared in the transparent gauze of the Broadway production and—as Williams said in explaining why the device was cut—the auratic power of Laurette Taylor's performance. Williams thought enough of the idea to want it in the published manuscript, but actually, even if the legends and titles had been used, they would have occurred in the form of magic-lantern slides, an effect of mood as well as meaning that may have been dominated anyhow, as in *Streetcar*, by the chiaroscuro of lighting and music. Augmented thus, the magic-lantern would have lent a certain romantic atmosphere to any effects of alienation, "emotion, nostalgia, which is the first condition of the play" (133)—a condition that, to the point of hallucination in *Streetcar*, seemed a considerable distance from the politics and techniques of Brecht.

If we thought of Williams then as an evocative writer with the susceptible delicacy of his glass figurines, he eventually seemed to become, as he might have said of Blanche DuBois but actually said of himself, "a definition of hysteria" (quoted in Kalem 53). It may seem an appropriate justice that the early plays were forgotten, but as we rethink the later work on the jaundiced ground of "the postmodern condition," as cultural productions or social texts, it's probably good to remember that the first things produced were overtly left-wing dramas about union busting, a prison strike, and a flophouse for what we would call street people today. One of them, *Candles to the Sun*, had not only a premonitory touch of the poet but, in the character of Birmingham Red, a conspicuous touch of Marxism. And in a period whose dominant playwright was Clifford Odets, the opening performance ended, according to a review in the *St. Louis Post-Dispatch*, like the legendary *Waiting for Lefty*, with the audience joining the actors in singing "Solidarity Forever."

About a week before the production of *Streetcar* on Broadway, *LIFE* magazine had a photographic feature on the House UnAmerican Activities Committee hearings (Olson), but by then Williams seemed immersed in "the broken world" of the epigraph to the play, as if the voice that was no more than "an instant in the wind" had no political content, and "each desperate choice" now made (239) was, far from being collective, increasingly solipsistic. Nor was gay pride ever sufficient in Williams to entirely overcome self-contempt, no less to arouse a sexual politics in a participatory mode. Yet the homosexuality of Williams was hardly a trade secret, and there are those who have believed—putting aside the stereotypic, if not homophobic, revelations about Blanche's young husband—that if he "covered the waterfront" in his personal life (which he told David Frost in 1970[40]), the homosexuality suffused the conception of *Streetcar* in more or less ambivalent, surreptitious, or overheated ways, most especially, so far as the production confirmed it, in the sullen charm and narcissism of Brando's performance as Stanley. Whatever the gender constructions, they were not likely to be thought of in political terms, as they may very well be now; if not in the theater, surely in theory, with Williams seen (if still in the closet then) as an undercover agent of eventual critique. He later made statements about all good art being revolutionary, but so far as most of us knew in the late forties, his ideological past was not as vulnerable to the other McCarthyism as that of the director of his play, Elia Kazan, who later named names before the committee, or that other most promising playwright of this period, Arthur Miller, who refused. Despite the gestures at "social background" in *The Glass Menagerie*—"the huge middle class matriculating in a school for the blind," Guernica in Spain, labor disturbances at home, "the fiery Braille alphabet of a dissolving economy" (145)—the social conscience of Williams seemed to have dissolved into the psychosexual Braille and sometimes fiery (or purple) passages of the drama of lyricized loners.

As for the critical conscience of Mary McCarthy, she wrote of *Streetcar* in *The Partisan Review*, whose own Marxism was shaken and diminishing in the New York intellectuals' anti-Stalinist wars. Given the state of our theater at the time, where not only Williams's radical plays but Brecht himself was virtually unknown, ideas of any kind were at a premium, and one might have welcomed an ideological debate. But sadder by far than McCarthy's assault upon Williams was that the deflection or sublimation of his politics appeared to have little to do with the withering retrospective of her most plenary contempt: "His work reeks of literary ambition as the apartment reeks of cheap perfume; it is impossible to witness Williams's plays without being aware of the pervading smell of careerism" (134).

What beguiles me now, aside from the raw gratuitous virulence of the judgment, is the anachronism of its piety on the postmodern scene, where it's hard to imagine anyone, either artist or critic, getting so worked up over the sweet smell of success. Or mortified by it either, as Williams apparently was, with no Southern Comfort for the residual puritanism, "sweet, so sweet!... terribly, terribly sweet" (*Streetcar* 382)—as if the emotional perturbations and fragile beauty of Blanche, "*which must avoid a strong light*" (245), had been exposed to the glare of publicity and, even before Marilyn or Jackie or Liz, silkscreened by Andy Warhol. After all, according to the cultural logic of late capitalism, where it's more or less taken for granted that the arts are merging with fashion, even subversion and transgression have become equivocal functions of success, and in the libidinal flow of commodified exchange, it's possible to think of the streetcar named Desire as a sort of Duchampian readymade, like the urinal named Fountain, or—depending on "the epidermic play of perversity" (Foucault 171),[2] the lubricity of performance—the Deleuzian desiring machine.

This may have little to do with Williams's intentions, nor is it a preface

to a schizoanalysis of a neurasthenic play, which, in passing from the political unconscious of its author to the hysteria of its heroine, seems to
have acquired a hyperrealism that, in its simulation of the truth of desire—passing by way of the Cemeteries to the Elysian Fields—is dangerously on the edge of kitsch, like the song Blanche quite improbably
sings, a paper doll testament to the loss of the real ("Not sold—*lost,
lost!* [273]) in what we have come to think of as an "economy of
death." That economy, with its sadomasochistic array of specular seductions, is just about literalized by Blanche, with the "Blue Piano" growing
louder behind her, in her manic obsessive defense of the loss of Belle
Reve, as if she were herself, iteratively, the body of the dream: "I, I, *I*
took the blows in my face and my body! The long parade to the graveyard!... You didn't dream, but I saw! *Saw! Saw!* And now you sit there
telling me with your eyes that I let the place go. How in hell do you think
all that sickness and dying was paid for?" (262). So far as intentions are
concerned at this late date in the dominion of deconstruction we may, I
trust, pass over them in peace without any damage to the manifest content
that has, in scholarship and performance, been only too much rehearsed.
As for the latencies in the text, so far as they are psychological, they are
perhaps better left to the actors, who will—unless the production is radically
revisionist or brazenly parodistic, like the gender-bending version by Bloolips and Split Britches retitled *Belle Reprieve*—give us variations on the
characters not unlike the precipitations of color and slippages of figure, or
reversals of light and shadow, on the cultural icons emulsified, rephoto-
graphed, engraved, and blurringly replicated by Warhol himself, who also
serigraphed a "Silver Marlon."

For all that, it will continue to be, with whatever blurred contours of a
possibly bleeding psyche, a familiar surface. With Brando in particular as
the referent for Stanley, in an almost preemptive performance now me-
morialized on film (the form that, as the theater can't, reproduces desire in
a "body without organs"), the fact is that the play itself, with its self-
consciously sensuous dramaturgy, is an icon of popular culture, drawn to
begin with from popular culture. This is true even when the source appears
to be high art, as in the stage direction alluding to "*a picture of Van Gogh's
of a billiard-parlor at night.*" If the kitchen then suggests "*that sort of lurid
nocturnal brilliance, the raw colors of childhood's spectrum*" (286), that is
the spectrum broadly and regressively inhabited by all the denizens of the
Quarter and the elements of the play. Williams constructed it of already
charged and precoded materials, from the classical nineteenth-century hys-
teric as aging southern belle to the poker night and its master stud to the
French Quarter itself, with its boozy rhythms and local color, which—like
the "*infatuated fluency of brown fingers*" on the keys—invests the scene
with "*a kind of lyricism [that] gracefully attenuates the atmosphere of
decay.*"

If an elitist like Mary McCarthy could spurn this "raffish charm" (243) a generation ago, it's unlikely that a sophisticated critic with a modicum of cultural theory would be much put off today by the lurid effects of a drama with a seductive dose of kitsch. Since the drama of Williams was the paradigm of much of what we see on television, it is no wonder that *Streetcar* might be perceived today as generously endowed with soap operatic qualities, including the enticements of a voyeuristic style. If the figures of the play seem to have come, then, from the marketplace of signs, it's as if Williams had realized before the intensified consciousness of the mediascape of the postmodern that it is only as readymades that they can function mythologically. As for the elements of the drama that, from the day I first saw it, always seemed factitious, like the vaguely Faulknerian concoction of the "epic fornications" of Belle Reve or the inscription of Mrs. Browning's sonnet on Mitch's cigarette case, they exist somewhere between the provenance of dreams and the fantasizing of history.

Speaking of which, there is always the adventitious circumstance in which history affirms the degree to which it requires fantasy, as it did in the city that is the setting of the play. About a week before the opening, there was a cover story in *Time* on the New Orleans mayor Chep Morrison, who was described as Blanche might have described her savior Shep Huntleigh, as a "symbol of the bright new day which has come to the city of charming ruins." Morrison seemed to embody at the time the postwar energy in all the nations' cities. (As the play was about to open, they were debating welfare reform in New York, so that they could put employable people back to work; the army was making final indictments at Nuremberg; Molotov and General Marshall were feuding over the German treaty; and the first phases of the Cold War were creating jobs at home.) We may look back at that now with a certain nostalgia, as we dwell with increasing dismay upon the brutalizing reality of what seems at times irreversible decay, which has polluted our cities and filled the streets with those who can hardly depend, like Blanche, upon the kindness of strangers.

If in this perspective we insist on doing the play by interiorizing its characters, there are some aspects of the drama that might be reconsidered psychologically, like the period in which Blanche, on the edge of desperation, was going it alone, with nothing really to help her but the wiliness of dispossession. By whatever lies and deceits, and whatever illusory pathos at the end, Blanche has by no means been without a sense of reality that came, with a certain tough-mindedness, from the experience of decay. The narrative of that experience may be, at need, revised to fit the occasion, as it is under the scrutiny of Stanley, who plots her departure (and punishment) so that in another kind of fantasy he can, once more, got those little colored lights going. (Stanley's own narrative is a little tenuous in the play, like his being a traveling salesman for the machine tools plant in which Mitch makes precision parts.) When they have their first encounter over Stanley's urgency about the Napoleonic code, she sends for a lemon Coke "with plenty of chipped ice in it" and abruptly cools the repartee between them: "All right now, Mr. Kowalski, let us proceed without any more double talk" (280). That it's not quite an equal match shouldn't deter the actor from refusing to invest her performance entirely in the conspicuous symptoms of panicked excess or the *"uncertain manner...that suggests a moth"* (245). It's not that Blanche can no longer see the truth but that, with all the fictions upon which her reality has been constructed—those she inherited and those she contrived herself as the inheritance fell apart—she can no longer do much about it, to the point of hallucination.

Meanwhile, as we rehearse the fantasies upon which the play is predicated, it may turn out that those of Blanche are, as we see women today after the Clarence Thomas hearings, to be weighed against those of Stella or, for that matter, the neighbor Eunice, who after all appeared on the scene before the battered-wife syndrome gained public attention. When she runs down the stairs crying out for somebody to call the police, a conventional audience is on the whole, including the women, still likely to laugh. We may or may not laugh when Stanley abuses Stella and calls her back with animal cries, but it is she who returns us to the illusions understood by Ibsen and O'Neill, and focused most recently through Anita Hill, who was not only abused by the men who questioned her but disbelieved by a majority of women whose own lives, perhaps, depend not so much on the kindness of strangers but on fidelity to the phallic order of things, or investment in the family, with some helpless dependency on the authority of their husbands. Stella sobs at the end *"with inhuman abandon"* (419), but as she prepared for Blanche to be taken away, we have a version of the woman whose future depends, for whatever reason on readymade desire, on *not* seeing the truth: "I couldn't believe her story and go on living with Stanley" (405). Eunice advises her, for better or worse, never to believe it. "Life has to go on. No matter what happens, you've got to keep on going" (406).

The lines are old and shopworn, and the very truth on which they rest becomes ugly and squalid, the state of becoming that is, inevitably, its own violation. Surely she knows better, but what would most lives be if they ever depended on that?

NOTES

1. The article on success seems to have been of some importance to Williams. Written for *The New York Times* Drama Section, 30 Nov. 1947, it was first reprinted as the introduction to the Signet edition of *A Streetcar Named Desire* (New York: NAL, 1951) n.pag.

2. The phrase was used by Michel Foucault to describe the performative logic of a phantasmic movement of mind in the discourse of Gilles Deleuze.

WORKS CITED

Foucault, Michel. "Theatrum Philosophicum." *Language, Counter-Memory, Practice: Selected Essays and Interviews*. Ed. Donald F. Bouchard. Trans. Bouchard and Sherry Simon. Ithaca: Cornell UP, 1977. 171.

Frost, David. "Will God Talk Back to a Playwright? Tennessee Williams." *The Americans*. New York: Stein and Day, 1970. 33–40.

Kalem, Ted. "The Theater: The Angel of the Odd." *Time* 9 Mar. 1962: 53+.

McCarthy, Mary. *Theater Chronicles 1937–1962*. New York: Farrar, Strauss, 1963.

"Old Girl's New Boy." *Time* 24 Nov. 1947: 26–29.

Olson, Sidney. "The Movie Hearings." *Life* 24 Nov. 1947: 137–48.

Williams, Tennessee. *The Glass Menagerie. The Theatre of Tennessee Williams*. 7 vols. to date. New York: New Directions, 1971. Vol. 1: 123–237.

———. *A Streetcar Named Desire. The Theatre of Tennessee Williams*. 7 vols. to date. New York: New Directions, 1971. Vol. 1: 239–419.

———. "The Catastrophe of Success." *The Theatre of Tennessee Williams*. 7 vols. to date. New York: New Directions, 1971. Vol. 1: 135–41.

3

Marginalia: *Streetcar*, Williams, and Foucault

William Kleb

They never met, and though contemporaries (they died a year apart), there is no indication that either was aware of the other's work, but reading Michel Foucault and Tennessee Williams at the same time, one is struck again and again by a remarkable thematic and methodological kinship. If *Histoire de la folie, Discipline and Punish* and the first volume of *The History of Sexuality* had preceded Williams's great period (1943–1961), instead of immediately following it, a case for influence as powerful as those linking Williams to Crane, Lawrence, and Nietzsche might even be made.[1] Reading the other way around—looking at Williams's work as a kind of imaginative prefiguration of Foucault's theory—an exploration of the common points of perception between the two can still be illuminating and rewarding. Like those of Genet, Williams's plays construct and animate the same shifting ontological landscape mapped out by Foucault; situated at the margin where death, madness, and sexuality intersect and interact, they focus, as does Foucault in his most important texts, on the struggle to control (through the power of knowledge and the manipulation of "truth") a definition of the Same and the Other.[2] The correspondence between Williams and Foucault is pervasive, but nowhere is it clearer or more useful from a critical point of view than in Williams's masterpiece *A Streetcar Named Desire*.

What is peculiar to modern societies, in fact, is not that they consigned sex to a shadow existence, but that they dedicated themselves to speaking of it *ad infinitum*, while exploiting it as *the* secret (Foucault, *HS* 35).

In *The History of Sexuality*, Foucault maintains that modern discourse on the subject has been dominated, incorrectly, by what he calls "the repressive hypothesis" (2). According to this hypothesis, a lax, free-form attitude toward sexuality, common in Western culture during the seventeenth century ("the classical age"), was subsequently redefined by the rising bourgeoisie (for religious and economic reasons) in terms of the "conjugal family." Sexuality was thus moved into the home, where it was carefully confined to the serious function of reproduction. "The legitimate and procreative couple laid down the law." Illegitimate sexualities were "driven out, denied and reduced to silence." Or, if "places of tolerance" were provided for these outcast desires, they had to be elsewhere—the brothel or the mental hospital (3–4).

Foucault sees the matter differently: since the late eighteenth century, he argues, when the human sciences and the concept of social welfare began to emerge, there has been in the West a "proliferation of discourses concerned with sex" (18). This proliferation has concerned itself primarily with managing and normalizing sexuality through the examination, the classification and, ultimately, the treatment of a wide range of "peripheral sexualities" (39) now considered "abnormal" (110). The key figures around which these investigations have coalesced are the hysterical woman, the sexual child, the "perverse adult" (the homosexual in particular), and the "Malthusian couple" (105). Although adults and children may have been "deprived of a certain way of speaking about sex, a mode that was disallowed as being too direct, crude or coarse," this was only the counterpart of many other newer forms of discourse, and perhaps the condition necessary for them to function most effectively (30). The repressive hypothesis, therefore, plays only a "local" and a "tactical" role in this larger "mechanism" of power; it is, in fact, a "ruse," actually an *"incitement"* to discourse (12). If sex is *the secret* that must be revealed—or "confessed," as Foucault puts it (58–63)—for the health of the individual and of society (the Freudian argument), speaking of sex in an atmosphere of presumed repression becomes an essential transgressive move, an act of (sexual) revolt (129–30). "If repression has indeed been the fundamental link between power, knowledge and sexuality since the classical age, . . . nothing less than a transgression of laws, a lifting of prohibition, an irruption of speech, a reinstating of pleasure within a whole new economy in the mechanisms of power will be required" (5). The repressive hypothesis, then, sex as secret, contributes to the proliferation of discourses on sexuality that has characterized modernity (35).

According to the most recent "empirical enquiry" published by the Kinsey Institute, the idea of sexual revolution has "enjoyed a vogue at various times not only in our past but in the histories of other societies" (Klassen et al., 3). Such an idea seems to emerge in conjunction with unsettling social changes, for example, during and after wars (4). It became a "powerful cultural reality" in America in the 1960s (5), but the origin of this "revolution" is generally traced to the late 1940s (post–World War II), in fact to the publication of the first of Alfred Kinsey's two books on American sexuality, *Sexual Behavior in the Human Male* (January 1948). Although

Foucault does not mention Kinsey in *The History of Sexuality*, the efforts of the American sociobiologist surely provide a vivid example of Foucault's "*scientia sexualis*" (67) at work for the welfare of society. Packed with statistical evidence drawn from thousands of hours of (confessional) interviews, Kinsey's analysis focused, at least in the minds of the American public, on "peripheral sexualities" (in particular, on homosexuality and the sexuality of children), and it was promoted in terms of the repressive hypothesis. Kinsey, according to one commentator, "found the whole subject entangled in a mass of taboos and repressions that gave it the appearance of an impenetrable jungle. He wondered why human sex habits couldn't be studied with the same scientific objectivity and recorded with the same detached precision as were the sex habits of lower animals" (Deutsch 5). The report was called a "light" shed on the "behavior of the great body of the nation . . . a start toward realism in dealing with social problems" (Ernst and Loth 16). And it "exploded like a bombshell" (Kirkpatrick 391). Considered a major breakthrough by many (Kinsey himself was compared to Darwin, Freud, and Copernicus), the report was attacked by others as an "amoral, mechanistic, dehumanized approach to the sacred subject of sex and as a menace to the stability of the American family" (Deutsch 2). Within a few weeks of publication, it was near the top of the best-seller list, and it provoked a blizzard of commentary: reviews, symposia, digests, articles, books, and naturally countless references (many satiric) in the popular media. Public discourse concerning human sexuality suddenly became a national pastime—even, it seemed, an obsession. One month prior to the appearance of Kinsey's book, *A Streetcar Named Desire* opened on Broadway (December 3, 1947).

Williams's play is art, not science, but it can certainly be read as a "discourse on sexuality," and as such it, too, lends itself to an analysis from Foucault's point of view. If, for example, Kinsey proved that sexual desires (and practices) generally considered rare and/or abnormal were not, in fact, peripheral, but common, lodged in the average home and the normal heart, Williams dramatized this point on stage.[3] Like Kinsey, his central strategy was talk, self-revelation; the structure of *Streetcar* can be seen as a series of confessions, some forced, others voluntary, in which the marginal figure (Blanche) is reclassified as an object of purely sexual knowledge. Public response to the play was also remarkably similar. Like *Sexual Behavior*, and for many of the same reasons, *Streetcar* was perceived initially in terms of sexual transgression—a "*Glans Menagerie*" in George Jean Nathan's famous phrase (163), in which all forms of human sexuality (decent and indecent) were publicly exhibited, celebrated and (according to some) exploited. Eric Bentley, for instance, reported that "early audiences . . . fairly licked their chops over the sexiness of the play" (88). Finally, such incitement was attacked on religious and political grounds and defended on sociological and psychological: what on the one hand represented obscenity and moral decadence, became, on the other, an example of honesty, truth, a light turned on, a frank and open exploration of sexual maladjustment. In any case, the framework of perception was the same: repression. In short, both Kinsey's book and Williams's play exemplify the "peculiar" strategy by which modern Western societies use abnormal sexuality (along with other forms of marginal behavior) to formulate and institute "technologies of power" (HS 35, 82). There is, however, a difference: reading Kinsey, one can see these power relations at work in the abstract, fully deployed in the domain of sexual science; watching Williams's play, one can learn *how* they work and what they mean in human terms.

The history of madness could be described as the history of the Other, of what is for a culture both internal and foreign and therefore to be excluded (so as to exorcise the internal danger). But this is done by shutting it away (so as to reduce its otherness). The history of the order of things could be described as the history of the Same, of what is for a culture both dispersed and related, therefore to be distinguished by kinds and collected together into identities (Foucault, *Order* xxiv).

It is surely one of the great moments in modern world drama, the first encounter of Blanche DuBois and Stanley Kowalski. "You must be Stanley. I'm Blanche." "Stella's sister?" (265). Of course: What other Blanche could she be? But Stanley is not satisfied, and his first simple question begins a quiet, casual, but increasingly charged interrogation that ends minutes later with Blanche about to be "sick," forced to speak of the central, agonizing event of her past, the death of her boy-husband Allan Grey ("The boy— the boy died" [268]). The shape of this short scene mirrors the overall dramatic shape of Williams's play (Blanche's exposure and defeat); employs its central interactive strategy (interrogation and confession); and states the major dramatic question: Who is this strange woman—moth-like, *"incongruous"* (245)—who has arrived unannounced and uninvited, at night, claiming kinship and a place at the hearth?

Situated at a moment in American history in which the sexual limits of the culture came sharply and vividly into focus, it is not surprising that audiences and critics alike first answered this question in sexual terms. Blanche was immediately and widely perceived as a sign for sexual maladjustment, whatever the response evoked or required. For many she was simply a prostitute, a nymphomaniac, or both.[4] Ironically, such a reading, at the *sexual* limits, has serious limits of its own. Most important, it can obscure an understanding of the power relations at work in Williams's play by restricting awareness of the true scope of Blanche's power. Surely sexuality is a key term in Williams's configuration of the otherness of Blanche DuBois, but it is by no means the only term, and it becomes, in fact, the term that finally *limits* her power, allows her to be contained, silenced, excluded, and confined. To read Blanche's character principally as a study of sexual abnormality is, simply, to read it clinically, to read it from the point of view of the Doctor and the Matron who take her away.

The process of exclusion and confinement of the Other is a central theme in all of Foucault's work, and he examines it by looking at the origins (in the late eighteenth and early nineteenth centuries) of three modern institutions: the clinic, the prison, and the asylum. Each operates by dividing individuals into categories: sick/healthy, criminal/law-abiding, mad/sane—and each internally uses similar "disciplinary" techniques.[5] Each also shares a common ancestry in the "houses of internment" of the seventeenth century (HF 57, 38). These earlier institutions, however, had a very different profile and purpose: They were "prisons of moral order" whose task was to protect society (HF 94). Anyone regarded as a threat to society at any point or level might be confined: the poor, the unemployed, the sick, venereals, homosexuals, prostitutes, the sexually promiscuous, blasphemers, witches, profligates, free thinkers, libertines, the insane, even violators of family order (in France, for instance, by simply obtaining a *lettre de cachet en famille*). This latter group might include noisy women, prodigal sons, and daughters whose passions were overexcited by reading too much romance literature (HF 97–134). And all were housed together; there was no separation. To the modern mind, this "process of exclusion" seems indiscriminate, irrational, even incomprehensible, but Foucault explains it as a product of the Age of Reason (a term he uses interchangeably with "the classical age"). From this "mode of perception," a moral society required the rational mind: the ability to arrive at true judgment and correct conduct (HF 66–67, 92). Refusal to behave in a socially acceptable manner (and this was a matter of will, not incapacity) not only violated the social contract, it separated the individual from the category of Reason. Thus, alienation from Reason, its absence, Unreason, was the coherent and unitary category that subsumed the behavior of all the inmates in the houses of internment of the classical age (HF 100–6). It also accounts for the cruel manner in which they were treated: during this period, the distinction between Reason and Unreason was equally a distinction between human and nonhuman (HF 190). Unreason, then, was a huge, polymorphous, all-encompassing term for otherness—anything and everything that threatened the Same (HF 436).

This is what Blanche DuBois really represents. Frail, delicate, she enters the Utopian world of Elysian Fields like a ghost and simply expands; endlessly talking, she gathers and multiplies images of disruption and discontinuity until they threaten to consume the family, the community, the house, the stage itself. Her symbolic power becomes immense, but her strategy is simple: to defend herself by taking control of the Same; to reconstitute her otherness (her difference) as sameness. She attacks at three major points—Stella, Mitch, the flat itself—and at each point Blanche's otherness organizes itself around different modalities of Unreason.

At first, she is a powerful symbol of indigence. Homeless, jobless, she enters with a valise (245), and her trunk contains everything she owns (281). Not only is she a "destitute woman" (396), she is the archetypic "poor relation" (337), and it is these two factors, her poverty and her kinship (not her sexual history), that make the strongest claim on Stella and put the most pressure on her marriage. The sexual tension that undeniably exists between Blanche and Stanley from the beginning is much less important in the early scenes of the play than Blanche's confession of the loss of Belle Reve. Stanley, fooled by her glamorous wardrobe, immediately suspects her of fraud; he dismisses her flirtation and concentrates on the fact that under the Napoleonic Code, whatever belongs to Stella belongs to him. Property is the issue. Blanche's poverty becomes his own (280–84).

Even more disturbing is the relationship between Blanche and Stella. Blanche is "my sister" (416) and Stella, of course, must take her in, but Blanche's presence reconnects Stella to her past, to Belle Reve and to what it represents: "sickness and dying" (262), profligacy, "epic fornications" (284). Alcoholic, hysterical, sexually "flighty" (364), Blanche stands for Stella's psychological inheritance: a threat not only to her marriage but to the baby in her womb. To protect her family from this morbid legacy, Stella must reject Blanche and reaffirm her new life with Stanley. This she does in the famous climax to the drunken Poker Night, a scene that begins with the two sisters tightly bonded against the men in the kitchen and ends with Blanche outside the flat (whose walls have become opaque), separated from the site of healthy sexual union, the Kowalski marriage bed (305–7). From this moment on, until the very end of the play, Stella is firmly allied with Stanley. Williams establishes this clearly and decisively in the scene that follows. Although it contains Blanche's strongest appeal to her sister ("Don't hang back with the brutes"), at no point is Stella's allegiance to her husband in question, and at the end of the scene, she embraces him *with both arms, fiercely, and in full view of Blanche* (323–24). Throughout Stella is unequivocally the loyal wife, defender of conjugal "love" (321), sacred repository of *new maternity* (310). Although the imagery Williams uses to describe Stella in the stage directions that open this scene may be ambiguous (for instance, the *choral chant* from the street combined with Stella's book of *colored comics*), the difference between Stella and her sister is not. *[Blanche's] appearance entirely contrasts with Stella* (310). Within the site of the family, Blanche has failed to take control of the Same; her otherness has been firmly reestablished and contained. At this point, the first movement of the play ends, and the figure of Blanche/Unreason is reconstituted around the dominant modalities of sex. The second pressure point is Mitch, the unmarried male friend.

When he first appears, Mitch is with Stanley, and Williams stresses their sameness—both are *about twenty-eight or thirty years old, roughly dressed in blue denim work clothes* (244). Later, we learn that they work together at the same plant, bowl on the same team, and served in the same "outfit" in the war (365). Mitch is Stanley's "best friend" (366). There is also something different about him. Blanche recognizes this instantly, and says so (292), but Williams establishes Mitch's difference even before the two meet, from the moment the poker game begins. "I'm out" are Mitch's first words in the scene (he repeats them twice more), and this out-ness is clearly connected to his unmarried status and to his "sick mother" (286–94). Stanley accuses him of being a momma's boy ("We'll fix you a sugar tit" [288]) and there is even a sexual undercurrent to his teasing ("Git y'r ass off the table, Mitch" [287]); this is picked up by Stella when she tells Blanche that she doesn't think that Mitch would be a "wolf" (292). Mitch's sensitivity, then, immediately puts his manhood into question. "Hello!" Blanche says, as Mitch steps "*uncomfortably*" through the portieres. "The Little Boys' Room is busy right now" (296).

Just as Stella is linked to Blanche by their literal kinship, Mitch, it turns out, is linked to Blanche by a kinship of temperament. He is shy, modest, with romantic yearnings and an (unformed) aesthetic sensibility—as Blanche puts it, a "natural gentleman" (348). And as she does earlier with Stella, Blanche attempts to forge this common difference into sameness; again, to take control of the Same—Mitch's bond to Stanley and his community of men. But if Stella's kinship to Blanche connects her to the legacy of Belle Reve, Mitch's connects him to the symbolic value of Allan Grey. Williams foreshadows this linkage when Mitch, in their first meeting, tells Blanche the story of his silver cigarette case (a gift from a "very strange girl" who was dying) and insists that she read the inscription from Mrs. Browning: "I shall but love thee better—after—death" (297–98). The connection becomes explicit when Blanche tells Mitch (and only Mitch) the story of "the person I loved" and "lost" (353–55). It is Mitch's finest moment; as he hears Blanche's confession, he seems to gain in stature and substance; he matures and becomes, for a moment at least, a man of strength and compassion; in her eyes, a "God" (356). Blanche's miraculous salvation (religious imagery stresses the point) is, of course, an illusion; ironically, it is also the moment in which Mitch is most at risk. At the root of Blanche's sexual disorder is Allan Grey's homosexuality, not her sentimental rationalization about "deliberate cruelty" to others (397), and around this terrible secret Williams develops a complex cluster of references to other forms of deviant behavior: promiscuity, prostitution, sexual obsession, and pedophilia, in addition to homosexuality. Mitch's temperamental sameness to Blanche clearly implies the possibility, at least, of a sexual sameness, and in their growing attachment (which promises to end in marriage), that possibility is thrown into sharp relief. Unmanly sensitivity, disease, arrested adolescence, even sexual confusion, have all symbolically planted their seeds in Mitch; Blanche's presence threatens to make these seeds grow. In short, there are actually two major questions dominating the Blanche-Mitch movement of Williams's play: one, whether Blanche will succeed in getting Mitch to marry her; the other, whether Mitch will escape the sexual fate she represents, with its connections, finally, to madness and death.

Mitch's escape, of course, is actually a rescue. As he did with Stella, Stanley steps in. The pattern of action repeats itself: confession, interrogation, physical violence, sexual dominance. Just as earlier Blanche confesses her loss of Belle Reve to Stella (206–62), she now confesses her loss of Allan Grey to Mitch (353–55). These acts of contrition fail to save her; in each case, a second confession is demanded. Stanley conducts the first of these himself (about Belle Reve); he stage manages the second. If the model for Blanche's initial confession to Mitch is religious, with Blanche as penitent and Mitch as priest, the model for the second is judicial. Just as Stanley does in scene 2, Mitch becomes Blanche's interrogator (and torturer). Using evidence supplied by Stanley, he forces Blanche to confess the whole truth about her secret sexual life, and this confession elicits not compassion, forgiveness, the promise of salvation, but severe physical punishment—rape. It is carried out by Stanley after Mitch is unable to do it himself. If Blanche's strategy is to reconstitute her difference by taking control of the Same, Stanley's task is to defend his control of the Same by reaffirming Blanche's difference.[6] This he does decisively at the end of the second movement of the play by redefining the "truth" about Blanche solely in terms of her sexual misdeeds (258–64). In short, he transforms her from an exploding symbol of Unreason to a contained sign (the rape is the signifying act) linking sexual promiscuity and madness. According to Foucault's view of Western social history, this is precisely what happened at the end of the eighteenth century: The broad category of Unreason was divided up and replaced with new, narrowly defined categories and classifications by the modern disciplinary institutions of the nineteenth century (HF 557–612).

Finally, Stanley's rape of Blanche not only pins her down as a sexual object, but also wrests the house itself (and the stage) from her control. From the beginning, Blanche moves decisively against the flat, the space, and the world of the play. First she tries to establish its difference (from Belle Reve), then she tries to transform it, and finally her mind, her imagination, threatens to consume it. It is this movement, overriding the other two, that reveals the deep sources of Blanche's power as a figure of Unreason, its roots in the supernatural.

When Blanche enters, Williams has already established the sameness of the setting—a place of perfect happiness, a romantic, sexually frank, and healthy playground where the races intermingle easily, a lyrical "*Blue Piano*" plays in the background, and overhead "*a tender blue sky gracefully attenuates the atmosphere of decay*" (243). Historically and realistically, the French Quarter of New Orleans should be a perfect final resting place for Blanche DuBois (one of the famous American bohemian enclaves, it served for two hundred years as a kind of grand bordello for the Mississippi Valley), but Williams mutes its marginality in this opening scene, creating instead an idealized tableau of urban working-class life. It is only with Blanche's appearance that the darker connotations of the place emerge, that we learn its name, Elysian Fields (the abode of the blessed after death), and the names of the streetcars, Desire and Cemeteries (246), she had to take to get there. These details, in fact, seem as much a part of Blanche's symbolic presence as they do of the setting, and they foreshadow her attempt, when Stella returns, to reconstitute the place as different from Belle Reve—as a "horrible" nightmare, as "the ghoul-haunted woodland of Weir" (251–52).

This move fails. Belle Reve, after all, is gone, and in any case, its value as a point of reference against which to measure the difference of Stella's new home is immediately undercut by Blanche herself as she tells the sad and sordid tale of its loss: "the long parade to the graveyard" (261). Forced to live in the present, and in the Kowalski's two-room flat (indeed, like Cinderella on a pallet in the kitchen), Blanche proceeds to take it over and to make it over. By scene 2, she has requisitioned the bath (it and Stella's dressing table, with the mirror, become her special places for the rest of the play), and she turns Stanley's bedroom (her trunk now stands there, prominently placed) into a dressing room; her new *"flowered print"* dress even lies across his bed (269). This is the first of a series of transformations. While she redecorates—a Chinese lantern over the naked light bulb (300), a new bedspread (382), new upholstery (379)—she redefines. Her imagination changes the bedroom into a peep-show (296), a Left Bank artists' cafe (344), a ballroom (391). The dominant metaphor throughout is theatrical: as Blanche feminizes Stanley's flat (makes it, in Mitch's words, "a house with women" [303]), she theatricalizes it, subverting its reality, even altering time and space. When the Young Man (who's collecting for the *Morning Star*) steps through her portieres, he is, in a sense, stepping into Blanche's dream[7]—"a little piece of Eternity" (338). This point becomes dramatically explicit in the rape scene. Essentially realistic, Williams's play uses a series of expressionistic devices to reveal Blanche's emotional interior. The most obvious of these (and the first used) is the music she hears whenever she remembers the death of Allan Grey. But there are others, visual as well as auditory, which become increasingly prevalent as Blanche becomes increasingly unhinged. Many of these are drawn from reality (the locomotive, for instance), but under the influence of Blanche's neurotic presence, they become subjectified.[8] Finally, in scene 10, they take over the stage. This scene, the climax of the play, begins realistically enough. Blanche, to be sure, is dressed outlandishly in a faded white satin ball gown and rhinestone tiara, drunk and talking about "taking a moonlight swim at the old rock-quarry" (390). But the *"spectral admirers"* she addresses are invisible, and when Stanley returns, he pulls her roughly back into the real world by ridiculing her behavior ("What queen do you think you are?") and exposing her lies (398). As Blanche's terror grows, however, her imagination (her subjective reality) asserts itself, and the style of the scene shifts from realism to expressionism: Blanche's mind takes over the space. Suddenly *"inhuman voices like cries in the jungle fill the night, shadows and lurid reflections move sinuously as flames along the wall space"* (399). Finally, the line (the limit) between inside and outside collapses as the walls of the flat disappear and a tawdry vision of life at the sexual margins materializes. Surely these images reflect the intensity of Blanche's fear, her sense of being trapped and under attack, but if madness is a kind of fury that threatens not only to consume the mind but to destroy the world (as the Age of Reason said it was), this moment reveals Blanche at her most dangerous (HF 136, 189).

It also exposes, literally, the primal source of her power, its subconscious or preconscious roots in the irrational, its spiritual pedigree. In the course of the play, Williams connects Blanche to several famous romantic hero-ines—among them Strauss's Marschelin, Mae West, and Camille—but these are only modern impersonations of a sisterhood that stretches further back and finds its origins in fable and myth. Behind the pathetic refugee (real-istically drawn), Williams creates an expanding symbolist shadow—the pri-mordial feminine Other in its most threatening and entrancing (to the male) aspects: enchantress, witch, and faery queen.[9] He develops this relationship poetically, through a dense, complex, at times ironic and witty pattern of imagery. In brief, Blanche may be looking for a "cleft in the rock of the world" (387), but figuratively she is all air, fire, and water. Her planet is the moon (355, 360, 391); her time of day is night (384); she prefers darkness to light (383); she wears *"flowery dresses"* (391), and seems "light as a feather" (347). She calls herself a "witch of a woman" (279) and later writes to Shep Huntleigh of her "summer on the wing, making flying visits here and there"; she threatens to "swoop down" on him in Dallas (325). Her age is indeterminate (352). She is a virgin ("Virgo" 329), an "old maid" (300), a wife, a widow (364). She even seems to change her shape at will: "Who is this sister of yours," Stanley demands, "a deep sea diver?" (274). Like Ondine (the nymph who had to marry a human to gain a soul), she seems to live in water: she spends hours "soaking in a hot tub" (269); the Kowalski bath is her magic well (374). Her dominant color is spectral white (ironic symbol of purity), but underneath, in private, she wears red (276, 297). Childless, avid for love, her gaze eroticizes the male body (on stage) and binds it to fantasies of adolescent sexuality: the army makes men of boys; Blanche makes boys of men (285). Finally, as reality closes in on her ("She'll go *Tuesday*!...Her future is mapped out for her" [367]), fire be-comes her figure; she threatens to burn down the house (390, 399). It is this huge shadow, then, this ancient Soul—desperate, lost, and out of time—that ultimately challenges Stanley's power, and it goes with Blanche as he carries her to bed.

It seemed to me interesting to try to understand our society and civilization in terms of its system of exclusion,... in terms of what it does not want, the limits, the way it is obliged to suppress a certain number of things, people, processes, what it must let fall into oblivion, its repression-suppression system. (Foucault, "Conversation" 192)

Anxious about meeting her sister's new husband for the first time, Blanche questions Stella about Stanley. "Is he so different?" she finally asks. "A different species," Stella replies (257–58). Different, obviously, from the men of Belle Reve. In the world of Elysian Fields, on the other hand, Stanley represents the Same, the organizing principle around which life is centered and revolves. This principle is defined throughout the play in predominantly sexual terms. Described at different times as an "ape" (323), a "pig" (371), a "goat" (his sign is Capricorn [328]), a "*baying hound*" (306), a "survivor of the stone age" (323), Stanley is also "*the gaudy seed-bearer*" (265), father of Stella's "son" (395). (No one assumes that their child will be anything but male.)[10] Stanley's "animal force" (319) promises to regenerate the decadent DuBois genseo. He is, on the most basic level, an icon of male heterosexual power. He is also something more. If the "classical" figure of Unreason can help to illuminate the true range and reach of Blanche's power, then another key figure (according to Foucault) from this same period can throw additional light on Stanley—the absolute monarch, the source of all *political* power.

Williams makes the metaphoric connection clearly. Stanley may be the "unrefined type" (268), but he speaks with "*lordly composure*" (269); he may be "on the primitive side" (279), but he also has "an impressive judicial air" (281); he may not have been a "very good English student" (267), but he still represents the Law, and he summons the Napoleonic Code to support his case for a stake in Stella's property (280–81). In short, Stanley is "the king around here" (371), the Huey Long of Elysian Fields. He is also, as Blanche puts it, "my executioner" (351). This, too, is a typical motif of the figure of the king as described by Foucault. In brief, at the same time that the houses of internment were confining a broad range of social misfits under the category of Unreason, criminal acts (infractions of the Law) were more often dealt with not by internment but by immediate punishment, in serious cases by the public infliction of bodily pain (DP 3–31). The reason for this was that every violation of the law was regarded as a kind of regicide. Publicly staged corporal punishment, "*supplices*," thus became a juridico-political reassertion of sovereignty (DP 33, 48–49). This was an essential characteristic of the *ancien régime* of punishment. It is also the way that Stanley operates against Blanche. Reform, treatment, understanding are simply not in his conceptual vocabulary. He lives in a different (premodern) world, where the "will to knowledge" is exercised through interrogation, and punishment is registered physically. Stanley's rape of Blanche, then, is simply one of a series of moves (beginning with the nausea induced by his questioning) in which the power of the king is inscribed, literally and figuratively, on Blanche's body. The culmination of this, in fact, is not the rape but the final scene, a kind of *supplice* staged by Stanley in which his people are brought together (thus the problematic poker game at such an odd moment) and made to witness a final demonstration and reassertion of the king's power and control. In it, Blanche is displayed, humiliated, and punished—symbolically raped *twice* (once when Stanley rips down her Chinese lantern [416], as Mitch does earlier [384], and again when the Matron wrestles her to the floor and announces that her nails must be trimmed [417]). The staginess of this final scene (to which Bentley objected [88]) is intentional. The end of the play refers, metatheatrically, to countless earlier stage executions, complete with weeping but impotent friends and relatives at the foot of the scaffold. Blanche's romantic fantasy of a death at sea, as she dresses for her long walk (back and forth across the stage in the Kazan/Mielziner version) ironically foreshadows and underscores this theme (410).

Despite his central role in Blanche's *supplice*, however, Stanley is not in total control at the end of Williams's play. There are other power relationships at work, one represented by Stella, the other by Blanche. It is Blanche, indeed, who has the final move. To return to Foucault: By the late eighteenth century, he argues, modes of punishment founded on spectacle and physical pain were gradually being replaced by the reformist penal institutions characteristic of modern society—institutions based on continuous surveillance (discipline in the original sense of the word), sites for the observation, analysis, and instruction of confined individuals (DP 7–16, 218–28). The object of punishment, therefore, shifted from the body of the condemned to the personhood, the soul. This humanization of the penal system, which occurred as the social sciences emerged, was apparent in other institutions as well: the factory, the army, the school, the hospital, and the asylum. The asylum, of course, figures prominently at the end of Williams's play. Stanley may be staging a demonstration of his victory over Blanche in the final scene, but technically, at least, the prisoner is being handed over to a different, newer "technique of power" (DP 148), the mental institution. Its representatives are the Doctor and the Matron, and they have been summoned to the house not by Stanley but by Stella—"I don't know if *I* did the right thing" (405) and "What have *I* done to my sister?" (416 [emphases mine]). Her anguish at this moment, and her earlier, minimal pleas for tolerance (358) notwithstanding, Stella clearly regards herself throughout the play as Stanley's partner, and it is her love for him that validates his role as husband and father-to-be as well as his rule as the king. Stanley's brutality to her is diffused by the powerful images of physical health, sexual vitality, and procreation in which they both participate as one. (This oneness is the point of their coming together at the end of the fight in scene 3, and it is restated at the end of scene 4.) Also, Stella's allegiance to Stanley helps to attract the allegiance of the audience, and it is a powerful factor in defending Stanley's control of the Same. In the final scene, however, something about this relationship seems to have changed. As Stanley gloats, Stella sobs cathartically (*"inhuman abandon"* [419]), and it is surely possible to regard her as the one who has rescued Blanche from Stanley's *ancien régime* of corporal punishment, as the character who now stands for a more humane (and modern) disciplinary modality, one that sends Blanche not back to Laurel (or to the streets) but to a safe haven in a home for the mentally disturbed. Such a reading, however, seems questionable. What, for example, has been "the system of exclusion" ("Conversation" 193)? As Bentley says, "Can a sister just send someone to an asylum without any medical advice? If so, which of us is safe? And even if Blanche is mad at this moment, will she remain so?" (88–89). In other words, can her rescue really be seen in humanistic terms, or is it simply a question of a *lettre de cachet en famille*, another version of Stanley's way, updated and made more palatable to modern sensibilities? As Foucault sees it, internment, whatever the rationale, is always a kind of exorcism, a rite of purification, an emblem of anxiety (HF 210, 429–39). Here these ritualistic elements are dominant. As the church bells chime out over the Quarter, Eunice (whose name means "good victory" and who is the central choric figure in the play) pronounces Stella's absolution and Blanche's epigraph: "You done the right thing, the only thing you could do. She couldn't stay here; there wasn't no other place for her to go" (416–17). At the same time, Williams shows what Blanche has ahead of her. In *Histoire de la folie*, Foucault describes the new reformist techniques of the asylum as a process whereby the mentally ill (as they then came to be known) were freed from the chains of classical internment only to be subjected instead to a new regime of power, one which used the threat of corporal punishment to enforce *moral* authority (psychological constraint). Inmates then were urged to enact a cure (become rational) by assuming the personae of acceptable social types (HF 581–90). This is precisely what happens in the scene between Blanche, the Matron, and the Doctor (417–18). First, Blanche is freed from the Matron's physical constraint by the humanistic intervention of the Doctor. Then the Doctor's moral authority reconstitutes her as "Miss DuBois." Finally, she responds (as she must or risk further restraint by the Matron) by reassuming her genteel social role ("the kindness of strangers"). Such a "liberation," Foucault argues, is a "myth"—one technique of control has simply been exchanged for another (HF 558, 579, 581–604). Williams would seem to agree. Placed within the context of Stanley's *supplice*, this scene shows Blanche's institutionalization (and Stella's intervention) for what it truly is—not a promise of salvation or redemption, but simply a different style of subjugation, one that takes its victims out of sight (off stage) and substitutes psychological discipline (a kind of "moralising sadism" [*Mental* 87]) for the infliction of bodily pain. On this point at least, the apparent difference between Stanley and Stella is revealed to be no difference at all. Both are guardians of the Same.

There is another moment, however, at the very end of the play, in which Stella's relationship to Stanley is ambiguously defined. Blanche's ritual subjectification and her transfer from one modality of power to another surely may be seen as the final defeat of Unreason in the play: the reestablishment of the safety, stability, and sanctity of the family, a reaffirmation of the need for vigilance and action against the forces of discontinuity and rupture. The final moment between Stella and Stanley might even be played as an eroticized Nativity Scene, complete with the Kowalski babe wrapped in a *"pale blue blanket"* (418). And yet there is something troubling about this tableau, at least as it appears on the page—a sort of separation between Stella and Stanley, even as he *"kneels beside her"* and feels for her breast (419). It is more implied than stated, and yet (if Stella's reticence, her lack of response to Stanley's move, is played) it points to a sense that something in their relationship has been fundamentally redefined or lost. And of course it has: Blanche has come and gone, and she has not, after all, burned down the house, but she has changed this world.

A central thesis runs in varying ways through much of Foucault's work: The individualizing mechanisms of modern civilization are focused on figures situated at the margins of society. Thus, he writes in *Discipline and Punish*, "When one wishes to individualize the sane, normal and law-abiding adult, it is always by questioning how much of the child he has within him, by what secret madness he is inhabited, what fundamental crime he has wished to commit" (195). This describes the central thematic strategy of Williams's play (indeed, of his entire work). Williams opens *Streetcar* with a vision of Utopia, brings Blanche/Unreason into it, and then moves her, literally, to the center of the home. At first, like Eunice, the audience perceives Blanche as an outsider, but when Eunice is sent away, and Blanche begins to inspect Stella's kitchen, she gathers our gaze and we begin to see the world through her eyes. From then on, no matter how her difference is defined and displayed, something of this point of view remains. As each of Williams's "normal" characters responds to Blanche's presence, she individualizes him or her in terms of what she represents, aspects of her condition and character. Her perceptions uncover and reveal the "secret" elements within: who each truly is (or might become). At the heart of Stella's love (her loyalty and devotion), Blanche locates sexual addiction and infantilism. In Mitch's natural gentility, she reveals a mother fixation, moral cowardice, and the potential for sexual assault. Finally, she reconstitutes Stanley's paternalism as a kind of domestic tyranny where rape and adultery are male prerogatives. The rape scene demonstrates this process at work: Ironically, just as Stanley (defender of the Same) pins down Blanche (proliferating Other) as a controllable sign for sexual lunacy, she pins *him* down as a sexual outlaw. She implants her otherness *in him*. It is this that stands between Stella and Stanley at the end of Williams's play. Stella may not "believe" Blanche's accusation (405), but she knows it as a possibility. She reads Stanley differently now—in terms of Blanche. This is Williams's project, as it is Kinsey's and Foucault's—to relocate the Other within man's own nature, within the Same. "Only passing through" (413), Blanche leaves us "with a broken world" (239), fractured and haunted by "secrets" of its own.

In *Histoire de la folie*, Foucault defines the modern asylum as an analytical space in which the judges of normalcy consider the question of the marginal figure—examine and evaluate behavior considered antisocial if not illegal (599–603). In a way, Williams's theatre does the same, inviting a psychoanalytic response. Although Stanley and Stella subjectify Blanche as a manageable sign linking sexual abnormalcy and mental disorder, the audience, relieved, can now focus simply and safely on the psychosexual pathology of Blanche DuBois—and her creator. The theatre itself becomes the asylum to which Blanche, and Williams, are condemned. Reading *A Streetcar Named Desire* by way of Foucault can help to free the play, and its author, from this ironic confinement, this "disciplinary" site. And it can return them both to the dangerous, disruptive, and marginal world where they both belong.

NOTES

1. This relationship might also be demonstrated using other texts by Foucault, most notably *The Order of Things*, but I have chosen to focus on these three key works because the correspondences here seem most direct and most resonant. Foucault suggested that his writing be viewed as a "tool box" containing a variety of ideas and strategies that might be used when appropriate and without regard for a totalizing system ("Des supplices"). The English translations of *Surveiller et punir* (*Discipline and Punish*) and *Histoire de la sexualité, T 1*, (*History of Sexuality*) are complete and adequate, and I have used them throughout. The English translation of *Histoire de la folie* (*Madness and Civilization*) has been radically abridged, and I am thus using the original, keeping the title in French; the English translations from this text are mine. Where necessary, I use the following initials to indicate the work cited: *Histoire de la folie* (HF); *Discipline and Punish* (DP); *History of Sexuality* (HS).

2. Throughout his work, Foucault urges the adoption of a "limit-attitude," an analysis of and reflection upon the limits. "The Kantian question was that of knowing what limits knowledge has to renounce transgressing," he writes in "What Is Enlightenment," "[but today it seems that the] critical question...has to be turned back into a positive one: in what is given to us as universal, necessary, obligatory, what place is occupied by whatever is singular, contingent, and the product of arbitrary constraints" (45)? This is also Williams's central question and strategy.

3. A passage from Foucault that develops this idea seems remarkably relevant to Williams's play and deserves to be quoted, at least in part. "In the family, parents and relatives became the chief agents of a deployment of sexuality which drew its outside support from doctors, educators and later psychiatrists.... Then these new personages made their appearance: the nervous woman, the frigid wife, the indif-

ferent mother...the impotent, sadistic, perverse husband, the hysterical or neurasthenic girl, the precocious and already exhausted child, and the young homosexual
who rejects marriage and neglects his wife. These were the combined figures of an
alliance gone bad and an abnormal sexuality; they were the means by which the
disturbing factors of the latter were brought into the former; and yet they also
provided an opportunity for the alliance system to assert its prerogatives in the order
of sexuality....from the mid-nineteenth century onward, the family engaged in
searching out the slightest traces of sexuality in its midst, wrenching from itself the
most difficult confessions, soliciting an audience with everyone who might know
something about the matter, and opening itself unreservedly to endless examination.
The family was the crystal in the deployment of sexuality..." (HS 111).

4. See, for example, Richard Watts, Jr. *New York Post* 4 Dec. 1947: n.p.;
Howard Barnes, "O'Neill Status Won by Author of 'Streetcar'," *The New York
Herald Tribune* 14 Dec. 1947: V1; John Mason Brown, "Southern Discomfort,"
The Saturday Review 27 Dec. 1947: 22–24; *Newsweek* 15 Dec. 1947: 82–83; *Time*
15 Dec. 1947: 85; Nathan 163.

5. Foucault uses the word *discipline* in the sense of *training*: "Instead of bending
all its subjects into a single uniform mass, it [disciplinary power] separates, analyses,
differentiates, carries its procedures of decomposition to the point of necessary and
sufficient single units" (DP 170).

6. Stanley also reclaims Mitch's sameness, a fact that Williams stresses by having
Mitch appear in scene 10 in the same blue denim work clothes (379) that he and
Stanley both wore at the beginning of the play. Blanche also recognizes this change
when she explicitly refers to Mitch's "different" behavior (381) and their "different"
backgrounds (397).

7. The ambiguous reality of this scene, its position (slightly) out of time, somewhere between dreaming and waking, is clearly indicated by Williams's stage direction. *"Her eyes fall shut and the palm leaf fan drops from her fingers. She slaps
her hand on the chair a couple of times. There is a little glimmer of lightning about
the building"* (336).

8. It is possible to trace this process of subjectification for each of the major
audiovisual signs, the Blue Piano (with its growing accompaniment of trumpet and
drums), the locomotive, the thunder and lightning, the fire. The key transitional
moment is the scene with the Young Man. Prior to that—with one exception, the
"dissonant brass and piano sounds" (305–6) that accompany Stanley in Scene 3—
all these effects are rooted in reality, despite their relevance as expressionistic subtext.
After this scene, the expressionistic (nonrealistic) element becomes dominant; they
are located primarily in Blanche's mind.

9. To understand more fully Blanche's symbolic relationship to the archetype
of the faery queen, see profiles of this figure in the following: A. D. Hope, *A Mid-
summer Eve's Dream: Variations on a Theme by William Dunbar* (New York:
Viking Press, 1970); Maureen Duffy, *The Erotic World of Faery* (London: Hodder
and Stoughton, 1972); Laurence Harf-Lancer, *Les fées au moyen âge* (Paris: Editions
Champion, 1984).

10. There are two references to the sex of the Kowalski child; both occur before
its birth. "Blanche: Oh, I hope candles are going to glow in his life and I hope that
his eyes are going to glow like candles..." (373–74). "Stanley: When the telephone

rings and they say, 'You've got a son!' I'll tear this off and wave it like a flag!" (395).

WORKS CITED

Bentley, Eric. *In Search of Theatre*. New York: Alfred A. Knopf, 1953.

Deutsch, Albert. "Kinsey, the Man and His Project." *Sex Habits of American Men: A Symposium on the Kinsey Report*. Ed. Albert Deutsch. New York: Prentice-Hall, 1948. 1–38.

Ernst, Morris L., and David Loth. *American Sexual Behavior and The Kinsey Report*. New York: Greystone Press, 1948.

Foucault, Michel. "A Conversation with Michel Foucault." *Partisan Review* 38 (1971): 192–201.

———. "Des supplices aux cellules." *Le Monde* 21 Feb. 1975: 16.

———. *Discipline and Punish*. Trans. Alan Sheridan. New York: Pantheon, 1977.

———. *Folie et déraison: histoire de la folie à l'âge classique*. Paris: Plon, 1961.

———. *The History of Sexuality, Volume I: An Introduction*. Trans. Robert Hurley. New York: Vintage Books, 1980.

———. *Mental Illness and Psychology*. Trans. Alan Sheridan. Berkeley: UP of California, 1976.

———. *The Order of Things: An Archeology of the Human Sciences*. London: Tavistock, 1970.

———. "What Is Enlightenment?" *The Foucault Reader*. Ed. and trans. Paul Rabinow. New York: Pantheon, 1984. 32–50.

Kirkpatrick, Clifford, Sheldon Stryker, and Philip Buell. "An Experimental Study of Attitudes Towards Male Sex Behavior with Reference to Kinsey Findings." *Sexual Behavior in American Society: An Appraisal of the First Two Kinsey Reports*. Ed. Jerome Himelhoch and Sylvia Fleis Fava. New York: W. W. Norton, 1955. 391–404.

Klassen, Albert D., Colin J. Williams, and Eugene E. Levitt. *Sex and Morality in the U.S.: An Empirical Enquiry under the Auspices of The Kinsey Institute*. Middleton: Wesleyan UP, 1989.

Nathan, George Jean. *The Theatre Book of the Year: 1947–48*. New York: Alfred A. Knopf, 1948.

Williams, Tennessee. *A Streetcar Named Desire. The Theatre of Tennessee Williams*. 7 vols. to date. New York: New Directions, 1971. Vol. 1: 239–419.

There Are Lives that Desire Does Not Sustain: *A Streetcar Named Desire*

Calvin Bedient

Tennessee Williams thought of himself as the Dionysus of modern American theater. He was more its Orpheus, I think, and what he could not bring back from the underworld, intact, was simplicity, unity, and purity—Apollonian virtues. With respect to persons, his Eurydice was a compound of his mother (Edwina) and his sister (Rose). Hades was his father (Cornelius), a virilized Dionysus, drunken and wanton.

How to get the women up without exposing them to Hades' death-bearing wrath? Indeed, how to escape the whole male community's vengeance for what looks like an incestuous compassion—for a melting complicity with women?

In Williams's play *Orpheus Descending*, Val, the snakeskin-jacketed hero, befriends two older married townswomen. One is a visionary primitive painter who believes that the Son has looked down on her from the sky and put his hand to her bosom; her husband sees her placing Val's hand there in imitation. The other, Lady, is a storekeeper maternally linked with food (her pet scheme is a confectionery, which on the stage, so Williams instructed, is "shadowy and poetic as some inner dimension of the play" [*Tennessee Williams: Four Plays*]); *she* becomes pregnant by him and is shot by her malignant, invalid husband, who is "death's self" (141). Eventually, the townsmen torch him alive as a menace to local decency. So it is that the play plays with the fire of nostalgia for the legendary union of mother and son. But this antisocial passion is forbidden; it offends the territorial rights of husbands. It is the serpent after it has left Eden.

Williams kept writing variants of this plot, trying to get it right. How to exorcise his own guilt both for being so attached to the family women and for hating them for it? If *A Streetcar Named Desire* is one of his stronger plays, the reason, in part, is that here Orpheus is missing. A more or less minor character, Mitch, has the opportunity to lead the heroine, Blanche

DuBois, out of her hell but muffs it. He is still too much of a boy, and too much a bungler, to be a hero. Blanche herself innocently directs this mother's boy to the "Little Boy's Room" soon after meeting him (296); his friends tell him that he needs a sugar tit; he carries a carnival statuette of Mae West upside down (some way to treat a lady); and his relationship to the regenerative sparagmos of the torn-apart god is a mock one: He works at the "precision bench in [a] spare parts department" (292). In this play, there is no one with whom the playwright could want to identify. To put it quite another way, he'd almost rather be Stanley Kowalski, Blanche's ultimate destroyer (though she has done most of the work of destruction herself), than Blanche. He keeps his balance; the snakeskin jacket, Orpheus's sign, stays in the closet.

Eurydice, then, is left to the mercy of her brother-in-law, Stanley, who rapes her in order to show her which sex is the master sex. There is some Dionysus in him: his sign is the Goat, he drinks, and he's a *"gaudy seed-bearer"* (265). But when he finds it convenient, he respects Apollonian law (though his rape violates it), and he is offended by what he takes to be Blanche's immoralism. In all, he acts out the playwright's own would-be potent vengeance against his castrating mother and sister. He is the Phallus through which going ahead is possible. How condemn him without cutting out one's own chance for an escape from women? How, on the other hand, condone his brutality?

Here, Williams is suspended between wanting to forgive his mother (who is more Blanche than Blanche is, a monster of Southern gentility, affectation, and affectless garrulity) and wanting to uproot her from his psyche. The play is more an elaboration of his quandary than its catharsis. The ending, in fact, is crushing. To cart the mother/sister away to a grim mental institution (Williams's sister was placed in several such institutions) is not a true purgation; on the contrary, it only darkens the guilt. So one leaves the theater or closes the book circumspectly, as if afraid to hurt further something already squashed. This something is a Eurydice who was not delivered from bondage but brought forward only to be sent back even more shattered, more hopeless, than before.

Blanche gets ground up between the mills of Williams's compassion and his condemnation. What is there to condemn? Primarily, the power of seduction—the archaic, maternal glamor that makes those seduced by it feel weak. It is against this unmanning seduction that Stanley declares his independence. His loudness, his drinking, his buddy system, all defend him against it. Who do women think they are, coming over one with their ball-busting pretensions to fragility, their contempt for a man's necessary, pushy virility? Turn the mother-woman out of the house. Slip your hand into your wife's blouse as she sobs luxuriously over the defeat of sisterhood and feminine sanctities. (Does she not secretly rejoice in the triumph of a harsh masculine order? After all, women, too, must fear the mother's seduction.) In sum, be a man.

The action of *Streetcar* consists of a masculinist rout of female abjection. Now, this is veritably *the* story of patriarchy. How well did Williams understand his own complicity in it? He is reported to have summed up the moral of his play as follows: "If we don't watch out, the apes will take over" (Quirino 88). But what Stanley really represents, in his brutish fashion, is the patriarchal order, and this order, in *its* fashion, stands as a bulwark against the primitivism of feminine abjection, the pull of the archaic mother. Because he is a speaking being, because he believes in "civilization," the playwright himself must oppose the abject identity-threatening corporeality that the mother, in her archaic guise, represents; more, he must fear the abyss on the far side of abjection—what Julia Kristeva calls "the archaic 'Thing,' the elusive preobject of a mourning that is endemic with all speaking beings" (*Black Sun* 152). Everyone buys into the "legal fiction known as symbolic activity," Kristeva adds, in order to "lose the Thing" (*Black Sun* 146). Only suicides and the depressive dumb or those who use words without any belief in them keep a kind of faith with the encrypted fantasy of the mother as the guarantee of her offspring's omnipotence.

Williams's plays stage ritual reenactments of the sacrifice of either the archaic mother or a mother-sodden son—the sort of sacrifice on which Western culture is based. I would argue that it was this very thing that helped ensure his power over his audiences. While the famed "poetry" of his theater uttered incest, his plots burned it at the stake.[1]

In the 1970s, Kristeva announced with revolutionary jubilation that theater in the United States was turning less resentful of "the ever-present constraints of power" in society. Instead, it was offering a "supple subjectivity, finding its catharsis in the deepest psychic clouds, . . . abreacting its death and its catastrophes." "The remaking of language," not communal interplay, had become its subject—the "reconstruction of the subjective space experienced by our modernity." This was accomplished, for instance, through "the silent theater of colors, sound and gestures," with its inclusion of the symbolic (that is, concepts) within the "semiotic" (that is, prelinguistic sensory phenomena) ("Modern Theater" 131–32).

Williams himself considered his words and thoughts subalterns to "the color, the grace and levitation, the structural pattern in motion" of his theater live. "*Dynamic*" was his mana-word for the stage (*Where I Live* 69). *Streetcar* is not only pervaded by snatches of music; it was originally called *The Primary Colors*, and the stage directions disclose the significance Williams placed in the stage colors. As if heeding Burke on the sublime, he sought strong hues reminiscent of Gauguin's and Van Gogh's aesthetic fundamentalism (i.e., primitivism). Did he hope thus to scare off the fainting moth of Blanche's real (as well as pretended) neurasthenia? Color Stanley green and scarlet, color Blanche scarlet and white: the two meet at a bloody intersection, as if in a painting in which the wildest colors had a "date with each other from the beginning" (402), in the words Stanley addresses to Blanche just before he rapes her.

Still, like the other Broadway playwrights, Williams did not contribute to the "most advanced experiments in writing"—those which, in Kristeva's words, "address themselves uniquely to the individual unconscious" ("Modern Theater" 131). In his list of the "dynamic" properties of his theater, he included "the quick interplay of live beings"—in other words, character. His own theater is, for all its "levitation," conventional or, to use a more honorific word, classical. Where he lived, the community still harried and brought down beautiful (that is, feminine) souls, urging the dogs of coarse sublimity against them.

As a boy, Williams himself was laughed at for his Southern gentility in St. Louis after the family moved there from Clarkesdale, Mississippi. Gangs of schoolboys followed him, calling "Sissy!"—or so he remembered. And he had been shocked by the "ugly rows of apartment buildings the color of dried blood and mustard"—depressive Van Gogh. It was in one such building that he lived.

"I am glad that I received this bitter education," he said, "for I don't think any writer has much purpose back of him unless he feels bitterly the inequities of the society he lives in" (*Where I Live* 59–60). But in Williams, social inequity is not a burning subject. *Orpheus Descending* and *Streetcar* (to stay with the two plays already compared) focus, instead, on the fragility of, respectively, an ingenuous and a disingenuous poetry of being, the false hope that the soft, mother-remembering soul can be spared from sacrifice.

To vary an earlier statement, Williams's plays enact the all-but-ritual purgation of abjection from the community. They would do for the audience and the playwright what his guitar does for Val, the hero of *Orpheus Descending*. "It washes me clean like water when anything unclean has touched me" (*Tennessee Williams: Four Plays* 50). In his foreword to *Sweet Bird of Youth*, he wrote:

If there is any truth in the Aristotelian idea that violence is purged by its poetic representation on a stage, then it may be that my cycle of violent plays have had a moral justification after all. . . . I have always felt a release from the sense of meaninglessness and death when a work of tragic intention has seemed to me to have achieved that intention. . . .

I would say that there is something bigger in life and death than we have become aware of (or adequately recorded) in our living and dying. And, further, to compound this shameless romanticism, I would say that our serious theater is a search for that something that is not yet successful but is still going on.

(*Three by Tennessee*, xii)

If Kristeva's piece on the new American theater leaves Williams covered by its avant-garde dust, her analysis of the "theological" sacrifice of the body in *Revolution in Poetic Language* points one to the cultural centrality of Williams's "tragic intention." More, *Powers of Horror: An Essay in Abjection*, her brilliant supplementation of Freud's (neglectful) discussion of incest, and *Black Sun*, her study of depression and its secret allegiance to the encrypted mother-Thing, help us to a view of the coherence and etiology of the ills in *Streetcar*, hence to an understanding of the play's jangly, if truthful, failed catharsis.

I shall leave the relevant arguments of *Revolution in Poetic Language* aside in this essay in order to concentrate on abjection and melancholy. To take up, first, the most difficult and unfinished of Williams's suggestions about serious modern theater, namely that it intimates "something much bigger in life and death than we have become aware of." Is this mysticism? If so, it is a mysticism of dread.[2] Williams brooded over "an underlying dreadfulness in modern experience." He intuited "something almost too incredible and shocking to talk about." But for that very reason, it is the one necessary subject, the one unavoidable truth. So Williams faulted Proust for not quite daring "to deliver the message of Absolute Dread." The atmosphere of Proust's work is "rather womb-like" (*Where I Live* 46).

Dread: life outside the maternal shelter? Life as a malady of grief, of death, because the disappearance of my omniscient beginnings, of my autoerotic fusion with the mother, "continues to deprive me of what is most worthwhile in me" (*Black Sun* 5). Dread, then, as the sensation of standing on the slippery lip of a depression (*Black Sun* 6):

The child king becomes irredeemably sad before uttering his first words; this is because he has been irrevocably, desperately separated from the mother, a loss that causes him to try to find her again...first in the imagination, then in words....if there is no writing other than the amorous, there is no imagination that is not, overtly or secretly, melancholy.

If this universal fatality of being a child seems, all the same, a *modern* malady, that may be due to the erosion of theological support for the symbolic order—the disappearance of consolatory myth. "As if overtaxed or destroyed by a too powerful a breaker," Kristeva writes in "The Malady of Grief: Duras" (*Black Sun*), "Our symbolic means find themselves hollowed out, nearly wiped out, paralyzed" (223)—which leaves more and more people prey to the mother-Thing, something prior to language and imperial enough to make a mockery of it, something maintained by jealously kept affects. A preobject, then, that keeps us from an attachment to objects, from the extroverted paths of desire, and that makes love implode into death, death into love.

Williams committed himself to the *truth* of unbearable anxiety. Blanche, accordingly, feels "a sense of disaster closing in on her," and she cries out: "Something has happened!—What is it!" (237). Near the end of the play, Williams assigns her a *"look of sorrowful perplexity as though all human experience shows on her face"* (407). She is the Mona Lisa of dread, the fragility and terror of the "I" exiled from the womb but still inside the mother-space where objects form in grief that this space should exist at all. Why does the world open if it then wants to fold up again? What a catastrophe should it revert back! *Let it do so!* No, *prevent it!*

What checks regression is, in Kristeva's view, the powerful horror of abjection: fear of the mother as murky and suffocating materiality, as mortally unclean. It is the (would-be) clean and proper "I" that conceives this dread of its own annihilation in mother-filth. Yet a lost maternal utopia nonetheless beckons to the fundamentally wounded, deficient, empty—that is, to everyone. Williams's "poetry" is, as already indicated, his wooing of it, the sign of his seduction by it.

What does Blanche herself have to respond to it with? She has "poetry" too—much to Stanley's contempt. But it is largely kitsch. Even to her, it is too little a thing to have. She also has alcohol, which she pours into the bottomless mug of her emptiness, betraying the presence in her of a little girl deprived of the breast. She has, in addition, the memory of the family estate, Belle Reve, but, splashed by several recent deaths within its walls, it has become hideous with abjection. Most of all, she has that involuntary fidelity to the mother-fantasy whose sign is an inability to feel desire. At most, she can only feel a desire for desire, or fake it.

Despite the play's title, Blanche is one of those whose lives, in Kristeva's words, "are not sustained by desire" (*Powers of Horror* 6). (In any case, in the play the streetcar named *Desire* is a poor, rattly thing and but leads to the cemetery). Desire is an object-seeking energy that exceeds our (necessary) narcissism; it is the "drive toward the other" (*Powers of Horror* 33). Blanche's narcissism lacks this sort of redirection, this egress from its self-absorption. If desire is abjection with its back turned, Blanche is too abject, too frightened at the shadowy borderland of subjective identity, to experience it. Her question is not "Whom shall I love?" but "How can I be?" As for her genteel idealizations, they are superficial, the glitter on a black body of water in which she is always about to drown.

To relax from the tensions and to escape the disgusts of abjection, Blanche takes long hot baths (these, however, are ambiguous, for they make her squeal with pleasure like a child as well as leave her feeling clean, purged of her fascination with the archaic mother). She also has her makeup and her fashionable or pretentious clothing, by which she treats herself as a mannequin, a static artifact—something as sculptural, faultless, bloodless, and seductive as the mother-idol that she has set up in a buried temple. By turning herself into an attractive *thing*, she both emulates and keeps a heartless distance from the fantasy of an inseparable (incarcerated) mother that her crushed omnipotence has fabricated.

How sedulously she seduces others! As if to keep from being seduced herself, to preserve herself intact and ready for the incestuous consummation that will restore her omnipotence. Far from committing her to others, her seductive airs cocoon her in a habit of make-believe. She will thus stay young, stay close to childhood! "For these last few remaining moments of our lives together," she says to Mitch, after a date that went poorly, "I want to create—joie de vivre. . . . We are going to pretend," and so on (344). Is not Blanche always in her last few moments, always pretending? Otherwise, she would have to say to life what she thinks men say to women who do not "entertain them"—"no dice!" (341).

Wherever she is, Blanche is already in a play; her existence in Williams's work is thus a sort of doubling of what she already is—an actress on a stage emptied of everything except the shadows of her fancy. Is she perhaps always playing to one hidden audience—a face blind, deaf, sublime, monumental as an Easter Island statue?

Given to continual self-creation and self-concealment, Blanche imitates her author. And, like Williams, she had a promiscuous interest in men, particularly young men: boys or boy-men (Mitch). For a homosexual male, other men can be loved as Narcissan reflections, or else as the Phallus the mother appealed to in asking the father-world to come and admire what *she* has produced, her child. But Blanche? Her psychology is more or less consistent with that of *feminine* depression as Kristeva presents it in *Black Sun*; to a depressed woman, eros is maddening, shattering. Virile Stanley is thus anathema to Blanche, like an alarm clock viciously clattering at the ear of Sleeping Beauty. If she pursues boys, it is doubtless because she can rule them, make toys of them, or use them as mirrors to her vanity. Any Prince Charming who calls her away from the mother *appears* only to wake her up. The youth who comes collecting for the newspaper (Blanche: "It would be nice to keep you, but I've got to be good—and keep my hands off children" [339]) is no more than a phallic statuette to match Mitch's plaster-doll Mae West, part of a Barnum and Bailey world.

Did Blanche really love her boy-husband, Allan Grey? All too desperately! All too idealistically! Evidently, she wanted a life above the flesh (Stella: "she thought him almost too fine to be human!" [364]). A life with that idealistic, if also regressive, being, *a poet*. But what was her aim—to *forsake* or to *recoup* the mother-Thing? The chance for recuperation consisted in the fact that her amorous idealization was trellised on an androgyne: "There was something different about the boy," Blanche says, "a . . . softness and tenderness that wasn't like a man's" (354). So her union with Allan was not a true break with the mother. Moreover, the boy seemed uncertain as to what he "needed" from Blanche, whether a liberation from, or an access to, his own encrypted Thing. She therefore had the power to destroy him, and she does.

First, Allan fails *her* by compromising his already equivocal status as the Phallus that can save her from the archaic engulfing mother. In having sex with an older man, Allan perhaps shows his own need for a father-rescuer. If Allan himself is not the Phallus, then is he not one with the abjection that the Phallus opposes with its law, its symbolizations, its dedication to form? "You disgust me," she says to him (355). Whereupon he shoots off the back of his head at the edge of darkened Moon Lake, as if in proximity to the nondifferentiating mother-matter from which his personal identity— terrified and unsure, both hating and loving its source—once arose. This lake is sister-water to Blanche's baths, her drinks, the perfume that she sprays like *eau de mysticism* even on Stanley's red-blooded American male- ness.

Once Allan dies, Blanche, it seems, can no longer desire; the experiment of getting outside herself fails. The only one who possesses her, and whom she wants to possess, precedes her—is "the impossible within" (*Powers of Horror* 5). But an attempt to disavow this impossible love can lead a woman "on a feverish quest for gratification" (*Black Sun* 77). Blanche's promiscuity has been of this desperate kind. Perhaps she might have said with Carol, a character in *Orpheus Descending*: "The act of love-making is almost un- bearably painful, and yet... to be not alone, even for a few moments, is worth the pain and the danger" (*Tennessee Williams: Four Plays* 75).

What keeps her from being pathologically depressed is hysteria, the same that makes her cast about nervously for new, satisfying (at last satisfying!) fictions about how happy life can be *out here*, in the father's sociosymbolic order. But this effort, being frantic, is no good. Besides, how can the social order compete with the sacred crypt in the ruined garden of her loss? Es- pecially if that order consists not of a beautiful aristocratic dream (*belle rêve*), but of a rowdy bunch on a street ironically named Elysian Fields?

In addition to dread, hysteria, and a lurking melancholy, Blanche illus- trates guilt. For Williams, "guilt is universal" (*Where I Live* 109):

I mean a strong sense of guilt. If there exists any area in which a man can rise above his moral condition, imposed upon him at birth and long before birth, by the nature of his breed, then I think it is only a willingness to know it.... [B]elow the conscious level, we all face it. Hence guilty feelings, and hence defiant aggressions, and hence the deep dark of despair that haunts our dreams, our creative work, and makes us distrust each other.

If the play flags Blanche's guilt in her history with Allan, Blanche is guilty, too, over the loss of Belle Reve, and this suggests that she *wanted* to free herself of the estate because it had become synonymous with the mother's lethal legacy of abjection, in particular the body's corruptibility. Protesting overmuch, she denies responsibility for its loss: "You're a fine one to sit there *accusing* me of it!" she says to Stella, who, however, hasn't said a word (261). "I stayed... and fought for it, bled for it, almost died for it!" (260). So, it was that important to her. "You came to New Orleans," she adds, "and looked out for yourself!" Blanche's tag for Stella—"Stella for Star" (250)—points to her sister's ability to detach herself and gain distance from the beautiful dream of her maternal and earthly origins. Blanche herself may have preferred to stay within the dream, until it turned to blood, "the struggle for breath." "Death is expensive, Miss Stella!" "The loss—the loss" of which Blanche murmurs is perhaps not just the estate, which was made over to its mortgagees, but the dream of a maternal sphere stronger than death. Which is to say that, for Blanche, *abjection*, with its horror and repulsion, had begun to dominate over the compelling mysticism of the Thing.

Still, in her ambivalent revolt against the mother, Blanche is a divided woman, part fluttery surface and part inner crypt in which lives an impossibly retained empowering mother. Over against the Southern decadence of the DuBois males (epic fornicators), Blanche poses as an immaculate Southern belle, complete with perfect manners, enchanting graces, pure principles, spotless dresses, a fresh-scented body, and clean hair. A drink is splashed on her white skirt; she shrieks. Mitch comes to call in his work-clothes; she scolds. Ironically, her constant pretence to purity makes her appear all the more unclean to others once it lies exposed. A woman free of the deathly crypt? Rather, a whited sepulcher.

Blanche can affect to make light of death: "You've got to dive where the deep pool is," she instructs certain phantasmatic suitors, "—if you hit a rock you don't come up till tomorrow" (91). But, really, she already belongs to death, and when a blind Mexican woman comes to the door with gaudy tin funeral flowers (the antithesis of Stanley's gaudy maleness), Blanche treats it as a sign of doom. She entertains a wistful fantasy of eating something unclean and sinking to the bottom of the sea—of giving in, after all, to a fatal abjection. The unclean edible? "An unwashed grape" from the Dionysian French Quarter, symbol of an intoxicated unselving. But she dreams of being "buried at sea sewn up in a clean white sack" (410). The sack is a fantastic protection from the Great Unclean that must, nonetheless, be re-entered. The ocean reclaims her own. She is death; but outside of her—that, too, is death.

Blanche attempts to stay afloat, not through love, but through seduction— a *glamor* of the surface. To seduce is neither to desire nor to love. Rather, as Jean Baudrillard says in his brilliant book on seduction, it is to challenge the autonomy of sex itself, to provoke desire only to deceive it, to show it as deluded about its power. To seduce is to appear weak so as to render others weak; to avoid the question of truth; to disappear in "the flickering of a presence" (one of Williams's early titles for the play was *The Moth*).

It is not to attach any meaning to what one does, for "what destroys people, wears them down, is the meaning they give their acts."[3] It is to turn one's body into a "pure appearance, an artificial construct with which to trap the desire of others"; it is to maintain a spectacular immortality through makeup, stylish clothes, gestures that gild the self-made idol.

Seduction, then, makes a mockery of the seriousness of the law, of productivity, of meaning. It is a theater in which only one player, Narcissan, is lighted, a softening paper lantern over the bulb. Why, even death must hesitate to break up this thespian's act, so mesmerizing is she, so polished.

A seductress whose style is antiquated and wearing thin, Blanche camps, in both senses, in southern coquettish refinement. (Unseen by Mitch, she rolls up her eyes when she protests her devotion to "old-fashion ideals" [348]. She plays him for a chump.) Her life-apart-from-meaning is moonshine, the moon itself pitted, cold. She's a Scarlet O'Hara in the wrong century (so it was natural that Vivian Leigh should play *her*, too). Besides, she drinks too much, and, though she is only thirty, she worries about aging.

If her game succeeds with Mitch for a while, it is useless against Stanley, who represents a "serious" male mentality—the ethic of production and above-board relations. (He is even suspicious of Hollywood glamor, which is hardly even American.) Stanley has his goaty sex—an industrial machine for producing both pleasure and a son (it must be a son). He has his work. And he has his competitive homo-social diversions with the boys (bowling and poker). Everything else is Mardi Gras tinsel and witchcraft (Blanche: "I cannot imagine any witch of a woman casting a spell over you." Stanley: "That's—right" [279]). Stanley has the a- or prehistorical sensibility of a hard-hat industrial worker of the north (never mind that he lives in New Orleans, of all the wrong places). A radical democrat, he sneers at the cloud Blanche trails after her, which is half rice powder and half dying star-fall of southern gentility.

To interest Stanley, as Blanche says, a woman would have to "Lay . . . her cards on the table" (279). But when Blanche wants to "kibitz" in the men's poker game (290), she's stone-walled. For, like masculine work, poker must not be contaminated by seduction—by feminine allure, by mother-magic. Its rules are transparent, are willingly adhered to, and lack imprisoning internalization. (Poker is serious: Stanley orders Mitch to get even his male ass off the table.) Poker supplements strict social law without falling into the feminine domain of obscure enchantment.[4] It is a deliverance from the law's guilt—an arbitrary ceremonial, a smoke-filled reprieve from meaning.

In poker, no one is allowed to be larger than the game. Masculine democracy, a cards-on-the-table sternness, restrains competitiveness. Unlike seduction, which is hieratical, hierarchical, poker is compatible with democracy and capitalism. Seduction is played with a trick deck. Only the seductress (or seducer) is allowed to win. Queen of Hearts, Queen of Diamonds (really rhinestones), Blanche flirts and sparkles. The role of the others is but to succumb. But Blanche secretly fears death, the Queen of Spades, hence the desperation underlying her airy ways.

To Blanche, Stanley is like death: He is nonseducible. Paradoxically, his primitive life force is death to her, because she cannot turn it into a game, her game. It is intolerably real. Stanley is male sun to her feminine mists. He is the only man around who will not let her say, without choking: "You may think you can crack me with desire, but, instead, I will make you bow to *appearances*." Fascinated as she is with so pure an opposite to herself, and envious as she is of her sister's pregnancy—to have a baby, to rejoin one's mother through one's child!—she cannot bear Stanley's phallic definiteness, his loud *finis* to her illusions. "The first time I laid eyes on him I thought to myself, that man is my executioner!" (351).

To be triumphant, a seductress must strangle her own psychology, neutralize fantasy. An advocate of seduction, Baudrillard disdains psychoanalysis for suppressing it and bringing upon itself the return of seduction through the Lacanian "imposture" (57). Blanche, however, is psychological, infested with guilty hallucinations. She's unable to exchange psychology for artifice. Finally, she loses her ability even to play with fictions. She becomes their pathetic plaything.

Even if Blanche were not up against the age's hostility to seduction (ours, Baudrillard says, is "a culture of the desublimation of appearances"), she is hopelessly fragile, afraid of being deserted, afraid of the future, afraid of the past, afraid to love, afraid of crowds, afraid of light, afraid of death. Afraid and guilty. She is, as well, the victim of male pride and paranoia. The men around her feel castrated by her Della Robbia blue; but the satiny scarlet in her history makes a whore of her (Mitch: "You're not clean enough to bring in the house with my mother" (390). Males are terrified of the possibility of being taken in by a mother-prostitute. The two elements must be kept distinct. With men, Blanche is at once fire and ice; dry ice. Even as she flirts with a man, she lays a prohibition on his genitals. Then to discover that, with *other* men, she has played the harlot!

Stanley takes his vengeance. It is, deep down, vengeance against the frightening mother. As Kristeva says, a virile man has to cross "over the horrors of maternal bowels" (*Powers of Horror* 53) to appropriate archaic maternal power. And here is Blanche, Miss White, attempting to *dismiss* Stanley's sexuality as apish. To Stanley, Blanche perhaps has a double significance: She is both the Phallic Mother and the abjection (the feminizing abjection) he fears in himself. She is the possibility that the phallus, at least his, is nothing. So she must be shown up, put down.

The opposite of the "quicksands" (354) into which Allan sank is phallic form, the law. Stanley is Allan's *positive* opposite. Many who have written on the play equate Stanley with sensuality alone, but Williams makes him dual; he represents the sociosymbolic order (in which he is, though a worker, a "king" [271]), as much as he does the bullying Phallus. In fact, the two are related, as the play illustrates. If the available alternatives are the Phallus or depression, abjection or the law, then Stanley makes the right, the only viable, choice. As phallic "one-eyed jack" (286), he defeats Blanche, Queen of Clubs, the Phallic Mother; that is, in a retrospective arrangement, the omnipotent archaic mother before the actual mother is found to be wanting in (masculine) potency.

This defeat recapitulates the violence against the mother-remembering *soma* on which every system of signs is founded. Of course, that Stanley triumphs over his fears in the swaggering conviction that Blanche wants to be mastered by him makes him repugnant. But what he stands for, even as he breaks it, is the social law and its accouterments: desire, objects, productivity.

The catastrophe arises from the collision between, on the one hand, the law and the violence that motivates it and, on the other, lawless seduction, which is itself a reach for power, in other words, between a "masculine" and a "feminine" assertion of strength. What seals it is the actual fragility of Blanche's hold on the world of objects. Each character is what the other must expel in order to keep going, to keep up the pretense of success in life.[5]

I suggest, then, that the play sacrifices Blanche, or "feminine" abjection, however reluctantly, in favor of the transparent social system. When the cards are down, the playwright prefers identity-sustaining law to the engulfing archaic mother.[6] He thus injures and humiliates part of himself, the unspoken part of every speaking being, hence, as I noted before, a final effect of sickening pain. "Is it not by signifying hatred, the destruction of the other, and perhaps above all his own execution," Kristeva asks, "that the human being survives as a symbolic animal?" (*Black Sun* 181).

What price survival? A *Streetcar Named Desire* both wins and loses its own game of seduction. "Violence," Williams said, "is purged by its poetic representation on stage" (*Where I Live* 109). Again, poetry utters incest; but just for that reason, the plot itself must oppose it. No poetry in the plot itself, only "realism."

What kept Williams from the avant-garde route was his need to purge "universal guilt." He used classical plot as a ritual for ridding the symbolic order of contaminants. But is Stanley's "deliberate cruelty" the same thing as a necessary social violence? Blanche calls such cruelty "the one unforgivable thing" and adds that it is "the one thing of which I have never, never been guilty" (p. 397).[7] Characteristically, she protests too much. She was cruel to Allan as, in turn, Stanley is cruel to her. Blanche shows contempt for a fake seed-bearer, a failed protector against the Phallic Mother, and Stanley shows equal contempt for the cock-teaser, Blanche. Of course, this parity between them, such as it is, does not excuse the cruelty of either. The question is: How *much* violence can be justified in keeping at bay the castrating Phallic Mother?

Williams's play does not attempt an exact measure. It has, thanks to Blanche, a wincing core that says any violence is too much. This makes for "serious" theater indeed. Yet for all that she represents "poetry," Blanche is not in any assured sense a positive heroine who offers a needed corrective to the unpoetic patriarchy. In *Orpheus Descending*, the symbolic order is mistaken in its enemy; Val, the snake-youth, is genuinely wholesome. By contrast, Blanche represents the deadly drag of the historical and, even more, archaic past. All the same, she is inescapable; she is the heart of abjection and the heartless depression in everyone. Williams understands that without condemning it. It is this that makes *Streetcar*, for all its heavy symbolism, a profound and powerful work of mourning—a stunning contribution to the modern literature of grief.

NOTES

1. On poetry as an utterance of incest, see Kristeva, *Desire in Language* 137.

2. "Those in despair are mystics—adhering to the preobject, not believing in Thou, but mute and steadfast devotees of their own inexpressible container" (*Black Sun* 14).

3. Baudrillard, *Seduction*; see especially "The Ecliptic of Sex" and "The Effigy of the Seductress."

4. For Baudrillard's discussion of poker and other games, see *Seduction* 132 ff.

5. "The abject has only one quality of the object—that of being opposed to *I*. If the object, however, through its opposition, settles me within the fragile texture of a desire for meaning, . . . what is *abject*, . . . the jettisoned object, is radically excluded and draws me toward the place where meaning collapses. A certain 'ego' that merged with its master, a superego, has flatly driven it away" (*Powers of Horror* 1–2).

6. Kenneth Tynan said that "when, finally, [Blanche] is removed to the mental home, we should feel that a part of civilisation is going with her. There ancient drama teaches us to reach nobility by contemplation of what might have been noble, but is now humiliated, ignoble in the sight of all but the compassionate." Tynan takes Blanche's impassioned speech on behalf of art at face value. I suggest that Blanche hollows culture out, betraying, as she does, a fundamental opposition to being conscious. See Tynan (263).

7. I take Britton J. Harwood's point (133) that Blanche's cruelty seems to burst from her and so to lack deliberation. Still, in uttering her words, she intended to hurt. Conversely, it is not clear that Stanley means to be cruel, as opposed to giving Blanche what he thinks she probably wants.

WORKS CITED

Baudrillard, Jean. *Seduction*. Trans. Brian Singer. New York: St. Martin's, 1990.
Harwood, Britton J. "Tragedy as Habit: *A Streetcar Named Desire*." *Tennessee*

Williams: A Tribute. Ed. Jac Tharpe. Jackson: UP of Mississippi, 1977. 104–15.

Kristeva, Julia. "Modern Theater Does Not Take (A) Place." *Sub-Stance* 18/19 (1977).

———. *Black Sun: Depression and Melancholia.* Trans. Leon S. Roudiez. New York: Columbia UP, 1989.

———. *Desire in Language: A Semiotic Approach to Literature and Art.* Ed. Leon S. Roudiez. New York: Columbia UP, 1980.

———. *Powers of Horror: An Essay in Abjection.* Trans. Leon S. Roudiez. New York: Columbia UP, 1982.

———. *Revolution in Poetic Language.* New York: Columbia UP, 1984.

Quirino, Leonard. "The Cards Indicate a Voyage on *A Streetcar Named Desire.*" *Tennessee Williams: A Tribute.* Ed. Jac Tharpe. Jackson: UP of Mississippi, 1977. 77–96.

Tynan, Kenneth. *Curtains: Selections from the Drama Criticism and Related Writings.* New York: Atheneum, 1961.

Williams, Tennessee. *Where I Live: Selected Essays.* Ed. Christine R. Day and Bob Woods. New York: New Directions, 1978.

———. *Tennessee Williams: Four Plays.* New York: New American Library, 1976.

———. *Three by Tennessee.* New York: New American Library, 1976.

———. *A Streetcar Named Desire. The Theatre of Tennessee Williams.* 7 vols. to date. New York: New Directions, 1971. Vol. 1: 239–419.

5

The Ontological Potentialities of Antichaos and Adaptation in
A Streetcar Named Desire

Laura Morrow and Edward Morrow

The classification of the constituents of a chaos, nothing less here is essayed.

Herman Melville, *Moby Dick*[1]

Streetcar is among the most bewitchingly simple (yet intricate), seductive (yet elusive) dramas of this century. Since the play's opening almost a half century ago, scholars have remained divided over *Streetcar*'s most fundamental elements: distinguishing the protagonist from the antagonist, identifying the play's generic form, discerning what Williams intended by a conclusion in which nothing is concluded. These issues were raised in the very first (tryout) reviews of *Streetcar* in October–December 1947 (Kolin). *Streetcar*'s plot is deceptively uncomplicated: Blanche, a woman who claims a better reputation and social position than she possesses, goes mad when Stanley confronts her with the truth. Though Blanche is self-centered, manipulative, and deceitful, she elicits our (reluctantly qualified) sympathy; and though Stanley is passionately devoted to truth-seeing and truth-telling (and to his wife), he elicits, at best, only reluctant praise. Scholars find it difficult unequivocally to distinguish the protagonist from the antagonist, or to identify the play's form: is this play Blanche's—or Stanley's? Is *Streetcar* a traditional Aristotelian tragedy or a modern, Milleresque threnody for the common man (or woman) or a metageneric idiosyncracy? Does *Streetcar* espouse feminist values, or is its vision more akin to that of *Iron John*? Or is Williams concerned here less with issues of gender than with those of class; is *Streetcar* a Social Darwinist drama of (dis)empowerment? The more we attempt to interpret the seemingly simple components of this play, the more complex we realize is the totality before us: Athens and Sparta subvert their own ideologies. Nevertheless, despite the multifarious and conflicting visions informing the play, its characters and plot convincingly represent human behavior. Once revealed, Blanche's and Stanley's actions seem deftly foreshadowed and psychologically consistent, their fates inevitable. They could not have acted, nor could we have interpreted, otherwise; we, too, have had this date from the beginning.

Required for any further revelation of the assumptions informing Williams's text is a more comprehensive critical paradigm, a paradigm that accounts for the orderly disorder/disorderly order of *Streetcar*. Heretofore, *Streetcar* scholarship has frequently been partial and sentimental, according to Adler's brief survey of *Streetcar*'s critical reception. Critics tend to write *apologia* for Blanche rather than detached, objective assessments of her character and actions (see Tischler or Berkman). Blanche's flaws and Stanley's virtues are afforded disproportionately little attention (or are misperceived as virtues), for these subvert the theoretical, political, and sociological assumptions underlying most interpretative stances. Other methodologies offer partial answers to *Streetcar*'s essential dilemmas, but no single approach accounts fully for the elements subverting its own thesis, for the generation of disorder within a given rational, critical order. Feminist critics (for example, Kathleen Hulley or Anca Vlasopolos) frequently ignore the extent to which Blanche is culpable, the degree to which she seduces Destiny—and Stanley. *Streetcar* scholarship demands a methodology that recognizes and accounts for the interpenetration of order and disorder.

Chaos Theory, we believe, offers such a paradigm.[2] Although this theory is, admittedly, not especially accessible to those untrained in mathematics, the enchanting world of "strange attractors," "folded-towel diffeomorphisms," "smooth-noodle maps," and "Butterfly Effects" offers insights into the arts as fresh as those it affords the sciences. To our knowledge no one has yet to explore Williams's work in light of this theory. Certainly it forms no part of recent books on *Streetcar* by Brenda Murphy or Thomas P. Adler. Chaos Theory studies discontinuous, erratic, and disorderly systems of behavior (e.g., patterns of the weather, of heart fibrillation, of turbulence). Chaos Theory teaches us that simple equations can generate complex outcomes (the Butterfly Effect, for example, in which minute changes produce chaos from an apparently orderly system). Similarly, fine playwrights like Williams perceive intuitively that the interaction between a few apparently simple characters can generate a complex and compelling work of art. Antichaos Theory (which is subsumed in, rather than opposed to, Chaos Theory) clarifies the determinism within chaotic systems, demonstrating through mathematical modeling that certain behaviors will deterministically arise and even "freeze" (in the terminology of computer science systems theory) in a particular formation, given a particular input array.

Chaos Theory is, we believe, a useful methodology for approaching that most discontinuous, erratic, and disorderly of systems—human behavior, particularly that giving rise to or manifested in artistic creation. "All living things," as Stuart Kauffman tells us, "are highly ordered systems.... the thousands of genes regulating one another within a cell; ... the billions of neurons in the neural networks underlying behavior and learning; the eco-system webs replete with coevolving species" (78). *Streetcar* can be viewed as a series of embedded and overlapping systems exhibiting various degrees of order and disorder, for example, the large system of New Orleans society; the smaller system of the poker group; the triad (Blanche, Stella, and Stanley); the pair (Stella and Stanley; Blanche and Stanley; Blanche and Mitch; Mitch and his mother; Eunice and her husband). And whereas these groupings consist of characters, one might execute a Chaos-based study of other conceptual groupings, such as semantic units, themes, the structuring of incidents, costuming, music, acting style, and more.

Scientists once assumed that the world was composed of systems that "could be reduced to a few perfectly understood, perfectly deterministic laws ... [whose] long-term behavior would be stable and predictable" (Gleick 303); those systems whose behavior defied such reduction were dismissed as irrelevant or intractable. (Similar assumptions underlie much contemporary literary and psychological theory.) But many scientists now acknowledge, after years of experimentation with meteorological, computer, economic, and biological systems (among others), that systems are neither as stable nor as simple as previous paradigms indicated: "Simple systems give rise to complex behavior. Complex systems give rise to simple behavior ... and [t]he laws of complexity hold universally (Gleick 304). Complex systems, moreover, contain local features, that is, interconnected often inter-influential elements. Clearly, the most significant of the complex systems in *Streetcar* is that formed by Blanche, Stella, and Stanley; the network connecting them is Desire. Through an examination of the rules governing this system's operation in *Streetcar*, we can better understand the treatment of order and disorder, or determinism and free will, or adaptation and evolution in the play.

Chaos Theory is inherently interdisciplinary: it cuts across scientific disciplines, viewing each system from a more holistic perspective than that of more traditional approaches (e.g., subatomic particle physics), which concentrate unnaturally upon isolated, disparately functioning components of a whole system. Since its emergence in the 1960s, Chaos Theory (like its recent offshoot, Antichaos Theory) has afforded new insights in formerly intractable areas, areas heretofore considered impossible to model (e.g., meteorology, mathematics, physics, physiology, and computer science systems theory). Chaos/Antichaos Theory developed as an effort to understand the nature and degree of determinism in complex systems (e.g., weather systems, fluid dynamics, snowflake formation). Edward Lorenz, the first Chaos theorist, detected "order *masquerading* as randomness" in weather systems. Fascinated by "systems that almost repeated themselves but never quite succeeded," Lorenz found in chaotic systems points of "fine structure hidden within a disorderly stream of data" (Gleick 22, 29).

As Roderick Jensen explains, Chaos Theory examines "the irregular, unpredictable behavior of deterministic, nonlinear dynamical systems" (Gleick 306). The word *chaos* is, however, something of a misnomer, for "the technical definition of chaos . . . carries with it an image of order in the midst of disorder. That definition contrasts with normal usage, wherein we mean by chaos either a state of utter confusion or a state in which chance is supreme" (Peterson 144). *Chaos*, in this theoretical context, does not, necessarily, imply total instability: "Any system," as Gleick argues, "could have both stable and unstable behaviors in it. . . . A chaotic system could be stable if its particular brand of irregularity persisted in the face of small disturbances" (48). But *Chaos* describes only a portion of the behavior of complex systems; in the phenomenon designated Antichaos, "some very disorderly systems spontaneously 'crystallize' into a high degree of order" (78).

Considered from this perspective, the world of *Streetcar* constitutes a complex system, with Blanche and Stanley (like the play's other individual characters) each functioning as a complex system networking with other systems. Through concepts such as "attractors," "self-organization," "frozen elements," and "canalizing functions," we can trace some of the orderly/disorderly systems that shape these characters in order to assess the degree of determinism informing them (thereby, perhaps, to mitigate or emphasize their responsibility for their own and others' tragic actions).

That complex system called "Stanley" follows simple rules that, like those in Chaos Theory, give rise to complex behavior. Stanley believes that the relationship between man and woman is supposed to be productive financially, spiritually, and physically. One of his chief rules derives from the Napoleonic Code, a complex system of justice remarkable for its attention to women's property rights. Stella, who should be aware of, if not in control of, her personal finances, says casually (regarding Blanche's explanation of the loss of Belle Reve), "Oh, it had to be—sacrificed or something" (Williams 270). Stanley thus must do the financial planning for them both. In asserting Stella's claim to property indisputably hers, Stanley's aim is neither to impoverish nor to exploit Blanche but to ensure that he, his wife, and, most importantly, their unborn child are being treated equitably (Williams 284). However insensitive his actions, Stanley is legally and morally right, as their property is communally held: "What belongs to the wife belongs to the husband and vice versa" (Williams 272).

Stanley also believes, naively, that words and numbers accurately and sufficiently model reality. That Stanley finds numbers compelling evidence of Truth is made evident the first time he appears. In response to Steve's comment that a mutual friend "hit the old weather-bird for 300 bucks on a six-number-ticket," Mitch comments, "Don't tell [Stanley] those things;

he'll believe it" (263). Similarly, Stanley wants to examine the papers regarding Belle Reve (Williams 271), especially the bill of sale. Stanley's assumptions *do* lead him to some partial truths: for example, though he inaccurately assesses the value of Blanche's clothing and jewelry, Blanche acknowledges the validity of his assertion that she could not have paid for her things "out of a teacher's salary" (Williams 278). But Stanley's rules are too few and too absolute to represent reality with unfailing accuracy: he *invariably* values substance over form, truth over illusion, and fixed, quantifiable fact over unfixed, mercurial fiction, demanding (and offering) as much technical detail as is possible. Stanley's logocentrism and numerocentrism are unequivocal, uncompromising, and insufficient in pursuit of any fuller truth. In having few rules, Stanley reveals his philosophical provincialism and naivete; he is one who discards or destroys that which conflicts with his simplistic assumptions.

Blanche's behavior, like Stanley's, obeys Antichaos Theory, in which patterns derive from but are not planned by a structure (just as smoke arises from fire but is not, in any Darwinian sense, selected by it). Certain behaviors, according to Antichaos Theory, are caused by the very nature and complexity of their organization of the system; they are inherent in that structure but are not causally related to it. Thus, though the rain falls from the sky, it is not caused by the sky; though Blanche comes from a decaying South and is destroyed, that environment neither *causes* her to be what she is, nor does it determine her fate.

We can understand the development of Blanche's character better if we can identify her "attractors." Stability within a Chaotic system arises from "attractors," which are "nonperiodic" in that they do not repeat themselves (Gleick 138). When plotted mathematically, attractors form nonrepeating patterns. "Under certain conditions," Peterson tells us, "nonlinear differential equations generate trajectories...that form peculiar shapes.... Such objects are called *chaotic*, or *strange*, *attractors*' " (146). Perhaps the most familiar example of a "strange attractor" is the Lorenz Butterfly, whose whorls form a shape reminiscent of a butterfly, or of the Lone Ranger's mask (Peterson 146–47). The Lorenz Butterfly is a stable, nonperiodic system, one that approximates but never replicates itself. Different attractors may be present simultaneously within a system: "A particular system may also have several attractors. Different initial conditions drive the system to a different attractor. The set of points going to the same attractor is called a basin of attraction" (Peterson 146), which, in a state cycle, is stable. What is modeled in the basin of attraction, then, is a sort of approximate psychological and social determinism. History is iterative: Blanche will always seduce whomever she can.

Blanche's attractors are illusion and seduction, both emanating from words; her "basin of attraction" consists of her seducing men with her body and herself with her dreams, repeating the same, would-be-ameliorative pattern in an endless cycle. Though the men's faces change, her devotion to illusion and her commitment to rewriting history remain constant. Significantly, Blanche never alludes to her former lovers as prospects for marriage, nor does she recall them with any of the romanticized nostalgia she affords her suicidal mate. And though she is often read as psychologically fragile and pitiable, there is also something relentlessly vampiric in her: she employs her sexuality as a tool with which she can rewrite history, engaging in relations with strangers, strangers who are no more than sex objects toward whom she will feel neither any sentimental attachment nor any responsibility should tragedy recur. Through these intentionally meaningless encounters, Blanche hopes to iterate and emend her first, lethal relationship. But in so desperately trying to make her sexuality function "right," Blanche regards men not as individuals with needs and feelings but as mere objects. In her objectification of desire, Blanche strikes an unhappy but an even bargain with her lovers, whom she uses every bit as much as they, presumably, use her.

Blanche can be identified as the protagonist of *Streetcar* when we consider her use of language in the context of Chaos Theory. Rather than attempt to derive or generate clear, rational, orderly meaning, Blanche (not unlike a poet or playwright) plays meanings against each other, hovering about an idea in vaguely concentric patterns rather than directly apprehending and communicating it; she uses language, as it were, chaotically. Blanche self-consciously tries to raise language and life to the level of art, which signifies on multiple, often conflicting, levels. This is consistent with Gleick's assertion that "the disorderly behavior of simple systems acts as a *creative process*. It generates complexity: richly organized patterns, sometimes stable and sometimes unstable, sometimes finite and sometimes infinite" (43). Blanche's "randomness"—her wandering through men and dreams—is the source of both her creativity and her destruction: her use of language enhances the world but distorts it, and the distortion perpetuates her self-destructive pattern of seduction.

Neither Stella nor Stanley uses language thus. Unlike her sister, Stella is creative only in the physiological sense; Stella is as verbally uninteresting as Stanley. And Stanley, the only other viable contender for the title of protagonist, eschews chaotic speech; for him, such imprecision merely distorts, not enhances, reality.[3] His language is as direct and precise as language can be. Stanley's basin of attraction is power, essential to which are, for him, mathematical and verbal precision. Stanley uses language pragmatically, not decoratively, to seek or communicate facts, to dispel illusion.

We may also better understand the interactions between Blanche, Stella, and Stanley by recognizing the similarity between their behavioral patterns and those in Boolean $N = K$ networks. Stella and Stanley's New Orleans society operates like an autonomous random Boolean $N = K$ network. Such networks "consist of N elements linked by K inputs per element; they are autonomous because none of the inputs comes from outside the system" (Kauffman 80). Stella and Stanley's New Orleans society is similarly closed (autonomous), and each member of their network interacts with and responds to the others, singly or collectively (small networks are linked to or combine to form larger networks). The individual networks are linked in many ways, for example, through sexual desire, family ties, male bonding (bowling, poker). Conflict arises when Blanche tries to change the K (the inputs), that is, to dissolve the existing network elements and links and replace them with more "refined" components. Blanche thus attempts to redefine and reprogram the system, introducing disruption both overtly (e.g., by criticizing relentlessly Stella's choice of spouse and home, which, unasked, she redecorates) and more subtly (through struggling for power through flirtation).

How can we account for Stella's and Blanche's having chosen different networks—or is it even appropriate to suggest that they "choose" their networks? According to Antichaos Theory, "Cell types differ because they have dissimilar patterns of genetic activity, not because they have different genes" (Kauffman 79). By analogy, then, all human beings—Stella, Stanley, Blanche, Mitch—share roughly the same "genetic instructions," the same impulses, appetites, and fears. What determines individuation for human beings, as for cells, is which variables, which "genes," become activated: "The dynamic behavior of each variable ... is governed by a logical switching rule called a Boolean function. ... Each combination of binary element activities constitutes one network 'state.' ... [Boolean networks] have a finite number of states. ... Because its behavior is determined precisely, the system proceeds to the same successor state as it did before ... [cycling] repeatedly through the same states" (Kauffman 79–80).

In the analogy above, each individual character is compared to a cell, and together these characters form a network. But one might also argue that each individual human being comprises networks of cells; in this case, the cells of a network can be the various aspects of that individual's character and behavior. One of the especially intriguing aspects of the Chaos model is that it can be applied with equal validity to both the internal functions of individual characters and to the external (behavioral) functions of groups of characters.

Let us, then, consider the individual behavior of Stella, Stanley, and Blanche in light of this schema. In the Boolean OR function, for example, if any input variable is active, then the variable itself will be active; with respect to the AND function, however, variables remain inactive unless *all* inputs are active. OR and AND functions are analogous to the ability to function within other systems. Considered thus, Blanche seems governed by the OR function in that, with minimal input, each of her actions iterates a characteristic pattern. This becomes more significant when we recall that the OR function is a type of "canalizing function," wherein "at least one input has a value that can by itself determine the activity of the regulated element" (Kauffman 83). Sometimes, this canalizing function causes elements within a system to become fixed, or "frozen"; the system is consequently "partitioned into an unchanging frozen core and islands of changing elements," wherein "changes in the activities of one island cannot propagate through the frozen core to other islands" (Kauffman 81).

Although Kauffman is speaking of mathematical constructs, the general principles he articulates describe rather strikingly the behavior of Blanche: she is "frozen" into a system of undiscriminating, compulsive, self-destructive seduction. Blanche keeps returning to the homeostasis of sensuality, despite her turbulent memories of Laurel, memories that might perturb a noncanalized system. So ineluctable is her pattern that Blanche tries to seduce even her pregnant sister's husband. Unlike Stanley, Blanche repeatedly forms casual networks approaching randomness.[4] She is trapped by her promiscuity in an unhealthy recursive network. Her sensuality is the source of her sense of power (however weak) and identity (however shameful).

Similarly, Stanley's behavior is frozen: in his marriage, for example, he is locked into a series of conflicts with Stella, battles for dominance in which he commits violent excess, is punished by her and/or the law, and is, ultimately, forgiven by Stella. Stanley's behavior with Blanche is also "canalized": given her nature and values, and given his nature and values, a tragic conflict (as in a Euripidean tragedy) was inevitable. Consider, for example, his rape of Blanche. From the outset of the play, Blanche has been trying to seduce him, to seize power from Stella and Stanley and become the dominant member of the household. She flirts with Stanley through her false delicacy (Williams 267, 277) and (partially) pretended insecurity about her looks (277), her elevated diction, her frequent state of undress, and her dispatching Stella for a soda while she declares her admiration for Stanley and sprays him with perfume (281). Both Stanley and Blanche are fully aware of Blanche's attempt to gain dominance through seduction (as Ann-Margret's teleplay performance makes especially apparent).

Blanche's seduction of Stanley has, of course, no more to do with love or sexuality than does Stanley's rape of her: this action is the manifestation of a tragic power struggle. The victory each seeks is over the other's soul, not the other's person. Without countenancing rape, we must remember that Stanley does not recognize Blanche's mental fragility; there is no evidence that he is aware that the woman who refers to him by a dehumanizing ethnic slur ("Polack") (374) is mentally ill. This normally faithful husband recognizes that Blanche is determined to control and turn against him everything he values: his wife, his marriage, even his friends. Blanche attempts to displace Stanley as the master in his household; to alter the language, values, and actions of his wife and friends; to undermine his marriage. Stanley rapes Blanche to demonstrate his power to her, that this is and will remain *his* household, not hers. Blanche has repeatedly ignored Stanley's warnings, that he knows her to be other than what she pretends. From *his* perspective, she is an opponent against whom the war cannot be won other than absolutely.

The rape scene poses an especially difficult problem in interpretation, for our attitudes toward and assumptions concerning rape have changed markedly since *Streetcar* opened. Distasteful as we would find such an argument today, the audience of 1947 no doubt blamed Blanche partially, if not primarily, for her rape; given contemporary assumptions about rape, the 1947 audience would have had few other interpretative options. Blanche has been acting seductively toward Stanley, and when he advances on her, she does not scream (which she *does* do to rid herself of Mitch's unwanted attention). Blanche offers little resistance to Stanley, despite the fact that he is unarmed and that he neither threatens, nor beats, nor otherwise physically injures her. At first, Blanche has a broken bottle in her hand, but she ultimately drops it and falls passively at Stanley's feet, having first moved into the bedroom. Today, of course, we know that rape victims often neither scream nor resist out of terror; one might well argue that Blanche is able to scream when Mitch makes sexual advances because he is never powerful enough to evoke paralyzing terror. But we must not allow chronocentrism to distort amelioratively our interpretation of Blanche as she was originally conceived and perceived; we must not discard earlier interpretations merely because they are not congruent with the received truth of later days. If we really wish to recover what *Streetcar* meant to Williams and his audience, then we must consider his work from the tragic misconceptions of the era during and about which the play was written. Williams intends us, at least in part, to blame the victim, to conclude that, with horrible irony, Blanche's attempted seduction of Stanley ultimately succeeds.

But why do Blanche and Stella, who were reared in the same environment and who share the same heredity, respond so differently to life? Why, unlike her sister, is Stella able to adapt to a male world as different from Belle Reve as that which Blanche encountered? Perhaps an answer to that question can be discovered through an analogy with Boolean algebra. Some complex systems exhibit order in a manner that can be modeled on the microcosmic scale of Boolean algebraic computation; similarly, within the microcosm of a Williams play, we can describe how selection orders the behavior of individual characters. Chaos Theory directs us to some useful questions about determinism, evolution, and adaptation, especially the relationship between adaptation, rigidity, and randomness. Is adaptation attributable more to environment than to heredity? To what extent is behavior deterministic, and what factors produce determinism?

The evolution of culture, of art, or of human psychology, like the evolution of a cell structure, is shaped by the reproduction of successful patterns and mutations of those patterns. Natural selection provides an ordering principle not only within cells, but also within individuals, works of art, or societies. Let us, for a moment, reconsider the conventional, evolution-based Social Darwinist reading of Stanley in light of Antichaos Theory. Merely because natural selection results in survival, argue Antichaos Theorists, we ought not equate selection with the ability to adapt: the native "capacity to evolve and adapt may itself be an achievement of evolution" (Kauffman 78). Stanley's having been "naturally selected" to survive does not bespeak any greater ontological coherence on his part. In other words, merely because Stanley survives and dominates his world (in contrast with Blanche, who, at least spiritually, is ultimately destroyed and dominated), he is not, for all his endurance, the more adaptable of the two: the fittest may survive, but they do not necessarily adapt.

"Because of chaos . . . [i]nitial conditions that are very much alike may have markedly different outcomes" (Kauffman 78). Unlike Blanche and Stanley, Stella is adaptable because she is not frozen in the pattern of either Blanche's or Stanley's canalization. Stella adheres to no predetermined pattern, to no specific behavioral canal but responds randomly to Blanche and Stanley. As Kauffman argues, "Systems poised between order and chaos come close to fitting many features of cellular differentiation during ontogeny" (84), that is, are most receptive to adaptation. Unlike Blanche, Stella recognizes the appeal of getting "off them columns" (Williams 377) at the same time that she shares Blanche's "Belle Reve" values. One of the factors that make Stella's behavior stable (though her choices remain randomized) is the complexity of her network, which is sufficiently complex and stable to sustain her, for "the stability of an attractor is proportional to its basin size" (Kauffman 81). Stella's social circle, her ties to others in the New Orleans basin of attraction, is essentially stable.

Evolution, Antichaos Theory maintains, relies not merely upon selection but upon self-organization as well. As "an innate property of some complex systems," self-organization is predetermined, for within a system, "networks typically return to their original attractor" (Kauffman 78, 81). Similarly, characters tend to return to an approximation of a familiar pattern (to the original attractor) after their functioning is disrupted. Consequently, Blanche insists on utter dominion over Stella, on treating her just as she had as the dominant member of the pair back in Belle Reve.

The image of the streetcar is especially appropriate in this play: The route of a streetcar is predestined, fixed, a "canalized function," as it were. Once on board the streetcar, one may see where it's headed; but howsoever evident may be the terminus of the network of track, one cannot change the direction of its course. It is, we believe, significant, that Blanche is of Huguenot ancestry (Williams 299); as Protestants in a Catholic-dominated country, they, too, disrupted the accepted order (albeit for altruistic reasons) and thereby brought suffering on themselves.

Might there have been any hope for Blanche? Clearly, in her original environment (Laurel), there was no hope for change; Blanche's state cycle remained constant, and she was continuing on a downward trajectory. But, Kauffman tells us, if perturbation/change "pushes the network into a different basin of attraction, the trajectory of the network will change: it will flow into a new state cycle and a new recurrent pattern of network behavior" (80). Given a new basin, given refuge in her sister's home or with Mitch, Blanche has an opportunity for real change: but, given the frozen state of her psyche, it is improbable, if not impossible, for any change to occur. Perhaps Blanche's system, like that of her deceased spouse, is overloaded by input, is unstable due to maximal perturbation ("damage").

The generic form of *Streetcar* is, then, close to that of Euripidean tragedy: the fates of the characters are predestined, predestined not by fate but by a combination of their inherited psychological makeup and the values to which they are exposed in their basins of attraction. Indeed, one might argue that the situation is fated to come out a certain way by the character types assembled, despite the particular individuals who are in that situation. Sensitive, reflective people (e.g., Blanche and her late husband) are like systems that exhibit antichaotic behavior: they tend to freeze into canalized functions as a result not of any tragic flaw, but simply because such freezing is an inherent property of complex systems. Williams offers here all the inexorability of Greek tragedy, but without a pantheon of gods determining fate according to their conscious, deliberate conception of justice.

The interpretation offered herein must, like all scientific and interpretative conclusions, be necessarily tentative and limited, given the evolutionary status of Chaos Theory. Nevertheless, this paradigm provides a useful perspective from which to consider playwriting and playtexts, serving as a reintegrative nexus for the arts and sciences. As physicist Mitchell J. Feigenbaum observes, "[A]rt is a theory about the way the world looks to human beings. . . . With [painters] Ruysdael and Turner, if you look at the way they construct complicated water, it is clearly done in an iterative. There's some level of stuff, and then stuff painted on top of that, and then corrections to that" (Gleick 186). Certainly, the potential applications of Chaos Theory to Williams studies are many. One might, for example, consider from this perspective Williams's biography; or his process of artistic creation; or the evolution of his work over his lifetime; or the evolution of Williams's sense of generic form or thematic preoccupations within a specific historical and/or (sub)cultural context; or, as we do here, one might employ this theory to interpret aspects of a single play, especially its treatment of order and disorder, or determinism and free will, or adaptation and evolution. Chaos Theory may thus help us clarify, if not answer, essential questions and assumptions underlying interpretation.

NOTES

1. Gleick (301) directs our attention to this quotation.
2. The terminology of Chaos/Antichaos Theory is still evolving; not all scholars

involved in this highly theoretical study are in full agreement as to the definition of individual terms. Interpretations based on different assumptions about Chaos/Antichaos will, necessarily, differ. For additional information, see especially John Briggs and F. David Peat, *Turbulent Mirror: An Illustrated Guide to Chaos Theory and the Science of Wholeness* (New York: Harper & Row, 1989).

3. One can easily conceive of a play in which all the characters use speech with Blanche's distinctive self-consciousness and elasticity; one has difficulty, however, imagining an effective drama modeled on Stanley's speech patterns.

4. It is impossible for anyone to be, in scientific terms, randomly promiscuous; to do so, one would have to sport with lovers of either sex chosen by a roll of the dice from a telephone book—and even this method excludes individuals with unlisted numbers.

WORKS CITED

Adler, Thomas P. *A Streetcar Named Desire: The Moth and the Lantern.* Twayne Masterwork Studies No. 47. Boston: G. K. Hall, 1990.

Berkman, Leonard. "The Tragic Downfall of Blanche DuBois." *Modern Drama* 10 (Dec. 1967): 249–57.

Gleick, James. *Chaos: Making a New Science.* New York: Viking, 1987.

Hulley, Kathleen. "The Fate of the Symbolic in *A Streetcar Named Desire. Themes in Drama 4.* Ed. James Redmond. Cambridge: Cambridge University Press, 1982. 89–99.

Kauffman, Stuart A. "Antichaos and Adaptation." *Scientific American* 265, no. 2 (August 1991): 78–84.

Kolin, Philip C. "The First Critical Assessments of *A Streetcar Named Desire*: The *Streetcar* Tryouts and the Reviewers." *Journal of Dramatic Theory and Criticism* 6 (Fall 1991): 45–68.

Murphy, Brenda. *Tennessee Williams & Elia Kazan: A Collaboration in the Theatre.* Cambridge: Cambridge University Press, 1992.

Peterson, Ivars. *The Mathematical Tourist: Snapshots of Modern Mathematics.* New York: Freeman, 1988.

Tischler, Nancy M. *Tennessee Williams: Rebellious Puritan.* New York: Citadel, 1961.

Williams, Tennessee. *A Streetcar Named Desire. The Theatre of Tennessee Williams.* 7 vols. to date. New York: New Directions, 1971. Vol. 1: 239–419.

Vlasopolos, Anca. "Authorizing History: Victimization in *A Streetcar Named Desire.*" *Theatre Journal* 38 (Oct. 1986): 322–38.

6

"We've had this date with each other from the beginning": Reading toward Closure in *A Streetcar Named Desire*

June Schlueter

As Anca Vlasopolos has shown, the strategy of Tennessee Williams's *A Streetcar Named Desire* is to implicate the reader in "violent processes of historiography—the processes of constructing a narrative of the characters' pasts" (322). *Streetcar* presents competing narratives, inviting the reader regularly and climactically to assess the authority of the storytellers. The play, as Vlasopolos notices, is "made up of acts of 'reading,' of interpretations of texts that range from documents and inscriptions—the Belle Reve papers and the words on Mitch's cigarette case—to pictures and people" (326). The text that becomes central to the struggle between Stanley and Blanche and to the construction and the reading of the play is Blanche's past, which, since the devastating death of her young homosexual husband, has included a succession of sexually needy and interested men. Blanche styles herself "a priestess of Aphrodite" who slipped outside to answer the calls of young soldiers; Stanley casts her as "the male joke about insatiable fallen women" (334).

Blanche's story might have found endorsement in scene 10 with her acceptance of Shep Huntleigh's invitation to the Caribbean, but the play makes it clear that she has fabricated this most recent chapter in her history and that Shep will not appear. On the other hand, scene 10 validates Stanley's story of Blanche's past through the "rough housing" that will culminate in rape, the ultimate expression of male authority and the consummate male joke. Understanding the direction that the plot he has been narrating must pursue, Stanley scripts the climactic scene between himself and the "whore," tellingly accounting for his behavior by explaining, "We've had this date with each other from the beginning" (402). The scene involves the reader in the most complex reading moment in the play, for even as she or he responds to this dramatically intense and emotional encounter, she or he is invited to assess its place not only within the scenes preceding it but also within the two narratives. Stanley's arresting recognition implicates the reader, as it has Stanley, in both a moral and an aesthetic retrospective reading toward closure.

Retrospective reading necessarily locates the reader within the critical discourse of reader response theory, a critical practice that, inhibited by W. K. Wimsatt and Monroe C. Beardsley's New Critical caution against the Affective Fallacy, did not come of age until the 1970s. Still, the reader's complicity in dramatic closure was already proposed by Aristotle in the fourth century B.C. Predicated on the assumption of the imaginative and emotional need for a unified whole, which, Frank Kermode points out, still informs the ways in which we structure both experience and fiction, the *Poetics* is instructive in its acceptance of the human penchant for pattern, shape, and design. This desire, Aristotle implies, is implicated in an ending: The reader takes pleasure in the sure progress of the action and in the completion of the whole.

The principle of affective response that Aristotle teases in the *Poetics* (he also speaks of reader response in terms of "pity" and "fear" [20]) receives fuller treatment in Wolfgang Iser's work on the act of reading. Describing more generally the process that the reader undergoes, Iser locates the meaning of a work of literature in the interaction between text and reader. Rather than accepting the historically defined reader sought by critics involved in *Rezeptionstheorie* or *Rezeptionsgeschichte* (in theory or history of reception), however, Iser proposes a theory of aesthetic response, a *Wirkungstheorie*. For Iser, the literary text is a prestructure, which, through its intentions and strategies, "anticipat[es] the presence of a recipient" and "designates a network of response-inviting structures" (34). In place of the "ideal reader" (Culler), the "superreader" (Riffaterre), the "informed reader" (Fish, "Literature in the Reader"), or the "intended reader" (Wolff), Iser postulates an "implied reader" who "embodies all those predispositions necessary for a literary work to exercise its effect—predispositions laid down ... by the text itself" (34); the implied reader is a literary construct, actualized by the real reader. As W. Daniel Wilson puts it, "The implied reader ... can be defined as the attitudes and judgments demanded of the real reader by the text" (856).

Iser's comments help clarify the problematic nature of Aristotle's affective response, which provocatively suggested, two millennia before reader response theory was formulated, that the reader's reaction is essential to the definition of tragedy. For both Aristotle and Iser, the play is structured so as to orchestrate responses; it is attentive to how a reader feels as he or she proceeds through the play and, most important for our purposes, to how the reader feels at play's end. Author, text, and reader all "know" that dramatic closure is a collaborative act that cannot occur without the reader's consent.

Building on Iser's insights, Hans Robert Jauss, also a leader of the Konstanz school of *Rezeptionsästhetik*, divides the reading process into two hermeneutic acts: understanding and interpretation. A first reading of a literary text, he suggests, involves the reader in an aesthetically perceptual reading, an immediate constitution and understanding of the work as aesthetic object. Because the first reading does not provide the reader with fulfillment of form until the final line, however, Jauss suggests that "analysis cannot begin with the question of the significance of the particular within the achieved form of the whole; rather, it must pursue the significance still left open in the process of perception that the text, like a 'score,' indicates for the reader" (141). Only in the "second" reading, which follows and is activated by the end of the first, can a reader understand the ways in which each segment of the text and each reading moment contributes to the whole. The second reading—not to be confused with a rereading—involves the reader in a reflective, retrospectively interpretive performance. As Jauss describes it, "The experience of the first reading becomes the horizon of the second one: what the reader received in the progressive horizon of aesthetic perception can be articulated as a theme in the retrospective horizon of interpretation" (143). The second, retrospective reading speaks to the reader's need to establish the "still unfulfilled significance retrospectively, through a new reading...in a return from the end to the beginning, from the whole to the particular" (145). In practice, that reading, though dependent on the achievement of the first reading and necessarily successive, becomes synchronic once the artistic whole is achieved.

Umberto Eco speaks of this prospective and retrospective process in terms of the *fabula*, which is "not produced once the text has been definitely read: the *fabula* is the result of a continuous series of abductions made during the course of the reading" (31). Forced at many points to face a "disjunction of probabilities" (31), the reader asks questions and forecasts, accepting tentative answers based on expectations established both within and outside the text—and certainly within (overcoded) intratextual frames. As Eco puts it, "The end of the text not only confirms or contradicts the last forecasts, but also authenticates or inauthenticates the whole system of long-distance hypotheses hazarded by the reader" (32).

Throughout the early and middle scenes of *Streetcar*, the reader has sustained an ongoing critical posture, witnessing Blanche's attempts to legitimize her construction of self through memorializing her life of refinement at Belle Reve and Stanley's attempts to deconstruct that past, to impose his own interpretation upon the formation she and others provide. Not yet committed to either version of the past, the reader has periodically though tentatively evaluated the two historiographers' claims. Now, with Stanley's recognition of the inevitability of his "date" with Blanche standing in sharp relief, the reader is prompted to reassess the competing claims of the "cultivated woman" of "intelligence and breeding" (396) and the "sub-human" man with "an animal's habits" (323), to choose between Blanche's story and Stanley's.

The first meeting between Blanche and Stanley, though not yet styled in the competitive mode, anticipates the contest between them, the achievement of the aesthetic whole. For Stanley's questions, though innocent—"Where you from, Blanche?" "You're a teacher, aren't you?" "What do you teach, Blanche?" and, critically, "You were married once, weren't you?" "What happened?" (265–68)—leave Blanche feeling ill. Though she proves herself the skilled and selective respondent, one wonders how she would fare were Stanley's questions about her past not so well intended.

The reader anticipates just such a circumstance when Stanley learns from Stella that the family estate has been lost. His insistence on seeing the papers so he can claim his share under the Napoleonic Code and his subsequent rummaging through Blanche's wardrobe trunk, offering assessments of the financial value of each item and questioning how she acquired gowns and jewels on a teacher's pay, sets the tone for the encounter with Blanche at the end of scene 2. Here Blanche uses her resources: "freshly bathed and scented" (276), she slips into a new dress, then asks Stanley to button it. Blanche sustains her refined speech and cheerful air even as she discovers that Stanley has examined her trunk. When she goes too far with her flirting, however, Stanley changes the tone, booming a command: "Now let's cut the re-bop!" (280). She tries a second time to gain ascendency through being playful, this time eliciting his confusion and anger: "If I didn't know that you was my wife's sister I'd get ideas about you!" (281). When Blanche at last offers information about Belle Reve, she does so seriously, from the perspective of one familiar with the history of the estate, leaving Stanley disadvantaged and needing assistance: "I have a lawyer acquaintance who will study these out" (284). Blanche is not far off when she boasts to Stella of how she handled the encounter:

We thrashed it out. I feel a bit shaky, but I think I handled it nicely. I laughed and treated it all as a joke.... I called him a little boy and laughed and flirted. Yes, I was flirting with your husband. (285)

Though the dialogue has come to an end, the reader anticipates its renewal and its intensification in subsequent scenes and doubts Blanche's ability to hold her own in future competitions. Though her manner was at first disconcerting to Stanley, she does not appear to be sufficiently prepared to keep the inquisitor at bay. At this point, an assessment of the status of the competition will entail a recursive reading: To balance her minor triumph, the reader will return to the opening scene, in which Blanche arrived at Elysian Fields. Her dislocation then was immediately apparent in the incongruity of her appearance and this New Orleans setting: Stanley's house is a two-story corner building in a poor section of Elysian Fields; Blanche is dressed *"as if she were arriving at a summer tea or cocktail party in the garden district"* (245). The reader has heard Stanley bellow at Stella, seen him heave a package of red meat at her, and watched him disappear around the corner with Mitch, *"roughly dressed in blue denim work clothes"* (244), a bowling jacket over his arm. Stanley has already established himself visually as a substantial and formidable presence, unlike the moth-like woman of *"uncertain manner"* and *"delicate beauty"* (245). Later, Blanche's conversation with her sister will reveal that Stanley is a "different species" (258), unlike the men they knew at Belle Reve. Yet this is the man who is challenging Blanche's story.

From the perspective of scene 2, the reader's forecasting will include two options: Either Blanche will get Stanley to understand how she came to lose the family estate and to rest his personal claim or Stanley will blame Blanche for her negligence or outright dishonesty and insist on his right to the property. Either way, both Stanley and the reader will need to know more about Blanche. The characters have begun their power play, each intent on gaining ascendancy through controlling the narrative of Blanche's past.

That narrative develops significantly in the middle scenes, when Stanley learns from his supply man in Laurel that Blanche has been associated with the Flamingo Hotel. Anticipating exposure, Blanche attempts to neutralize the story by warning her sister about "unkind gossip" and alerting her to difficulties at home. If the reader's tendency here is to accept Stanley's investigative work, Blanche's sad tale about her boy husband in scene 6 restores her dignity and reinstalls her as storyteller, capable of eliciting sympathy and understanding and, in effect, explaining the behavior that her brother-in-law could only dismiss with scorn. The reader will feel Blanche's desperation most acutely in scene 8 when, on her birthday, Stanley gives her a bus ticket back to Laurel; so also will the reader feel Stanley's brutish cruelty in this scene, for his cleaning of the table exceeds even the cruder behavior that has distinguished him all along. But the narrative competition has not yet been resolved: though Stanley has succeeded in upsetting Mitch with his version of Blanche's past, Blanche, ready with an alternative story, has left a telephone message for Mitch to call.

As the reader proceeds through the beginning and middle scenes, he or she is involved in periodic readjustments, necessitated by the placing of new events in the context of previous events. Despite temporary judgments on the reader's part and tentative endpoints, however, the impulse of this first reading is insistently prospective. As the reader asks questions about the competition between Blanche and Stanley—and its human booty, Stella and Mitch—she or he anticipates the end, the terminal event in the struggle between them and the completion of the aesthetic whole.

That event occurs in the play's penultimate scene, when the two narratives of Blanche's past come face to face to compete not only for priority but also for closure. Throughout the play, Blanche has seen the "miscellaneous" sexual encounters of her past as a means of filling an empty heart and of helping to satisfy the yearnings of lonely men; emotionally defeated by the suicide of her sensitive, homosexual husband and haunted by a succession of family deaths, Blanche has clung to the emotional debris, searching for kindness in strangers. Stanley, on the other hand, has shown little interest in the death of her husband or in the sacrifices she made at Belle Reve. Throughout the play, he has decontextualized her promiscuity, placing it outside the harshness of experience or emotional need. Like the people of Laurel, where "it was practickly a town ordinance passed against her!" (363), Stanley has been reading Blanche's sexual past not as a sad attempt to establish intimacies with strangers but as a repeated expression of raw, unbridled lust. Now, like Mitch, he is ready to collect what he has "been missing all summer" (389).

With Stella in the hospital and the two in the apartment alone, the narrative showdown begins. Blanche desperately tries to reach Western Union to wire Shep Huntleigh but fails. The millionaire Texas gentleman will not appear to claim her cultivated company. "Beauty of the mind and richness of the spirit and tenderness of the heart" (396)—all qualities she has said men admired in her—remain unconfirmed, inactivated within her ineffective story. Stanley, on the other hand, is able to complete his narrative—and becomes a participant in it. To Stanley, this wanton woman, who freely gave favors to soldiers and seduced a seventeen-year-old boy, has earned his treatment of her. The narrative line of Blanche's story of self fails at the same point that the narrative line of Stanley's story reaches its frightening conclusion.

However offensive Stanley's behavior, the reader now understands the force of his pronouncement of the inevitability of this "date." For Stanley's story, no less than Williams's play, has been pursuing the inexorable rhythm of tragedy: the rape, however repugnant, is the inescapable end of Stanley's narrative. Moreover, it affirms Blanche's story of Stanley as apeman, "grunting ... and swilling and gnawing and hulking!" (323). If Jauss is correct in his characterization of the aim of the prospective reading, the rape, as terminal event in both Stanley's and Blanche's narratives of each other, offers satisfaction, for it provides the reader with a sense of the aesthetic whole.

In the second reading, Stanley's story of Blanche has priority, for the reader now knows that it has prevailed. Her desperate effort to construct herself as a woman of breeding and refinement, of poetry and beauty, has yielded its credibility to Stanley's construction, which, the reader knows, has been legitimized through completion. Though in the first reading the reader may have wanted to understand Blanche's antisocial behavior and make allowances for it, he or she now knows that it is futile to do so, for scene 10 has secured the unsettling but incontestable fact that, as Vlasopolos puts it, "historical discourse depends on power, not logic, for its formation" (325). Having experienced the force of Stanley's script and its terminal action, the reader reevaluates Blanche's past in the prevailing author's (i.e., Stanley's) terms.

Now when the reader reviews earlier scenes, he or she realizes that he or she should not be surprised by the triumph of brutality in this climactic scene, for the force of Stanley's unrefined insensitivity has consistently determined the end of several encounters. Not only had his inquiry into her youthful marriage in scene 1 left Blanche physically sick, but also his examination of her love letters in scene 2 left her "*faint with exhaustion*" (283). In scene 8, his gift of a bus ticket back to Laurel left her clutching at her throat, coughing and gagging (376); and in scene 9, his exposure of her to Mitch left her crying wildly at the window: "Fire! Fire! Fire!" and then staggering and falling to her knees (390). These moments of physical disabling at the hands of Stanley are monumentalized in scene 10 in her inability to defend herself against rape. Scene 10 ends with the overpowered Blanche moaning and sinking to her knees: "*He picks up her inert figure and carries her to the bed*" (402).

The second reading will also reactivate a number of previous remarks: Stanley's "If I didn't know that you was my wife's sister I'd get ideas about you!" (281), Blanche's "Yes, I was flirting with your husband" (285) and her flippant invitation to Mitch, "*Voulez-vous coucher avec moi ce soir?*" (344) will no longer be comments without a climactic context. From the perspective of scene 10, these remarks have painfully self-fulfilling consequences. The reader will recall as well that in scene 6, when Blanche discussed Stanley with Mitch, she confessed that "the first time I laid eyes on him I thought to myself, that man is my executioner! That man will destroy me, unless—" (351). Now, one scene after Mitch has been disabused of the notion that Blanche is a "lily" and has withdrawn his marriage proposal (the "unless" of Blanche's proposition), the executioner performs his labor, graphically joining the deliberate cruelty that Blanche deplores and the sexuality that has been seething for months.

The reader involved in this retrospective reading will become aware of the extent to which his or her *prospective* reading was implicated in the play's generic character. For this play, as George Jean Nathan observes, commands interest comparable to that "held by a recognizably fixed prize-fight or a circus performer projected out of what appears to be a booming cannon by a mechanical spring device" (90). The pressure of the tragic form, the "continual rush of time, so violent that it appears to be screaming" (as Williams describes it in "Timeless" 49), is abruptly arrested in the moment before the blackout of the rape, providing the reader the opportunity to marvel at the force with which this streetcar has been careening to this stop. For the reader who has completed scene 10, reassembling the reading moments leading to the rape reveals the play's response-inviting design, which combines explicitly anticipatory events within an implicitly generic (i.e., tragic) mode.

The retrospective reading will also reveal that the interpretive process, though activated by the achievement of the aesthetic whole, is not wholly aesthetic. For in authorizing Stanley's narrative over Blanche's, the scene pressures the reader into a moral endorsement he or she might otherwise not have been willing to give. In agreeing to closure, the reader permits Stanley's taxonomy of female sexuality—Blanche must be either virgin or whore—to stand. The reader unwittingly becomes complicit in the text's "hidden determinism," a "gender-determined exclusion from the larger historical discourse" (Vlasopolos 325).

Moreover, in accepting Stanley's narrative as terminal event, the reader agrees to Blanche's future, for the narrative within the play has not only defined Blanche's past but also determined the outcome of the present dramatic action as well. In scene 10, Blanche, having exhausted her resources and Stanley's good will, is destitute. Moreover, if she is to have the support of her sister, she must rely on Stella's believing her version of this most recent event. But Stella has confided to her sister that Stanley's violence on their wedding night "thrilled" her (313), that "there are things that happen between a man and a woman in the dark—that sort of make everything else seem—unimportant," things that Blanche characterizes as "brutal desire" (321). How can Stella, who is not "in something that I want to get out of" (320), believe that, while she was in the hospital giving birth to their first child, her husband raped her sister? As Stella admits, "I couldn't believe her story and go on living with Stanley" (405). Hence, Blanche is exiled and institutionalized.

Vlasopolos is especially perceptive in her analysis of the final scene, which implicates the reader in the public endorsement of Stanley's achievement. Not only has the reader retrospectively reassessed both versions of history and realized the force of Stanley's reading, but now, with the others in Elysian Fields, he or she watches unobtrusively as events wind down and Blanche is removed, her version of her past silenced and ignored, her hope for the future denied. Attracted by the integrity and the pleasure of the aesthetic whole, the reader, in accepting Stanley's final fiction, has been seduced into a hegemonically masculine and conventionally generic reading of the play. The reader's "pragmatic shrug" (Vlasopolos 337) endorses the ideology implicit in both historical discourse and the tragic form.

But the text also provides for another implied reader, one who sees the final scene as an occasion to reassess rather than endorse the "pleasurable" reading activated by scene 10. At this point, that reader will have recognized his or her complicity in what can be described only as coercive closure. And, with Blanche, the reader will be demanding to know "What's happened here? I want an explanation of what's happened here" (408). Stanley's deliberate cruelty—his jeering at Blanche and tearing down the paper lantern—will seem especially gratuitous here, with Blanche already in defeat and minutes away from the asylum. Moreover, Blanche's reliance on the kindness of strangers, even as family and acquaintances assemble to witness, not to prevent, her expulsion, may alert the reader to how little kindness his or her own reading has shown her. For the reader uneasy about allowing the play to end so neatly, at Blanche's expense, yet another retrospective reading will deliver him or her back to scene 10, this time to question his or her own agreement to the closure it urged.

The comfort and discomfort implied in the strategy of scene 11 has clearly had an impact on criticism of the play, which has hardly offered a consistent reading of the end. Nor have the two film versions resolved the problematic final scene. In Williams's play, Stanley appears to escape accountability; the closing tableau finds him kneeling beside his wife to comfort her, his fingers finding the opening of her blouse. Elia Kazan's 1951 Hollywood film, however, under pressure from censors and the Catholic Legion of Decency, rescripts the end. In Kazan's final scene, Stella (Kim Hunter) reproaches her husband (Marlon Brando) as he tries to hold her: "Don't you touch me. Don't you ever touch me again." Stanley walks away from Stella, who stands watching the physician's car, with Blanche (Vivien Leigh) inside, pull away and round the corner. When her baby cries, she picks it up, and, as Stanley calls, "Stella, C'mon Stella," she resolutely insists, "I am not going back in there again, not this time. I am never going back. Never." Clutching the child, she runs up the stairs, with Stanley wailing her name like an animal in pain.

The retrospective reading of the Kazan version prompts an interpretation of its own, not only because of its morally stabilizing character but also because the director has tampered with the text throughout. Several of the lines that are activated by a retrospective reading of the text following scene 10 are left unspoken here: Stanley's "If I didn't know that you was my wife's sister I'd get ideas about you!", Blanche's "Voulez-vous coucher avec moi ce soir?", her narratives of her homosexual husband and the drunken soldiers who staggered onto her lawn. Most importantly, the precipitating line itself is gone: Stanley's "We've had this date with each other from the beginning."

John Erman's 1984 remake, by contrast, respects the original text. In Erman's scene 11, the camera follows Blanche (Ann-Margret), on the arm of her gentleman physician, past the poker players, out the door, and through the archway, then into the back seat of the car. As the car pulls away, Stanley (Treat Williams) kisses Stella (Beverly D'Angelo). She wraps her arm around his neck as he comforts her. The camera moves to Eunice, the upstairs neighbor, holding the baby, then back to Stanley and Stella as they walk into the house, arms locked in an embrace, past the poker game to the bedroom.

This production ends not with Stanley but with Blanche. The physician's car, with Blanche in the back seat, drives down a long road, at the end of which is a church. Once the car rounds the corner, the camera moves down the road as well and, when it comes to the end, moves upward to focus on the steeple. The bells sound in three echoing peals, ending the play and completing an association suggested earlier of Blanche with church bells. The peals rise above the cacophony of street sounds that accompany so many scenes, connect with the plaintive cry of the Mexican woman who sells flowers for the dead, and recall Blanche's "Sometimes—there's God— so quickly!" (356). They also complement Blanche's frequent association with candles, which are often arranged as though on an altar; her repeated baths, which are her daily attempts at spiritual cleansing; and the incessant New Orleans rain.

Erman's production responds to the text's suggestion of a sacramental context for Blanche's wish for purification. When the film ends with camera focused on the steeple and the three resonating chimes, Blanche's yearning seems fulfilled. As the camera rises about the New Orleans cityscape, the reader is left with the impression not of her sordidness or of her desperation but of the woman this lover of poetry and music and art wished herself to be. The final shot is a sad and powerful judgment on Stanley and the brutes. Blanche's own words in scene 4, when she responded to Stanley's "stone-age" bestiality, resonate: "Maybe we are a long way from being made in God's image, but Stella—my sister—there has been *some* progress since then!" (323).

The two film versions of the play, then, offer their own interpretation of desire in New Orleans. Both films present endings that explicitly invite the reader to lament the loss of Blanche's world of poetry, music, and art, of Greek-columned houses and rhinestone tiaras, of the woman who insisted "I don't want realism. I want magic!" (385). Though motivated by moral idealism, these reorchestrations of the final scene pressure the reader into a reevaluation of scene 10, permitting reflection on the aesthetic and ideological forces that enabled Stanley's narrative to prevail.[1]

Reading *Streetcar* from the perspective of reader response theory, as articulated by Iser and Jauss, directs attention to the end of the text, the anticipated point of the first reading, and the activating point for the second. Necessarily, such reading involves frustrations. Yet, as Barbara Herrnstein Smith points out, frustration is a necessary part of the gratification that characterizes literary closure: "Every disruption of our expectations causes some kind of emotion, and...the emotion is not unpleasant if we are confident of the presence of design in the total pattern" (14). For many readers, scene 11 will serve as a coda to a play brought to closure in scene 10. But those who understand scene 11 as the terminal event will recognize scene 10 as the point at which Stanley's narrative—not Williams's play— closes. Reading toward closure in *Streetcar* entails the final retrospective interpretation of the penultimate scene, once the whole of the aesthetic form has been perceived.

NOTE

1. My commentary on the two film versions previously appeared in "Imitating an Icon: John Erman's Remake of Tennessee Williams's *A Streetcar Named Desire*." *Modern Drama* 28 (Mar. 1985): 139–47.

WORKS CITED

Aristotle. *The Poetics. On Poetry and Style*. Trans. G.M.A. Grube. Indianapolis: Bobbs-Merrill, 1958. 3–62.

Culler, Jonathan. *Structuralist Poetics: Structuralism, Linguistics and the Study of Literature*. Ithaca: Cornell UP, 1975.

Eco, Umberto. *The Role of the Reader: Explorations in the Semiotics of Texts*. Bloomington: Indiana UP, 1979.

Fish, Stanley. "Literature in the Reader: Affective Stylistics" [1970]. *Is There a Text in This Class?: The Authority of Interpretive Communities*. Cambridge: Harvard UP, 1980. 21–67.

Iser, Wolfgang. *The Act of Reading: A Theory of Aesthetic Response*. Baltimore: Johns Hopkins UP, 1978.

Jauss, Hans Robert. *Toward an Aesthetic of Reception*. Trans. Timothy Bahti. Minneapolis: U of Minnesota P, 1982.

Kermode, Frank. *The Sense of an Ending: Studies in the Theory of Fiction*. London: Oxford UP, 1967.

Nathan, George Jean. Review of *A Streetcar Named Desire* [1947]. *Two Modern American Tragedies*. Ed. John D. Hurrell. New York: Charles Scribner's Sons, 1961. 89–91.

Riffaterre, Michael. "Describing Poetic Structures: Two Approaches to Baudelaire's *Les Chats*." *Yale French Studies* 36/37 (Oct. 1966): 200–42.

Smith, Barbara Herrnstein. *Poetic Closure: A Study of How Poems End*. Chicago: U of Chicago P, 1968.

Vlasopolos, Anca. "Authorizing History: Victimization in *A Streetcar Named Desire*." *Theatre Journal* 38 (1986): 322–38.

Williams, Tennessee. *A Streetcar Named Desire. The Theatre of Tennessee Williams*. 7 vols. to date. New York: New Directions, 1971. Vol. 1: 239–419.

———. "The Timeless World of a Play" [1951]. *Where I Live: Selected Essays*. New York: New Directions, 1978. 49–54.

Wilson, W. Daniel. "Readers in Texts." *PMLA* 96 (1981): 848–63.

Wimsatt, W. K., Jr., and Monroe C. Beardsley. "The Affective Fallacy" [1949]. *The Verbal Icon: Studies in the Meaning of Poetry*. By W. K. Wimsatt, Jr. New York: Noonday P, 1962. 21–39.

Wolff, Erwin. "Der intendierte Leser: Überlegungen und Beispiele zur Einführung eines literaturwissenschaftlichen Begriffs." *Poetica* 4.2 (1971): 141–66.

7

Perceptual Conflict and the Perversion of Creativity in *A Streetcar Named Desire*

Laurilyn J. Harris

If the doors of perception were cleansed every thing would appear to man as it is, Infinite.
>   William Blake, *The Marriage of Heaven and Hell*, 1790

The purpose of an artist's life is self-expression, but if that self is belittled and despised, if society insists it take a role incompatible to its nature, then knowledge of the self is impossible to attain, and hence impossible to express. To call that situation male chauvinism is to soften the impact. It is prejudice and it kills.
>   Kathleen Brady, "The Sexual Art of Judy Chicago," 1975[1]

Perception and creativity are interlocking phenomena, conjoined and commingled, and both are necessary to the production of art as each reinforces the other in a symbiotic relationship. But if perception, including perception of self, is skewed and devalued, and if the creative impulse is systematically thwarted and suppressed, the result is not creation but destruction, not art but a hollow caricature of art. So it is in the case of Blanche DuBois, whose fears and insecurities, deceptions and self-deceptions are trapped within the claustrophobic confines of the Kowalski apartment. There, in the simmering cauldron of a New Orleans summer, distorted perception and frustrated creativity ultimately combine to shatter her like glass.

Perception is a multilevel, multilayered phenomenon that colors human interaction and observation. It affects our attitudes, our preferences, and our conceptions of "reality." It can transform—and deform—the faces we see around us and the face we see in the mirror. And perception is at the heart of *A Streetcar Named Desire*, as Williams deals with the fundamental theme of the real versus the true.

Perception can be defined as "the relationship of sense-experience to material objects" (Quinton 61). The process involves the interaction between an organism and its environment, as that organism's conscious/subconscious mind attempts to extract and interpret information drawn from the surrounding welter of stimuli. Perception is "intuitive cognition, a flash of mental images produced by physical phenomena" (Harris, "Creative Differences" 14). The perceptual experience is "occasioned by the stimulation of sense organs" (Dennis 149), which in turn triggers "some kind of reactive or adaptive action from the individual" (Forgus 1). As Williams himself observes in his *Memoirs*, "Life is made up of moment-to-moment occurrences in the nerves and the perceptions" (250).

There is a considerable difference of opinion among various scientists, artists, and philosophers as they attempt to determine just how this process works. Is perception, as the older gestalt theory would have it, "a patterned message flashed from a carefully organized visible object" (Nemser, "Art Criticism" 329)? This approach implies that there is a "correct" way of seeing, one "accurate" perception of reality. However, it is not the stimulus *itself* that constitutes perception, but rather "the interpretation of the stimulus" (Dennis 149). Therefore, according to an increasing number of modern perceptual theorists, perception constitutes a highly idiosyncratic and personal filtering process influenced by factors such as past events, immediate environment, education, social sensitivity, biases, fantasies, and long-term mental and emotional response configurations. If this second theory is correct (and a good deal of evidence indicates that it is[2]), each person views phenomena through a screen woven of individual "concerns and awarenesses" (Donovan 76), and the process is so subjective that no two people ever receive exactly the same perceptual message from the same set of stimuli. Furthermore, this view of perception suggests an on-going, dynamic interaction between subject and stimulus, "a continuous tuning-in, amplification, suppression, and interpretation" (Dennis 150), which will in turn influence future perceptual activity. Perception thus becomes a "two way street" (Nemser, "Blowing the Whistle" 27), forcing us to reinterpret the past even as it conditions our response to the future, enabling us to "go beyond the conceptions of the present moment" (Goncharov). The perceptual process, therefore, "cannot be seen as separate from learning" (Nemser, "Art Criticism" 327), and the more we learn, the more personal our perceptions become, as we accumulate ever-increasing amounts of sensory baggage that make any attempt at objectivity or disinterestedness both implausible and impossible. As Barnes succinctly notes, "We are weighted creatures" (quoted in Diamond 2).

Many critics have interpreted the essential conflict in *Streetcar* as a clash between brutal reality, represented by Stanley, and romantic illusion, personified by Blanche. References to Stanley's "pitiless and probing realism" (Kernan 18) and his threatening "world of facts" (Corrigan 55) are juxtaposed with images of Blanche as a frail, fluttering, moth-like dreamer "revelling in her fantasies" (Corrigan 55). According to this reading of the play, Stanley destroys Blanche when he forces her to face "the essential and inescapable reality of things" (Riddel 31). However, the fundamental struggle in *Streetcar* is not between fantasy and reality, but between two radically different *perceptions* of reality. For if each person's interpretation of significant stimuli is to some degree unique, and if "perceptual activity supplies the materials from which the individual constructs his own personally meaningful environment" (Blake and Ramsey iii), an infinite number of disparate "realities" is possible. For example, both Blanche and Stanley see exactly the same visual phenomena, but sight and comprehension are not necessarily synonymous. To Blanche, Belle Reve is a crucial symbol of all she once was and of all she has now lost. To Stanley, Belle Reve is only "the place in the country" (270),[3] an old house glimpsed in a fading photograph. Blanche's reality is saving her sister from an abusive marriage to a subhuman brute. Stanley's reality is ridding his apartment of an unwelcome intruder bent on disrupting not only his home but also his relationship to a woman he genuinely loves.

Perhaps one of the most poignant moments in this tragedy of conflicting realities involves those few verbal exchanges in scene 2 when each of the protagonists makes a tentative, cautious attempt to understand the other and reach some sort of rapprochement: Stanley with his awkward, "sheepish" (284) semi-apology for "unpacking" Blanche's suitcase and for insinuating that she "swindled" Stella; Blanche with her wryly humorous explanation of how "the four-letter word deprived us of our plantation" (284). After the Poker Night, however, no truce, no shared perception is possible, for both Blanche and Stanley abandon all efforts toward conciliation and each sees the other only as the enemy. Both also unconsciously adopt the gestalt theory of perception: sterile, fixed, and narrow. They restructure reality to fit their preconceptions and prejudices, each willfully blinding himself or herself to even the smallest virtue his or her opponent might possess. Each perceives only the less creditable aspects of the other and takes that part for the whole. The morning after the poker party, Stella tells her sister that "you saw him at his worst last night." Blanche replies, "On the contrary, I saw him at his best!" (319). Blanche's Stanley is "common," "bestial," "ape-like." Stanley's Blanche is a hypocritical nymphomaniac "swilling down" his liquor. As Williams explains in his letter to Elia Kazan concerning the play:

Nobody sees anybody truly but all through the flaws of their own egos. That is the way we all see each other in life. Vanity, fear, desire, competition—all such distortions within our own egos—condition our vision of those in relation to us" (Kazan 329)

Neither Blanche nor Stanley can tolerate the other's "reality," and neither will compromise his or her rigid interpretation of the situation in the Kowalski home. The central issue of the play thus revolves around the question of whose perceptions, whose reality, will prevail and be accepted by the other, more malleable characters as authentic.

This is a struggle Blanche cannot win. She is mentally, physically, and psychologically exhausted, and her grip on her reality is too fragile and tenuous to match, let alone conquer, Stanley's vital, aggressive vision of himself and the world around him. He also has less need of what Kohut terms "responding mirrors" (41). Individuals tormented by fragile egos and minimal self-confidence need constant positive reinforcement from others. Their self-esteem rises and falls according to the image of themselves they see reflected in the eyes of those emotionally or spatially close to them. As R. D. Laing points out in *The Divided Self*, "Self-consciousness... implies two things: an awareness of oneself by oneself, and *an awareness of oneself as an object of someone else's observation*" (quoted in Lesser 14). A child looks into a mirror—or someone's eyes—hoping to see not merely an objective reflection, but something more, something that "reinforces the child's sense of self in any number of ways" (Lesser 16). Blanche's preoccupation with how she "looks" does not spring from narcissism or vanity, but from her crumbling sense of self-worth. As she grows more and more unstable under the pressure of Stanley's unrelenting contempt and his awareness of that part of her self she most wishes to hide, she frantically seeks to create a romanticized, reassuring self-portrait that she can study endlessly in the living mirrors within her sphere of influence—particularly Mitch and Stella. An image reflected in a real mirror is "the opposite of a self: an empty shell, a soulless illusion" that turns "warm tangibility into cold visibility" (Lesser 264). A living, sentient mirror has the power to give back idealized reflections, "faces other than those that look into it" (Lesser 264). But Blanche cannot maintain her hold on either her sister or her fiance.

Stanley's perception of "reality," while just as subjective as Blanche's, is backed by a much more dynamic, confident, and considerably less fragmented ego. Stanley too sometimes needs to reinforce his self-assurance by gazing into "responding mirrors": the image he projects to his friends, and particularly to his wife, is important to him, and he is enraged and hurt when Stella appears to see him through Blanche's eyes in scene 8. However, his response is to fight, to escalate the hostilities, to wear out his opponent until he can impose his perception of his sister-in-law on Stella, on Mitch, and, most tragically, on Blanche herself.

The other relevant phenomenon to be discussed, creativity, is more difficult to define in concrete terms than perception, because of the multiplicity of ambiguous and/or esoteric meanings attached to both the word itself and the process it implies. Indeed, few of those who consistently use the term actually attempt any sort of definition at all. How, then, does one find "an indicator of creative characteristics, thinking, and productions," as well as "a plausible measure of creative accomplishment" (Morse and Khatena 64)?

How can creative potential be assessed? What are the criteria of creativity? The data obtained from scientific experiments indicate that attributes such as quickness of mind, ingenuity, productive imagination, alertness, perceptual organization, and curiosity are essential characteristics of the creative personality (Morse and Khatena 59; Rawls and Slack 236). Reference sources stress the concept of originality: to create is to engender the growth of something new, to "bring into being, cause to exist" (*OED*. 1989 ed.), or to use something that already exists "in a new and imaginative way, to produce interesting and unusual results" (*Collins Cobuild English Language Dictionary* 1987 ed.). The creative product should exhibit "imagination as well as intellect" (*OED* 1989 ed.).[4] Williams emphasizes the "struggle" of creation as the artist attempts to translate "the experience of living...into pigment or music or bodily movement or poetry or prose or anything that's dynamic and expressive" ("Streetcar Named Success," viii-ix).

Is either of the protagonists in *Streetcar* truly creative? In Stanley's case, the answer is obvious: As the embodiment of fertility, the "gaudy seed-bearer" (265), his creativity is channeled into biology, and, in the final scene, the audience can witness the tangible evidence of his progenerative virility wrapped in a blue blanket. By contrast, Blanche's creative abilities are far less easy to categorize. Berkman attempts to refute the idea of perceiving Blanche "as representative of the artist" (34), citing her failure "to take a detached but energetic interest in observing an area of life hitherto unknown to her....to be attacked by Stan primarily for her desires to beautify, to transmit knowledge and experience, to make people more humane to one another," and, most tellingly, to "struggle on behalf of art" (34–35). In one sense, he is correct. Blanche does not symbolically epitomize the artist-as-martyr. Instead, because of factors such as her gender, education, social environment, and personal fears and frustrations, she embodies the artistic impulse thwarted, as, deprived of other outlets, her creative ability twists and turns back upon itself, fruitlessly expended on the only artistic medium readily available to her—herself.

Blanche possesses a number of the qualities and talents cited as essential to creativity by scientists such as Morse, Khatena, Rawls, and Slack: She is imaginative, perceptive, sensitive, and inventive. In addition, she has a gender advantage, for, according to the results of numerous complexity-simplicity experiments: (1) subjects rated high in creativity invariably prefer complex visual stimuli (Eisenman and Robinson 331; Taylor and Eisenman, "Perception" 242; Barron and Welsh 201; Eisenman and Johnson 113); (2) "sex and interest for visual complexity are significantly related" (Wiedl 152; Eisenman, "Birth Order and Sex Differences" 125); and (3) females tend to prefer more complexity than males (Eisenman and Johnson 116; Taylor and Eisenman "Birth Order and Sex Difference" 383–84; Looft and Baranowski 304). In test after test, replication after replication, preference for complexity has been linked to creativity, and women have expressed both a strong aesthetic orientation and a "striking" bias in favor of complex designs (Eisenman, "Complexity-Simplicity II" 171). These and other shape-preference studies indicate that many women not only have the potential for creative activity but also may even possess demiurgic abilities that out-weigh those of men (Harris, "Two Sexes in the Mind" 18). However, for women such as Blanche DuBois, the advantage of possessing what Virginia Woolf termed a "highly developed creative faculty" (91) is far outweighed by the disadvantage of living in a rigidly structured patriarchal society that allows that creative faculty minimal means of expression.

Perhaps in another historical or social context, Blanche might have re-ceived the comprehensive, intensive training that would have enabled her to channel her creative drive "into pigment or music or bodily movement or poetry or prose." Unfortunately, however, an adolescent girl from a socially prominent family during the second quarter of the twentieth century would have received an education differing little from that of any southern belle in the previous century, when a cultured young woman would have been expected to learn "accomplishments," but have no real vocation other than that of wife and mother. As Mrs. Ellis so admirably stated in her widely read *Family Monitor and Domestic Guide* (1844; quoted in Nochlin 28):

To be able to do a great many things tolerably well, is of infinitely more value to a woman than to be able to excel in any one.

The feminist movement, with its insistence on "the rights of individuals to choose occupations and interests based on personal ability, not gender" (Larsen and Long 1), will arrive several decades too late for Blanche. She is trapped in an earlier perspective, where "the insistence upon a modest, proficient, self-demeaning level of amateurism" militates against "any sig-nificant artistic accomplishment by women" (Nochlin 27). A girl like Blanche might take up some form of "art" as a hobby, a pastime, or a diversion—but *not* as a profession.[5]

Williams identifies "the passion to create" as "all that we know of God" (*Memoirs* 242), and declares that "it is only in his work that an artist can find reality and satisfaction ("Streetcar Named Success" viii). But Blanche is caught up in what Naomi Wolf labels "the beauty myth," which has as its basic tenet the assumption that female self-worth is determined by phys-ical attractiveness, and that "a high rating as an art object is the most valuable tribute a woman can exact from her lover" (171). A woman who accepts this premise remains forever vulnerable to outside opinion, and her satisfaction and self-esteem rise and fall according to the amount of male homage her beauty elicits. Naturally, Blanche, who has allowed her looks to define her life and the perceptions of men to determine her reality, is intensely preoccupied with her appearance and terrified of aging. She has fallen victim to one of the most repressive "cultural conspiracies" used to control women (Wolf 15). Even more depressing is the fact that she is to some extent aware of her own complicity in this conspiracy. After years of role-playing, she knows she has become "soft," not "self-sufficient enough" (332) to establish an identity of her own without relying on the judgment of others. Yet, even while despising herself for compromising her Self, she is still unable to break away and find "a new way to see" (Wolf 19). The beauty myth has become an integral part of her "reality," and she cannot bear to relinquish it. Even while she tells Stanley (396) that:

Physical beauty is passing. A transitory possession. But beauty of the mind and richness of the spirit and tenderness of the heart—and I have all of those things—aren't taken away, but grow! Increase with the years!

she is *"improvising feverishly"* and tragically incapable of believing her own words. Her perceptions and values contradict what she says. If she did believe in her "treasures," or could bring herself to believe in them, she might have been able to pull back from the brink of madness, and rescue herself from the "dark vein of self-hatred" (Wolf 10) that festers at the heart of the beauty myth. She does possess the tattered remnants of the qualities of mind and spirit that she describes: creative qualities that might have served as the foundation of a new, life-affirming reality. If she could nurture that reality, she would no longer need Mitch to transform her "paper moon." She could do so herself.

Those critics (both within and without the framework of the play) who seem perpetually exasperated by Blanche's petty vanities, her constant need of reassurance, and her inability to initiate a new and more productive reality, seriously underestimate the power of sexual stereotyping, a perceptual process that imposes upon its adherents a constriction of thought and behavior almost impossible to alleviate. The process apparently begins in the cradle, and "by the time boys and girls are 3 to 4 yr. of age they have already learned to make culturally expected sex-typed discriminations appropriate to their own sex as well as to the opposite sex" (Schell and Silber 385). As they grow older, children comprehend and acquire more and more gender-specific patterns of behavior, having learned that "incorrect" sex-typed choices can have unpleasant consequences, or can lead to perplexing misunderstandings. For example, "gender stereotypes and individual differences in sex type influence perceptions of emotional behavior" (Smith et al. 489). Anger, which is associated with aggression, is perceived as inimical to the "nurturing" aspect of the female stereotype, and is thus considered to have "more relationship costs, more life script costs" for women than for men (Smith et al. 488). More girls than boys are referred to children's mental health clinics "for being defiant and verbally aggressive" (Smith et al. 489). Mitch is astonished when Blanche reacts to his clumsy rape attempt with hysterical fury, and Stanley seems to regard her efforts to twist a broken bottle in his face as a form of sexual foreplay, causing him to accelerate his assault. Furthermore, Smith and his colleagues report that "the empirical literature on gender stereotypes and judgments of mental health indicates that deviant behavior is regarded by both professionals and laypersons as less serious when it conforms to gender stereotypes, and more serious when it violates these beliefs" (488). In other words, Blanche's promiscuity has earned her the reputation of a neurotic whore, while her male relatives were able to engage in "epic fornications" (284) with social impunity. The self-righteous and myopic citizens of Laurel, Mississippi, make no allowances for extenuating circumstances. A "decent" woman, a "lady," should be "sexually attractive, but not sexually available" (Tetreault and Barnett 3). Even Blanche's choice of a career is dictated by stereotypical sex-role considerations and community expectations. As a female member of the landed gentry, she "is trapped economically and socially" (Lant 228), having been trained for little else but looking ornamental and pleasing men. When she is forced to seek a job because of economic necessity, the only "genteel" occupation available to her is teaching, in which her grounding in literature can at least be of some use. Compounding her employment problems is her physical beauty that is, ironically, a hindrance rather than an asset as far as the job market is concerned, for "attractive women are rated as less qualified and therefore less likely to be hired into 'male' occupations than are unattractive women" (Spencer and Taylor 274). Since those "male occupations" traditionally offer higher salaries and more chances for career advancement, Blanche seems doomed to spend her life in a disheartening effort to teach "Hawthorne and Whitman and Poe" (302) to classes of bored high school students at a "pitiful salary" (262).

Under these circumstances, having no real vocation and no legitimate channel for creativity, Blanche pours out her creative energy on herself, attempting to re-create herself as an art object: a living embodiment of the ideal southern belle—young, lovely, genteel, flirtatious, and alluringly fragile.[6] She is engaged in an artistic reconstruction of reality, involving both her present and her past. She transmutes her perceptions and experiences directly into her "art" as a conscious and intentional creative act. Her whole public persona is a carefully structured role: life as performance art. Her choice of costumes, sets, and lighting are for the most part deliberately selected for theatrical effect. Berkman, questioning Blanche's credentials as an artist, notes that "even what might have been a sign of the artist, the Chinese paper lantern, symbolizes in the play less beauty than concealment" (35). However, that "concealment" is an important part of Blanche's self-directed "creation," vital to her effort to hide the unmistakable signs of strain and aging that are only too apparent in the merciless glare of the sun or a naked light bulb. She forbids Stella to look at her until she is "bathed and rested" (251), and insists that Mitch take her to dimly lit restaurants. As for Berkman's assertion that nowhere in the play is she struggling "as an artist" (35), Blanche does nothing *but* struggle throughout the whole drama to sustain the artistic life of her stereotypic fantasy self. What is really at issue is not the struggle itself, but the nature and value of the end product of her artistic endeavor. Specifically, is Blanche's "creation" worth such an impassioned struggle—a struggle that eventually costs her her sanity?

In his *Memoirs*, Williams states that "the chief endowment of any true artist is the honesty of intention" (24), and Blanche hampers and perverts her creative ability by using it to perpetuate an image of herself that is neither candid nor valid. The Fantasy Blanche that she tries to impose upon the world has, over the years, become a stale, hollow, almost-parody of what she may actually have been "a pretty long time ago" (365). Now she seems at times almost a caricature rather than a character. The "tender," "trusting" individual Stella knew as a girl has been buried under layers of artifice.

If the purpose of art is the recreation of oneself in another medium or, in the case of acting, the transcendence of oneself on the stage, Blanche fails as an artist. Tormented by her inner demons, she only plays the self she thinks others wish to see, seldom venturing publicly beyond the boundaries of the restrictive role she has assigned herself. The nature of stereotypes is prescriptive and reductive. They limit one's potential as well as one's "reality." "One's total personality is summed up in a few trite, easily identifiable behavior patterns. One or two obvious facets of character are developed at the expense of the whole being" (Harris, "Stereotypes" 4). Several empirical studies link "creativity with greater openness to experience" (Domino 114). By contrast, Blanche, trapped within the constraints of her stereotypic role and forever at the mercy of the perceptions of others, injudiciously clings to her protective camouflage and the sterile, frozen, misguided creation that eventually contributes to the destruction of her last chance for happiness and fulfillment. It is both pathetic and ironic that Blanche, who is so desperate for love and acceptance, thinks that she cannot attain them without trivializing herself by assuming a fictive and superficial identity. As her creator said in his *Memoirs*, "If you can't be yourself, what's the point of being anything at all?" (230).

Critics such as Kernan, Corrigan, and Lant see in Blanche a woman almost totally and pathetically "lost" (Lant 228) in a world of illusion and "romantic evasions" (Kernan 19). She would be better off if she were. But there is always a part of Blanche, a self-within-a-self, that is only too aware of the sordid travesty her life has become. She has moments of ruthless perception when she is disgusted by her own hypocrisy, wearily rolling her eyes as she plays the affable Mitch like a fish on a line with her talk of "old-fashioned ideals" (348). At such times, she sees herself not as a modern Scarlett O'Hara but as a combination of con artist and spider-in-chief of the Tarantula Arms. She is fragmented, unable to divorce herself completely from the "realities" of people like Stanley, or to amputate self from self

(Kolodny "Notes on Defining" 80) and compartmentalize the incompatible segments of her life. Even alcohol will no longer blur her duality of vision, or blot out her pain and guilt—guilt that apparently began with the suicide of her young husband.

Prior to World War II, many women "had been required to make only one big decision—[the] choice of a husband" (Chafe 175). Blanche's choice brings disaster on Allan Grey and on herself, as the past haunts the future. She has been much blamed by critics for not "responding compassionately" to the disclosure of Allan's homosexuality (Berkman 36), for not being supportive, for her failure to establish "an open and trusting relationship with him" (Cardullo 82) so that he might confide in her. Such criticisms view the past from the context of the present. What would a sixteen-year-old girl living in the second quarter of the twentieth century know of the psychological intricacies of the then-taboo subject of homosexuality? What would be her reaction when confronted with the graphic physical evidence of her idolized husband's sexual preference for a male companion rather than herself? The blow to her self-esteem and her confidence in her own attractiveness would be devastating. Yes, her fantasy of perfect, ideal love was unrealistic. Yes, her worship of Allan as someone "almost too fine to be human" (364) would have put an intolerable strain on a young man unsure of his masculinity. Yes, she blames herself bitterly, unceasingly for his death. But does she deserve to be condemned so harshly, deserve to be destroyed? Her husband expected more of her, a teenage girl hopelessly in love with him, than she could possibly give. He wanted her to "save" him somehow, to provide "a cleft in the rock of the world" he could "hide in" (387). She expects the same of Mitch, but neither relationship can stand the shock of altered perceptions.

Blanche is not a nymphomaniac. She is frustrated not in lust but in love, and her "intimacies with strangers" (386) follow a definite pattern. She invariably chooses, when she can choose, young men—army enlistees, high school students, a paperboy—all approximately the same age as her husband when he committed suicide. Even in the last scene, she envisions a romantic death at sea under the care of a "very young" ship's doctor (410). She feels the need to weave romantic fantasies about her conquests and near-conquests. The embarrassed paperboy looks "like a young Prince out of the Arabian Nights"; the soldiers are gathered up "like daisies" from the lawn at Belle Reve (389). But above all, they are "young, young, young" (339). It is as if she were trying to replicate her marriage again and again, hoping against hope for a happy ending each time, searching for proof that she is still young and desirable. Perhaps she is also seeking that part of herself she lost when she walked suddenly "into a room that I thought was empty—which wasn't empty (354). Her quest is, of course, inevitably doomed to fail. Time has stopped for Allan Grey but rolls relentlessly onward for Blanche DuBois.

Blanche says that she wants "magic"—eternal youth, beauty that never fades—but the unyielding surface of her mirror provides neither comfort nor reassurance. Her prolonged deathwatch in the tomb that was once Belle Reve[7] has made her terrifyingly aware of her own mortality; the art object upon which she lavished all her creative energy is "fading" (332), "played out" (387); and she is unable to sublimate completely her conscious awareness of the tawdry aspects of her life. She cannot reconcile her two self-images: the artistocratic lady from Belle Reve and the whore from the Flamingo Hotel. She is denied a sense of wholeness "in a world where other people have managed to achieve coherence" (Lesser 19). When she looks into a mirror, whom does she see: a doppelganger, the "self who is both our twin and our opposite" (Lesser 264); or, even worse, the "zero self" that represents the total loss of personal identity?

Why do schizophrenics stare into the mirror? What are they trying to do? The answer is obvious. They feel themselves crumbling and disappearing. By vision they are trying to see "No, I'm still there. I can see myself." But a mirror is cold. (Kohut 41)

Blanche is not a schizophrenic (at least, not yet), but she is on the brink of a complete mental and emotional collapse. She needs a mirror "in which the portrait one gets back is not the self one expects, but the lost self for which one searches" (Lesser 11). This is the reason that she needs the responding mirrors, the living *agents for self-confirmation, for self-approval*" (Kohut quoted in Lesser 14), who will validate the existence of her ideal Fantasy Self as her only self and thus make her whole. Solitude frightens Blanche, for then her "other" self begins to invade her consciousness, and the line between the two disparate images of her soul begins to blur. "I want to be *near* you, got to be *with* somebody," she cries out in panic to Stella, "I *can't* be alone!" (257).

It is in this precarious psychological state that Blanche DuBois seeks out her sister, hoping to find a refuge, a sanctuary where she can rebuild her broken life. Instead, she finds the "ghoul-haunted woodland of Weir" (252). Nothing in her experience has prepared her for Chateau Kowalski and the social and physical environment her sister now takes for granted. She might lament with Cassandra (for she is more Cassandra than the Madonna postulated by Schvey): "God of my destruction! . . . Through what streets have you led me now, to what house?" (Aeschylus 70). She is off-balance from the first, a stranger on alien ground. However, she soon discovers that though the landscape might be unfamiliar, the mindscape is not. The patriarchal system of the blue-collar working-class population of Elysian Fields is just as rigid as that of the aristocracy of Belle Reve. The only creative outlet recognized by the men as legitimate for their women is strictly biological, and even Stella, who as the second-born female sibling might have a creative potential even greater than that of Blanche,[8] is so acclimatized to this unwritten but very palpable code that she never questions it. In addition, the males expect their wives to be "straight" (385), sexually faithful to them while they themselves feel free to chase the occasional blonde " 'round the balcony" of the nearest bar (326), even though some of the females, like Eunice, are able to give vent to their rage and jealousy in ways far more physical than any lady of Laurel would consider proper.[9] Blanche, like John Proctor in Miller's *The Crucible* and like Williams himself (*Memoirs* 188), wants "to get [her] goodness back" and thus become whole again. To accomplish this, she expects to recuperate in a nonjudgmental atmosphere with the aid of her supportive, impressionable sister. To her shock and dismay, she finds herself trapped in the stifling atmosphere of a two-room flat dominated by Stanley, who sizes her up "at a glance" (265)—or thinks he does—and treats her with increasing scorn, rudeness, and hostility as the play progresses.

Starting with scene 2, Stanley picks up cues from Blanche's behavior that he believes are incompatible with his stereotypic image of a "respectable" sister-in-law. After she sprays him with her perfume, he voices his newly awakened suspicions: "If I didn't know that you was my wife's sister I'd get ideas about you!" (281). His "ideas" become certainties as the action builds to its inexorable climax and as the nature of his conflict with Blanche becomes more clearly defined. Bigsby calls Stella "the real hero of the play" (47). She is not; she is the prize, as is Mitch. Stanley and Blanche, both of whom are essentially egocentric, want to see nothing but unqualified veneration in the eyes of their two most accessible votaries. Such admiration is important (and in Blanche's case, vital) to their *amour propre*. Since their perceptions of reality are so radically discordant, however, each of the combatants must somehow persuade Stella and Mitch to accept her or his vision of reality as not just *a* valid perception of reality but as the *only* valid perception of reality. As the struggle escalates, the two antagonists come to regard each other as the physical embodiment of a threat rather than as a human being, thus objectifying and distancing the enemy. To Stanley, Blanche represents a threat to his marriage, a thief in his household who means to steal Stella's affection and turn her against him. In accordance with the prevailing masculine code, Stella is "his" woman. She belongs to him, he loves her, and Blanche's steady campaign to degrade him in her eyes is intolerable. Blanche's initial move against him, her "don't hang back with the brutes" speech (323), fails, but her long-term strategy to induce Stella to see him through her eyes is more successful. By scene 8, Stella is doing exactly what she asked Blanche not to do: compare Stanley's "unrefined," "common" manners and appearance with those of the "men that we went out with at home" (257).

As for Mitch, Stanley would resent the defection of any of his group of poker buddies, who obviously view him as their acknowledged leader. A defection to Blanche's "reality" would constitute a painful blow to his ego. Besides, he is sincere in his desire to save his "best friend" (366) from marrying a woman he considers little better than a prostitute. Blanche, for her part, considers Stella "all I've got in the world" (253), and, having been exposed to the supercilious disdain of "everybody . . . in the town of Laurel" (359), she is fiercely intent on retaining the only positive relationship she still has, basking in Stella's gentle reassurances and willingness to wait on her as she did at Belle Reve. Mitch, with his awkward but sincere admiration, not only helps to restore her battered faith in her attractiveness to men— the core of her self-esteem—but also offers her the refuge and respectability of marriage. The only person who stands in the way of her attainment of this goal is his friend Stanley, whose unfavorable opinion of her might demolish the image of the refined southern gentlewoman she has so carefully built up. Therefore, she employs the same insinuating tactics that are succeeding so well with Stella: constant but not ostentatious references to Stanley's coarseness, incivility, and "commonness" (351).

But, as previously noted, Blanche is no match for Stanley. He has "always smashed things" (312), and one of those "things" will be Blanche's precarious mental stability. Her "magic," her fading but still luminous beauty and charm, can ensnare Mitch and Stella only for a limited time. Her reserves of strength are almost gone, and she is neither tough enough nor angry enough to weather the barrage of Stanley's devastating concrete evidence. As her panic bubbles toward the surface, her performance grows increasingly forced and shrill, a cartoon Scarlett O'Hara. She lacks the mental toughness of O'Neill's Anna Christie, who can confront unflinchingly the embodiment of her sordid future in the person of Marthy, the waterfront hag. Nor can she muster the courage and resiliency of Beth Henley's Carnelle Scott, another "victim of broken dreams" (*Miss Firecracker* 106), who turns to promiscuity to bolster her shaky ego, but who in the end "can put aside her insecurity and self-hatred along with her romantic delusions" and get on with her life (Harris, "Stereotypes" 5).

As Stanley uncovers fact after damning fact, Blanche's only weapon is hysterical denial, and the battle is lost. Both Stella and Mitch initially brand Stanley's evidence as "lies," since an observer with very strong beliefs or preconceptions will tend to disregard or seriously doubt information that runs contrary to her/his expectations (Bond 113). But Stanley has acquired too much lethal ammunition. Stella, who knew "Blanche as a girl" ((376) reacts with pity and understanding, even when she realizes that Stanley's accusations might be more than just "partly true" (365). Mitch, disillusioned and bitter, rejects and denounces her. She is not "straight," not "clean enough" to marry (390). Blanche is guilty of that worst of crimes, deviation from accepted sex role behavior, and, when confronted with such deviations, "people will adopt explanations which require the least reorganization or change in their current conception, rather than use the information to alter their perception of reality" (Bond 114). Blanche's physical attractiveness doubly damns her, because "when attractive people fail to meet performance standards, that failure is attributed to internal factors [rather than to external circumstances] and is treated more harshly than that of others" (Spencer and Taylor 283). By scene 10, Blanche is alone, completely isolated, her last "responding mirrors" gone. At that point, as she teeters on the brink of insanity, the nightmare world outside crashes through both the flimsy walls of the apartment and the last feeble barriers protecting her reason, engulfing her in madness.

One of the true horrors of scene 10 is that the rape could easily have been avoided. Misperception is again the key factor. Stanley returns from the hospital in a jubilant mood, and his invitation to Blanche to "bury the hatchet" (395) and have a few drinks is probably sincere. As Cardullo points out, Stanley is not "maliciously intent on destroying his sister-in-law" (80), and he has every reason to be in a good humor. He and his wife are about to have a child (which he automatically assumes will be a boy), and his most irritating relative is leaving on Tuesday. Regrettably, a night that could have been spent in boozy camaraderie and that might in turn have led to some degree of mutual understanding, turns ugly and violent. Blanche's fear of Stanley is now so visceral that her only reaction to his heavy-handed approach is to retreat in terror, and Stanley, like any predator, can smell fear.[10] He begins to stalk her; his contempt for her and her illusions, which he interprets as "lies and conceit and tricks" (398) resurfaces. The words they exchange ("interfere," "roughhouse") become weighted with sexual meaning, and the scene culminates in a brutal rape.[11] Stanley's sexual assault is not part of a long-term, carefully planned campaign designed to drive Blanche mad, but it is more than an act of "uncontrollable drunken lust" (Cardullo 80), more even than an "expression of sexual dominance" (Larsen and Long 8; see also Nelson 140) or a "symbolic ravishing of the Apollonian by the Dionysian self" (Riddel 29). Stanley considers Blanche a whore and treats her like one, thus validating and reinforcing in his own mind his perception of her. He literally forces his "reality" upon her, bringing to the surface of her consciousness the terrible fear that his perception of her might be accurate, might be true. That, more than the humiliation and pain of the physical act itself, is the "awful thing" (401) she so feared would happen, and it is that which annihilates her reason so completely. Just for that short space of time, she sees herself through his eyes, and perhaps, in her guilt and wretchedness, she also sees the jeering faces of everyone she ever knew shouting the same words at her that she once hurled at Allan Grey: "I saw! I know! You disgust me . . . " (355). The only avenue of escape from that desolating vision is death or madness.

The last scene marks Blanche's final withdrawal into her own reality. By the end of that scene, she can ignore Stella's desperate cries of "Blanche, Blanche!" (418), not because she is angry at her sister's betrayal, but because she is in an almost literal sense "blind" to her (418), having blocked her and the rest of Elysian Fields out of her consciousness. For her, they no longer exist as she *"walks on without turning"* (418) out of their lives into an uncertain but probably harrowing future in the state asylum. As Miller explains, "Ego-defensive performance impairment may be in defense of self-perception" (490), and Blanche has been too bruised by life to regain any of her self-esteem except by severing all ties with any "reality" other than her own.

Much has been made of Blanche's "ritualistic epiphany" (Roderick 101) in scene 11, her progress from sinner to saint supposedly symbolized by the abandonment of her red satin robe in favor of a jacket of "Della Robbia blue. The blue of the robe in the old Madonna pictures" (409). Schvey, in particular, interprets "this change of costume" as a "casting off" of Blanche's "sensual side in favour of a new innocence, with strong implications of spiritual rebirth" (107). However, such interpretations do not take into account experiments dealing with "sex-related difference in the color lexicon" (Nowaczyk 261). In general, women seem to "possess more distinct internal representations for color than men" (Nowaczyk 257), and have a more extensive color vocabulary than men. Women are more color oriented than men (Caldwell 17). This, in turn, suggests that females may be more sensitive to nuances of color than males, and in addition may give more weight to any emotional overtones connected with individual colors. "A linguistic code for a color, the color word, is linked with a physical code for the color, the perceptual representation" (Nowaczyk 263). Since perceptual attitudes are expressed in preferences, the choice of a certain color represents a conscious or unconscious preference for that color. The Della Robbia blue jacket represents a conscious choice. Blanche, who tends to wear costumes rather than clothes, has planned her complete outfit for her rendezvous with Shep Huntleigh right down to her turquoise seahorse pin and artificial violets. In addition, it is she who verbally underlines the symbolic significance of that particular shade of blue and its connection to Renaissance religious paintings. On the other hand, the red robe has subconscious as well as conscious implications. It is interesting to note that although women in general seem to prefer lighter, less saturated colors than men (Child et al. 237), there is one exception: red. Indeed, even adolescent girls "seem more frequently than boys to prefer high saturation in a red" (Child et al. 241; see also Guilford 501). Thus, the dismissal of the red robe as a badge of harlotry is too simplistic. Blanche does indeed wear the red robe as a seductive device in scene 3 when she deliberately attracts Mitch's notice, but she also retreats to this particular garment when she feels lost and afraid, when, for example, her birthday party is ruined by Mitch's absence and Stanley's cruel "birthday remembrance" (375). Perhaps she clings to the robe because it reminds her of a period in her life when her beauty and seductiveness were beyond question. Perhaps the intense red,

red as the blood of a young man dead at the side of a lake, feeds her compulsive guilt. Above all, the robe has sacrificial overtones, for Williams emphasizes that it is in the red robe that she achieves *"tragic radiance"* (406). She is like Cassandra—raped, jeered at, and branded a liar when she tells the truth (Lant 233). Like Cassandra, Blanche too knows the identity of her destroyer, her "executioner" (351) well before the fatal catastrophe, and she too cannot escape destruction at his hands. Unlike Cassandra, she does not know the precise nature of the doom that awaits her when the doors swing shut behind her, but she goes with the same tragic resignation, realizing at last that "the time is full" and there is "no escape" (Aeschylus 79). The "spiritual rebirth" that Schvey and Roderick envision for Blanche may be an overly optimistic reading of the end of the play, given the grim conditions of the mental wards of that period. Completely surrounded by madness, she might forever lose her Self in her fictive self. She might eventually undergo the same type of prefrontal lobotomy that crippled the mind of Williams's sister.[12] In *Streetcar*, just as in *Agamemnon*, "no holy god of healing presides over this story" (Aeschylus 77).

A Streetcar Named Desire has often been labeled a tragedy of "misunderstanding," even by Williams himself (quoted in Kazan 330; see also Cardullo and Berkman). However, the essential tragedy goes beyond misunderstanding. *Streetcar* is a tragedy of misperception, thwarted creativity, and misplaced priorities. The central dramatic struggle involves two people so fundamentally incompatible that their individual "realities" can find no common ground upon which to build a relationship. Stanley emerges triumphant, his version of reality embraced, though not without profound regret, by his wife and his best friend. As for Blanche, although the nature of her internal and external value systems has prevented her from realizing any legitimate artistic potential she might once have possessed, nevertheless she is not merely pathetic, not just "a girl waiting in her best dress to go to the dance of life with someone who never came" (Godwin 145). She regains tragic stature as, calm and remote, she leaves the site of her final catastrophe. She has some dignity still, and, like Cassandra, she "shall not die/dishonored by the gods" (Aeschylus 78), even when the bleak walls of the asylum and of her own broken mind enclose her, wrapping her in a shroud of gray mist that the harsh, glaring lights of Stanley's reality will never again penetrate.[13]

NOTES

1. Quoted in Bastian (13).

2. See in particular Bastian; Blake and Ramsey; Dennis; Donovan; Eisenman and Johnson; Harris; Hess and Baker; Nemser; Nochlin; Register; and Snyder-Ott.

3. This and all subsequent quotations from Tennessee Williams's A Streetcar Named Desire are from the script printed in The Theatre of Tennessee Williams,

vol. 1 (New York: New Directions, 1971, and will be cited by page number in the text.

4. One might also wish to refer to the Torrance Tests of Creative Thinking (1974); Thinking Creatively with Sounds and Words (Khatena and Torrance 1973); or the Khatena-Torrance Creative Perception Inventory, known as the KTCPI (1976). Further research material can be acquired at the Annual Creative Problem-Solving Institute sponsored by the Creative Education Foundation at State University College in Buffalo.

5. It is interesting to note that, in a study examining the perceptions school children have about the visual arts, "over twice as many artists were drawn as male than female, and conversely twice as many art teachers were drawn as female" (Bastian 12). Children often derive their stereotypes from visible examples in our society, and, for the most part, in our culture, "women are expected to be neither serious nor taken seriously in art" (Hall 143). Women also have a tendency to devalue their own work, and, due to gender stereotyping, seldom "think of themselves as artists" (Whitesel 23), having internalized "restricting views of their creative potential" (Landy quoted in Diamond 21).

6. Unfortunately, women gain few real advantages in terms of status or power by adopting this type of societal role. As Fabes and Laner discovered in their study of how the sexes perceive each other (139), both males and females

perceived that social expectations regarding treatment of women, such as chivalry, courtesy, dating customs ... significantly favored females. However, the socially advantageous treatment of women was not perceived to reflect a greater degree of status for them. . . . These findings may suggest that the preferential treatment of women is a function of the male's perceived superior position of power and dominance.

7. According to Taylor and Eisenman, parental concerns and societal demands for conformity are heavier on the first-born female child than on later born sisters ("Birth Order and Sex Difference" 385). As the eldest unmarried daughter, Blanche would be expected to remain at home and care for her sick and dying relatives. After all, except for one brief, doomed interval, she has failed to achieve the central purpose for which she was reared: marriage. Even in a play such as Beth Henley's *The Miss Firecracker Contest*, which is set in the contemporary South, the primary goal remains unchanged. Elain, the family "beauty" bitterly remarks that, "When I graduated junior college she [her mother] said, 'You've had your spoonful of gravy, now go out and get a rich husband,' so I did" (39), thereby locking herself into a loveless relationship.

8. Several studies have shown that later-born females prefer "more complexity than first born females," and thus, at least in theory, have more creative potential than the eldest female sibling (see especially Eisenman, "Complexity-Simplicity: II. Birth Order and Sex Differences").

9. Note, however, that both Blanche and Eunice seek refuge in alcohol. After the initial discovery of her husband's infidelity, Blanche, Allan, and his lover drive out to the Moon Lake Casino, "very drunk and laughing all the way" (355). Eunice, after her initial fury at Steve has abated, seeks solace at the Four Deuces, "gettin' a drink" (327).

10. Scientists have discovered that, in the male consciousness, the potential for violence against women often lurks very near the surface. For example, in a study

of play constructions among college students, the tendency among male subjects was "to emphasize...potential disaster to women," whereas in the women's constructions, the theme of an insane or criminal man was universal" (Erikson 690). In similar studies involving young adolescents, girls tended to create enclosed interior structures and people them with families consisting mostly or entirely of women. When asked to introduce a disruptive force into such peaceful scenes, the intruding element was "always a man, a boy, or an animal" (Erikson 687).

11. During the rehearsal process, producer Irene Selznick suggested a change in the rape scene:

> I felt she [Blanche] would be destroyed more completely if, after resisting, she began to respond and then he changed course and repulsed her. It would be her fatal humiliation. I would have him fling her across the stage and just stand there, laughing savagely. I thought it would make the last act more valid.

Williams thought that the concept might be "dramatically sound," but Kazan vetoed the idea (Selznick 302).

12. Rose once said to her brother and his friends, "You must never make fun of insanity. It's worse than death" (*Memoirs* 121).

13. For additional relevant source material on perceptual and creative theory, see Carterette and Friedman, Clark, Mackinnon, Malchon, McDonald, Rosenthal et al., Six and Eckes, Snyder-Ott, and Warnock.

WORKS CITED

Aeschylus. *Agamemnon. The Oresteia.* Trans. David Grene and Wendy Doniger O'Flaherty. Chicago: U of Chicago P, 1989.

Barron, Frank, and George S. Welsh. "Artistic Perception as a Possible Factor in Personality Style: Its Measurement by a Figure Preference Test." *Journal of Psychology* 33 (1952): 199–203.

Bastian, Linda. "Women as Artists and Teachers." *Art Education* 28, no. 7 (1975): 12–15.

Berkman, Leonard. "The Tragic Downfall of Blanche DuBois." Bloom 33–40.

Bigsby, C.W.E. "Tennessee Williams: Streetcar to Glory." Bloom 41–47.

Blake, Robert R., and Glenn V. Ramsey. *Perception: An Approach to Personality.* New York: The Ronald Press, 1951.

Bloom, Harold, ed. *Modern Critical Interpretations: Tennessee Williams's A Streetcar Named Desire.* New York: Chelsea House, 1988.

Bond, Lynne A. "Perceptions of Sex-Role Deviations: An Attributional Analysis." *Sex Roles* 7 (1981): 107–15.

Caldwell, George. "Feminist Considerations in Theatrical Design." *Empirical Research in Theatre* 8 (1982): 15–25.

Cardullo, Bert. "Drama of Intimacy and Tragedy of Incomprehension: *A Streetcar Named Desire* Reconsidered." Bloom 79–92.

Carterette, Edward C., and Morton P. Friedman, eds. *Handbook of Perception.* Vol. 1, *Historical and Philosophical Roots of Perception.* New York: Academic Press, 1974.

Chafe, William H. *The Paradox of Change: American Women in the 20th Century.* New York: Oxford, 1991.

Child, Irvin L., Jens A. Hansen, and Frederick W. Hornbeck. "Age and Sex Differences in Children's Color Preferences." *Child Development* 39 (1968): 237–47.

Clark, Edward T. "The Influence of Sex and Social Class on Occupational Preference and Perception." *Personnel and Guidance Journal* 45 (1967): 440–44.

Corrigan, Mary Ann. "Realism and Theatricalism in *A Streetcar Named Desire*." Bloom 49–60.

Dennis, Wayne. "Cultural and Developmental Factors in Perception." Blake and Ramsey 148–69.

Diamond, Arlyn, and Lee R. Edwards. *The Authority of Experience: Essays in Feminist Criticism*. Amherst: U of Massachusetts P, 1977.

Domino, George. "Attitudes Towards Dreams, Sex Differences and Creativity." *Journal of Creative Behavior* 16, no. 2 (1982): 112–22.

Donovan, Josephine, ed. *Feminist Literary Criticism: Explorations in Theory*. Lexington: UP of Kentucky, 1975.

Eisenman, Russell. "Birth-Order and Sex Differences in Aesthetic Preference for Complexity-Simplicity." *Journal of General Psychology* 77, no. 1 (1967): 121–26.

————. "Complexity-Simplicity: II. Birth Order and Sex Differences." *Psychonomic Science* 8, no. 4 (1967): 171–72.

Eisenman, Russell, and Paul Johnson. "Birth Order, Sex, Perception and Production of Complexity." *Journal of Social Psychology* 79, no. 1 (1969): 113–19.

Eisenman, Russell, and Nancy Robinson. "Complexity-Simplicity, Creativity, Intelligence, and Other Correlates." *Journal of Psychology* 67 (1967): 331–34.

Erikson, E. H. "Sex Differences in the Play Configurations of Preadolescents." *American Journal of Orthopsychiatry* 21 (1951): 667–92.

Fabes, Richard A., and Mary R. Laner. "How the Sexes Perceive Each Other: Advantages and Disadvantages." *Sex Roles* 15 (1986): 129–43.

Forgus, Ronald H. *Perception*. New York: McGraw-Hill, 1966.

Godwin, Parke. "The Fire When It Comes." *Ghosts*. Ed. Isaac Asimov, Martin H. Greenberg, and Charles G. Waugh. New York: NAL Penguin, Incorporated, 1988. 115–58.

Goncharov, Andrei A. Address. Mayakovsky Theatre, Moscow. 30 March 1991.

Guilford, J. P. "A System of Color-Preferences." *American Journal of Psychology* 72 (1959): 487–502.

Hall, Lee. "In the University." Hess and Baker 130–46.

Harris, Laurilyn J. "Delving Beneath the Stereotypes: Beth Henley's *The Miss Firecracker Contest*." *Theatre Southwest* 14, no. 2 (1987): 4–7.

————. "Two Sexes in the Mind: Perceptual and Creative Differences Between Women and Men." *Journal of Creative Behavior* 23, no. 1 (1989): 14–25.

Henley, Beth. *The Miss Firecracker Contest*. Garden City, N.Y.: Nelson Doubleday, 1985.

Hess, Thomas B., and Elizabeth C. Baker, eds. *Art and Sexual Politics*. New York: Macmillan, 1973.

Kazan, Elia. *A Life*. New York: Alfred A. Knopf, 1988.

Kernan, Alvin B. "Truth and Dramatic Mode in *A Streetcar Named Desire*." Bloom 17–19.

Kohut, Heinz. *The Kohut Seminars*. Ed. Miriam Elson. New York: Norton, 1987.

Kolodny, Annette. "Some Notes on Defining a 'Feminist Literary Criticism.' " *Critical Inquiry* 2 (1975): 75–92.

Lant, Kathleen Margaret. "A Streetcar Named Misogyny." *Violence in Drama*. Ed. James Redmond. Cambridge: Cambridge U P, 1991. 225–38.

Larsen, Knud S., and Ed Long. "Attitudes Toward Sex-Roles: Traditional or Egalitarian?" *Sex Roles* 19 (1988): 1–12.

Lesser, Wendy. *His Other Half: Men Looking at Women through Art*. Cambridge, Mass.: Harvard U P, 1991.

Looft, William R., and Marc D. Baranowski. "Birth Order, Sex, and Complexity-Simplicity: An Attempt at Replication." *Perceptual and Motor Skills* 32 (1971): 303–6.

Mackinnon, D. W. "The Nature and Nurture of Creative Talent." *American Psychologist* 17 (1962): 484–95.

McDonald, Robert L. "Effects of Sex, Race, and Class on Self, Ideal-Self, and Parental Ratings in Southern Adolescents." *Perceptual and Motor Skills* 27 (1968): 15–25.

Malchon, Margaret J., and Louis A. Penner. "The Effects of Sex and Sex-Role Identity on the Attribution of Maladjustment." *Sex Roles* 7 (1981): 363–78.

Miller, Arden. "Performance Impairment after Failure: Mechanism and Sex Differences." *Journal of Educational Psychology* 78 (1986): 486–91.

Morse, David T., and Joe Khatena. "The Relationship of Creativity and Life Accomplishments." *Journal of Creative Behavior* 23, no. 1 (1989): 59–65.

Nelson, Benjamin. *Tennessee Williams: The Man and His Work*. New York: Ivan Obolensky, 1961.

Nemser, Cindy. "Art Criticism and Perceptual Research." *Art Journal* 29 (1970): 326–29.

———. "Blowing the Whistle on the Art World." *Feminist Art Journal* 4 (1975): 25–31.

Nochlin, Linda. "Why Have There Been No Great Women Artists?" Hess and Baker 1–39.

Nowaczyk, Ronald H. "Sex-Related Differences in the Color Lexicon." *Language and Speech* 25 (1982): 257–65.

O'Neill, Eugene. "*Anna Christie*." *Eugene O'Neill: Complete Plays 1913–1920*. Ed. Travis Bogard. New York: The Library of America, 1988.

Quinton, Anthony. "The Problem of Perception." Warnock 61–84.

Rawls, James R., and Gordon K. Slack. "Artists Versus Nonartists: Rorschach Determinants and Artistic Creativity." *Journal of Projective Techniques and Personality Assessment* 32 (1968): 233–37.

Register, Cheri. "American Feminist Literary Criticism: A Bibliographical Introduction." Donovan 1–28.

Riddel, Joseph N. "*A Streetcar Named Desire*: Nietzsche Descending." Bloom 21–31.

Roderick, John M. "From 'Tarantula Arms' to 'Della Robbia Blue': The Tennessee Williams Tragicomic Transit Authority." Bloom 93–101.

Rosenthal, Karen R., Ellis L. Gesten, and Saul Shiffman. "Gender and Sex Role Differences in the Perception of Social Support." *Sex Roles* 14 (1986): 481–99.

Schell, Robert E., and Jean Waggoner Silber. "Sex-Role Discrimination among Young Children." *Perceptual and Motor Skills* 27 (1968): 379–89.

Schvey, Henry I. "Madonna at the Poker Night: Pictorial Elements in Tennessee Williams's *A Streetcar Named Desire*." Bloom 103–10.

Selznick, Irene Mayer. *A Private View*. New York: Alfred A. Knopf, 1983.

Six, Bernd, and Thomas Eckes. "A Closer Look at the Complex Structure of Gender Stereotypes." *Sex Roles* 24 (1991): 57–71.

Smith, K. C., S. E. Ulch, J. E. Cameron, J. A. Cumberland, M. A. Musgrave, and N. Tremblay. "Gender-Related Effects in the Perception of Anger Expression." *Sex Roles* 20 (1989): 487–99.

Snyder-Ott, Joelynn. "The Female Experience and Artistic Creativity." *Art Education* 27, no. 6 (1974): 15–18.

———. *Women and Creativity*. Millbrae, Calif.: Les Femmes, 1978.

Spencer, Barbara A., and G. Stephen Taylor. "Effects of Facial Attractiveness and Gender on Causal Attributions of Managerial Performance." *Sex Roles* 19 (1988): 273–85.

Taylor, Robert E., and Russell Eisenman. "Birth Order and Sex Difference in Complexity-Simplicity, Color-Form Preference and Personality." *Journal of Projective Techniques and Personality Assessment* 32 (1968): 383–87.

———. "Perception and Production of Complexity by Creative Art Students." *Journal of Psychology* 57 (1964): 239–242.

Tetreault, Patricia A., and Mark A. Barnett. "Reactions to Stranger and Acquaintance Rape." *Psychology of Women Quarterly* 11 (1987): 353–58.

Warnock, G. J., ed. *The Philosophy of Perception*. London: Oxford UP, 1967.

Whitesel, Lita. "Women as Art Students, Teachers, and Artists." *Art Education* 28, no. 3 (1975): 21–26.

Wiedl, Karl Heinz. "The Relationship of Interest for Visual Complexity to Birth Order, Sex, and Personality Characteristics: A Genetic Analysis." *Genetic Psychology Monographs* 96 (1977): 143–62.

Williams, Tennessee. *Memoirs*. Garden City, N.Y.: Doubleday, 1975.

———. "On a Streetcar Named Success." *New York Times* 30 Nov. 1947. Reprinted Limited Editions Club *Streetcar* v–ix.

———. *A Streetcar Named Desire*. *The Theatre of Tennessee Williams*. 7 vols. to date. New York: New Directions, 1971. Vol. 1: 239–419.

Wolf, Naomi. *The Beauty Myth: How Images of Beauty Are Used Against Women*. New York: William Morrow, 1991.

Woolf, Virginia. *A Room of One's Own*. New York: Harcourt Brace Jovanovich, 1957.

8

Eunice Hubbell and the Feminist Thematics of *A Streetcar Named Desire*

Philip C. Kolin

A Streetcar Named Desire is filled with stories about women, both the women we watch on stage as well as those women we only hear about. What Kathleen McLuskie has said about the stories concerning Shakespeare's women, especially Desdemona and Hermione, applies equally well to *Streetcar*: The question of a woman's identity is often "locked" into stories about her, especially stories dealing with her sexuality (McLuskie 175). In *Streetcar*, to cite the most important and obvious example, multiple, conflicting stories circulate about Blanche. Stella portrays her sister as a kind, sensitive woman who has been deeply injured in love; Stanley digs up sexual information about Blanche's past to discredit and defame her. Confronting Stanley with his sordid narratives about her sister, Stella tells him: "I don't believe all those stories and I think your supply man was mean and rotten to tell them" (364). Of course, Stanley does not limit his stories to Blanche. He tells derogatory tales about women who would like to do their husbands out of their rights under the Napoleonic Code and about women who fish for compliments, though Stanley, of course, never takes the bait. Mitch, too, tells stories about women. He compounds Stanley's venomous narratives about Blanche by adding to their credibility; Mitch has done some investigative work about Blanche on his own.

In these male stories, women are often miscast, read unfairly, and fixed as betrayers (sexually sullied). Though not the subject of lewd, defaming stories in *Streetcar*, Eunice Hubbell, the Kowalskis' upstairs neighbor, is nonetheless the victim of male narrative strategies in the same way, though not in the same degree, as Blanche. Eunice's story has been dismissed or distorted because of the stereotypical roles she has been forced into by male characters in the play. Moreover, critics of the play seem to have been persuaded by those male characters. Speaking of Stella and Eunice "and the other women in their crowd," Thomas P. Adler believes that "despite occasional grumblings and defensive outbursts, [they] have few inner resources of their own" (61). And even though Kathleen Margaret Lant concedes that although critics blame Blanche for "refusing to face facts and . . . lying," it is really "Stella (and Eunice too) who constantly refuse to *look* at things, to listen to the truth, or even tell the truth" (229). As a consequence of this critical neglect or hostility, Eunice has been unfairly deprived of her special structural role and her authenticity as a character, both of which help define the masculine/feminine dynamics of *Streetcar*.

Eunice, I believe, has been stereotyped and thereby marginalized for two reasons: her so-called comic, minor role and her insistent femininity, attributes that canonical, patriarchal readings of *Streetcar* have used to dismiss or refute Eunice's importance. Criticism that mentions Eunice invariably depicts her and her husband Steve as the comic counterparts of Stanley and Stella; the Hubbells' quarrel in scene 5 of *Streetcar* is regarded as a humorous reflection of the more serious marital disturbance between the Kowalskis in scene 3, the ill-fated Poker Night. Gilbert Debusscher labels the Hubbells as the comic "upstairs doubles of the Kowalskis" (151). Though far more insightful than most readers who marginalize Eunice and her husband Steve as comic variations of the Kowalskis, Debusscher still minimizes Eunice's function by labeling the Hubbells' activities as the "satyr play" in *Streetcar*, the burlesque version of the tragedy in Greek theatre competition, and asks, "What is the tragedy, then, if not the story of Stella and Stanley?" (151). Consistent with the critical habit of seeing Eunice as a paramountly comic figure is stereotyping her as a shrew, the termagant, the wife who mercilessly pursues her henpecked husband. Even a widely praised feminist reading of *Streetcar* by Anca Vlasopolos fails to do justice to Eunice. According to Vlasopolos, Eunice lacks individuality, and together with the "other characters function[s] as a chorus, a fairly undifferentiated unit that is swayed by the exercise of authority" in scene 11 (328). Even less sympathetic toward Eunice is Vlasopolos's assessment that because Eunice witnesses Blanche's removal to the asylum with "consenting gaze" and "without protest," she becomes one of Stanley's accomplices.

I maintain that Eunice's role in *Streetcar* is neither minor nor predominantly comic; and far from being an accomplice in Stanley's brutal treatment of Blanche, Eunice is a central figure in directing our attention to its horror. The very behaviors that have allowed critics to write Eunice out of the script are the overriding concerns that establish her importance, as a feminist reading of the play demonstrates. Eunice's part may be small, but it broadcasts major implications for the tragedy *Streetcar* presents. Eunice is at the focal point of those issues that are most sacred to Williams: tenderness of heart, solicitude for self and others, and a sense of community. She is the positive model of all these virtues. In fact, Eunice, whose name means "Good Victory," is an exemplar of feminine community, which is not necessarily gender specific or restricted in Williams. Eunice is a bellwether character, a spokesperson for and representative of some fairly complex feminist issues affecting the other women (and the men) in the play. Hardly a flat character, she suggests multiple responses, some of them symbolically complex, as is customary in Williams's plays. There is a great deal of feminine power in the possibilities Eunice offers. Her detractors help to valorize Stanley's values/views of women expressed in his command to Stella: "Why don't you women go upstairs and sit with Eunice" (290). Behind Stanley's words lurks a dangerous ideology about the roles men assign women and about the male power structures that enforce such roles. For Stanley, women are ideologically situated by removing them upstairs. Women belong out of Stanley's way at important times and are expected to be silent and passive (just to "sit with Eunice"). Eunice thus becomes the symbol of such "out of the way-ness" for Stanley. A counter, more equitable view of Eunice is Stella's characterization of her as a friend, someone to lean on.

Eunice's relationship with her husband Steve, especially in their appearances in scenes 1 and 5, has a vital bearing on how we as an audience respond to Blanche, Stella, and Stanley. The Hubbells' relationship also underscores some major feminist themes. Near the end of scene 1, just before Stanley meets Blanche for the first time, we hear Eunice talking to Steve who is *"going upstairs"* after being out with the boys. She berates her husband for being late for dinner—in fact, missing it entirely—and for not letting her know that he would be late. Steve protects himself by protesting that he did tell Eunice at breakfast and even telephoned her. But when she retorts "never mind about that. You just get your self home here once in a while," Steve retaliates: "You want it in the papers?" (264). This short episode, when it is commented on at all, is treated as another comic interruption in the on-going plot, an insignificant interlude about a nagging wife and her less than accommodating husband who, once again, misses dinner.

But this exchange between Steve and Eunice has serious reverberations for both the Kowalskis and for Blanche. It is an early, albeit comic, rehearsal of some later, tragic events. Certainly, Eunice's complaint is justified, but it also points to her—and Stella's, too—just occupation with home life. Men like Steve and Stanley take their wives' caring for granted. As Steve disappoints Eunice, so Stanley disappoints Stella, and Mitch will later disappoint Blanche by not showing up in time for her birthday dinner in scene 9. And so it goes in the French Quarter and elsewhere. But these domestic tiffs have portentous implications in *Streetcar*. The fact that Steve disappoints Eunice begins a pattern that continues with Stanley and Mitch.

When Steve retorts, "You want it in the papers?" he, of course, is being sardonic about publicly announcing that he would be late or, perhaps, that he is judged wrong to disappoint his wife. Again, these lines can direct us to significant reverberations and analogues. The division of private quarrel and public disclosure is at the very heart of Blanche's victimization later in scene 11. As Anca Vlasopolos observes, "The private violence of the rape becomes the public violence of Blanche's flight from the Matron and the physical struggle with her" (335). Vlasopolos also correctly points out that by "making Blanche's expulsion public by having almost the entire cast on stage in the final scene," the "act becomes public and the woman is punished" (333). Steve's threat, comically hurled at Eunice, thus foreshadows Stanley's treatment of Blanche. Ultimately, Steve's behavior is a matter of a man's misdeeds done in private leading to a public disclosure at the woman's expense. Hence, it is fitting that the Hubbells' spat occurs immediately before "*Stanley throws the screen door of the kitchen open and comes in*" to find Blanche "*drawing involuntarily back from his stare*" (264–65). The Hubbells' exchange serves as a comic prologue to or analogue for how men (husbands) cause trouble for women (wives, sisters-in-law).

Scene 5—the "Paperboy Scene"—has been acclaimed as one of Williams's very best, but Eunice's role, according to the critics, has added little to the luster of that scene. Yet she functions significantly in it. Admittedly, we do not see Eunice for very long, and sometimes we only hear her in her lovers' quarrel with Steve. Such thinking, however, reflects the intention of critics who want to marginalize Eunice out of the script and who overlook the major implications of her role. Typically, her actions have been dismissed as a parody of the Kowalskis' fight and reunion in scene 3 earlier. Roger Boxill, for example, claims that the "row between the upstairs neighbors . . . suggests that the Kowalskis' quarrel need not be taken so seriously" (79). When viewed as a simple piece of comic relief, or dismissed as a comic interruption, Eunice and her fight are wrongly assumed to be unimportant and not terribly complex. But Eunice's actions contribute to the overall success of the scene and to the conduct of the play as a whole; in fact, Eunice's presence gives an even greater resonance and depth to this highly praised scene.

Certainly on one level Eunice and Steve's quarrel and subsequent lovemaking are analogous to Stanley and Stella's actions in scene 3. But, on another level, the behavior of Eunice and Steve in scene 5 calls into question the terms and conditions of Stanley and Stella's putative (troubled) reconciliation at the end of the play. Eunice's actions are still diminished, however, when they are judged solely against Stella's. The Hubbells' actions shed light, proleptically, on Blanche's predicament and eventual victimization. From a wider perspective, Eunice should be read against and through Blanche's actions. After all, Eunice's words and actions with Steve are literally—physically and in terms of stage time—embedded in the middle of Blanche's conversation with Stella about Shep Huntleigh and in her confrontation with Stanley who, for the first time, brings up her sordid past in Laurel. Or perhaps it might be more instructive to see things the other way around. Blanche finds herself in the middle of Steve and Eunice's quarrel and reconciliation. In either case, the juxtaposition is productive. By raising issues that are central to both the Kowalskis and to Blanche, Eunice's and Steve's participation in scene 5 alerts us to some potentially tragic disclosures found in both the larger contours of the scene and in its smaller details as well.

Structurally, scene 5 tells two stories with identical parts but with far different endings. The Hubbells' three appearances in the scene follow a definite course of action: a fight, or quarrel, followed by a highly charged (and amorous) pursuit, followed by a consummation and the joyous celebration of that event. Eunice accuses Steve of cheating on her; beats him and is beaten by him; she runs away and he chases her; she comes back with him, they make up and make love and then join their neighbors the Kowalskis at a local bar, the Four Deuces. The central theme and pattern of the Hubbells' quarrel and reconciliation—the pursuit of and for love—is precisely how scene 5 unfolds tragically for Blanche. She begins talking about Shep Huntleigh, battles with an angry Stanley, is chased (metaphorically) by him away from her opportunities for rest and love, is then met by the paperboy and Mitch, the man she wants to pursue her, as Eunice ultimately wants Steve to pursue her, and is then temporarily courted by Mitch, her "Rosenkavalier." But, unlike Eunice, Blanche will never capture the pursuing man. She never gains Shep, the paperboy, or Mitch. Though Blanche is situated in the middle of Eunice's pursuit and lovemaking, she is tragically unable to incorporate its closures into her life. Thanks to Eunice and Steve in scene 5, that point is made contrapuntally and painfully.

Again underscoring Blanche's tragedy, Steve and Eunice almost certainly have sexual intercourse when they return home from the Four Deuces. The stage direction suggests such conjugal joys: "*Steve and Eunice come around the corner. Steve's arm is around Eunice's shoulder and she is sobbing luxuriously and he is cooing love-words. There is a murmur of thunder as they go slowly upstairs in a tight embrace*" (330). We do not hear from the Hubbells for five pages of script (or about five to six minutes of playing time)—enough time for the proverbial quickie!—until Stanley appears and shouts their names whereupon there are "*joyous calls from above. Trumpet and drums are heard from around the corner*" (335). Eunice's happy sexual victory (recall the etymology of her name)—the inevitable goal of the amorous pursuit—has been denied Blanche in all of her relationships. Blanche was married to a homosexual; she was discharged by Mr. Graves for illicit sexual advances toward her pupils; and she certainly did not find a secure or satisfying sexual union with the soldiers from the local army base. Nor dare Blanche touch the paperboy collecting for the *Evening Star*. As events turn out, Mitch will want only "what I been missing all summer" (389), again, hardly the happy fruits of wedded bliss. And, finally, she is raped by the "*gaudy seed-bearer*" Kowalski. It is clear that Blanche cannot have the sexual happiness that she sees, both metaphorically and literally, all around her in the figures of Steve and Eunice. In the midst of Eunice's pleasure is Blanche's pain.

Parallel stage directions describing Eunice and Blanche further contrast the two women and thus force home the consequent involvement of Eunice in Blanche's tragedy. Near the end of scene 5, "*Blanche sinks faintly back in her chair with her drink. Eunice shrieks with laughter and runs down the step. Steve bounds after her with goat-like screeches and chases her around the corner*" (336). Eunice, active and vibrant, possesses what Blanche desires so deeply: lovemaking with a man who will care for and desire her, a man who will chase her into matrimony and give her safety. The differences between the two women are poignant; Eunice's "goat-like" passion counters Blanche's "butterfly wings." Unlike Blanche, Eunice has satisfyingly fulfilled her sexuality. So while Eunice is off to the bar, Blanche is left sighing, sinking faintly in her chair—"Ah me, ah, me, ah, me..."—reminiscent of love-starved maidens who desperately want a man in their lives. Blanche's loves on the horizon—the paperboy, Mitch, and, later, Shep Huntleigh—prove untouchable or fatal, never within her grasp. Her pursuit of love leads to the madhouse.

Eunice's accusations and her battle with Steve orchestrate, sometimes humorously to be sure, some of the tragic problems of infidelity confronting Blanche, Stella, and even Stanley. Shouting "*in terrible wrath*" (326), Eunice tells Steve that she "heard about you and that blonde!" and that she even saw Steve "chasing her 'round the balcony" (326). She hits Steve with some aluminum object—no doubt a pan—and shrieks so loudly that Blanche, who overhears this, asks: "Did he kill her?" When Eunice comes downstairs, "*in daemonic disorder*," she threatens to call the police and "*rushes around the corner*." The Hubbells' confusion does wreak of the traditionally comic husband-wife quarrel, pots and pans and all. But Eunice's battle with Steve also foreshadows (and asks us to compare with it) Blanche's similar predicament in defending herself against two aggressive males, Mitch and Stanley. Eunice cries out in wrath and in fear of a man, her husband Steve who threatens her. In scene 9, Mitch wants to rape Blanche and nearly assaults her. Repelling Mitch's angry advances, Blanche cries wildly and in hysteria (like Eunice in wrath), shouting "Fire" in an attempt to summon help from a legal system that she believes will protect her from the flames of Mitch's lust. Eunice, too, threatens to call for assistance—from the "police" and the "vice squad"—to thwart and shame an aggressive male. In scene 10, when Stanley closes in on Blanche, we hear a "*policeman's whistle*" (399) and Blanche's desperate cries to get help from the operator. But nothing will stop Stanley's "interfering" with her. With a knowledge of Eunice's actions and recalling her plight, an audience is encouraged to see a parallel with Blanche and to recognize that Blanche's feminine dilemma is not unique in Williams's fictional French Quarter, or in real life, for that matter.

Eunice's actions also parallel Stella's. Eunice's accusations leveled against Steve might very well be brought against Stanley by his wife Stella, but, of course, they are not. Stella will later have grounds to accuse her husband of chasing a blonde—her own sister Blanche. Following Jessica Tandy (the first Blanche), most Blanches have been blondes as well. One thinks of Claire Bloom, Ann-Margret, Blythe Danner, and Jessica Lange. In the British premiere of *Streetcar* in 1949, Vivien Leigh even dyed her hair blonde for the part of Blanche (Edwards 177). But unlike Eunice, Stella opts not to believe any stories about Stanley, while he, on the other hand, believes all the stories about Blanche. Reconciling with each other, the Hubbells come back to their apartment, Steve's arm around Eunice with her *"sobbing luxuriously"* and him *"cooing love-words"* (330). Similarly, in scene 11, Stanley puts his arm around Stella and moves his hand inside her blouse accompanied by the sound of Stella's *"luxurious sobbing"* (419). It is tempting to see in the Hubbells' reconciliation a parallel to the Kowalskis' earlier reunion at the end of scene 3 as much as a foreshadowing of Stanley and Stella's reunion at the end of the play. But Williams encourages no such easy, comedic ending and thwarts such attempts. In fact, Williams dissuades an audience, through his stage pictures, from transferring and thus comparing the Hubbells' sincere sexual happiness in scene 5 to the Kowalskis' in scene 11. It is important to remember Blanche when we want to compare and contrast the two couples in this context. Blanche is present in scene 5 when the Kowalskis join the Hubbells in sexual celebration at the Four Deuces. She is in the picture, so to speak, if only temporarily. But when Stanley attempts to be reconciled with Stella in scene 11, Blanche has been removed, physically and symbolically, carted off to the asylum. In scene 11, Stella is very much reminded of Blanche's absence; her sister is not standing before her. The absent sister blocks any future encounters at joyful lovemaking with Stanley. Thus, the resemblances between the Hubbells and the Kowalskis are as important for what they show as for what they leave out, for what they look back to as for what they do not anticipate.

Besides the analogical significance of her role, Eunice plays a major part in orchestrating the feminist issues raised in *Streetcar*. Eunice's female friendships in *Streetcar* are sincere and stalwart, a validation of female community. From the start of the play, she demonstrates her amiable nature, engaging in friendly conversation with the "colored" woman. Eunice's friendships know no racial barriers; she is living proof that there is a *"relatively warm and easy intermingling of races in the old part of town"* (243). Throughout *Streetcar*, from Blanche's entrance in scene 1 to her exit in scene 11, Eunice is a friend to the DuBois sisters, especially in their times of distress. As an exemplary female friend, Eunice's actions strongly contrast with the male friendships in the play. For example, in scene 3, the famous Poker Night, Stanley becomes so enraged that his friends have to force and pinion him amid *"grappling and cursing"* (303). The model for male friendship is the scuffle, the battle. Eunice does not battle with her friends, nor does she attempt to undercut them for selfish reasons. Her friendships remain intact, unlike the male friendships that end in bitterness and vilification. The last scene illustrates the horrifying division between male and female friendships. As Eunice compliments Blanche and consoles Stella, Pablo curses Stanley's "rutting luck," and Mitch, who believes that Stanley was responsible for Blanche's madness, berates his former friend with quintessential masculine insults: "You . . . you. . . . Brag . . . brag . . . bull . . . bull" (404). Later, Mitch *"lunges and strikes at Stanley"* in anger (417). Although male friends act out their aggression to vent their egos, female friends, symbolized by Eunice, are nurturing, protective, and sustaining. Eunice's mutuality opposes the men's menacing individualism.

Eunice's female friendship has a notable literary history behind it. Gilbert Debusscher has traced Eunice's lineage to nymphs and satyrs gamboling in the wild, sexual forests of the satyr plays. She can also claim kinship with some more recent literary models. Her ancestry can be profitably traced to the familiar female doubles, pairs of friends, found in Shakespeare, the Brontës, and Virginia Woolf. The female friends in Shakespeare and elsewhere are often a linked yet contrasting pair of women, one aggressive, assertive, and the other more reserved, sentimental, compliant (Williamson 108–9). In *As You Like It*, for example, the lively, assertive Rosalind balances the quieter, more reserved Celia, and, similarly, in *Much Ado About Nothing* the feisty Beatrice complements a far more docile Hero. Eunice is the outspoken Emilia to Stella's (or perhaps Blanche's) quieter, more resigned Desdemona. In her capacity as a commentator on and outspoken critic of Stanley's outbursts of violence and injustices, Eunice is, like Emilia, a feminine teller of truths, a witness to the misdeeds directed against other women who are unable to contain such attacks. In such an Emilia spirit, Eunice attacks Stanley at the end of scene 3, just after he beats Stella and just before she escapes to Eunice's (306):

> You can't beat on a woman an' then call 'er back! She won't come! And her goin' t' have a baby! . . . You stinker! You whelp of a Polack, you! I hope they do haul you in and turn the fire hose on you, same as the last time!

Emilia similarly defends Desdemona by pouring out her punishing judgments on Othello, who has justified his actions by claiming that Desdemona was false: "Thou art rash as fire, to say/ That she was false. O she was heavenly true" (5.2.139–40) and then lambasts him "O gull! O dolt!/ As ignorant as dirt;/ Thou hast done a deed—" (5.2.170–72). When Othello cries in agony on Desdemona's bed, Emilia proclaims with indignation: "Nay, lay thee down and roar/ For thou hast killed the sweetest innocent/ That e'er did lift up eye" (5.2.205–7). I am not arguing that Williams had *Othello*—or any other specific source—in mind when he wrote Eunice's excoriation of Stanley. What I am saying is that Eunice's role as witness and critic against the fate of a woman caught in a male trap is characteristic of the outspoken female friend dramatized in many literary/dramatic texts. Eunice's relationship to Stella and Blanche typifies the bonding of women in sisterhood.

Appreciating Eunice as a vital partner in a female friendship with Stella and Blanche ensures that she is not excluded from the main action but is instated as an important figure. Viewing her against the tradition of paired friends also sheds light on Williams's presentation of women to show their multiple roles, strengths, and bonds. Pairs of female friends emphasize such nurturing bonding and illustrate the spectrum of femininity, an antidote to the male stereotype of women as shrews and whores. Eunice thus challenges the cultural (male) aggressions that put women into passive roles.

As part of her role as friend, Eunice becomes a maternal caregiver, providing the maternal alternative to Stanley's destructive macho world in the French Quarter, what Robert Brustein has called "the dark masculine forces of society" (259). That maternal role is not an easy one to fulfill in *Streetcar*. When Blanche confesses to Mitch "my sister is going to have a baby," he refers to Stanley's assault on his pregnant wife: "This is terrible" (303). Maternity is under attack. Stanley does not think twice about beating his pregnant wife. In her capacity as a mother figure, Eunice performs admirably, though she, too, is often threatened. The casting for the original *Streetcar*, as well as the 1983 teleplay directed by John Erman, contributed to the presentation of the maternal side of Eunice's character. Peg Hillias, the first Eunice, was a number of years older than Kim Hunter's Stella, whom Eunice treats like a daughter or a younger sister. Similarly, in the teleplay, Erica Yohn's Eunice was much older than Beverly D'Angelo's Stella. In her maternal role, Eunice often comforts, advises, and embraces Stella. As Stella comforts Blanche in scene 5 about Mitch, Eunice comforts Stella about Blanche in scene 11. When Stella escapes from Stanley's wrath in scene 3, she runs upstairs to Eunice as a daughter would run home to her mother for protection and counsel. Stanley himself obliquely acknowledges Eunice's motherly role when he yells: "Eunice, I want my baby!" and then adds, "My baby doll left me" (305). Stella is Stanley's baby whom Eunice watches over. The metaphoric association of "baby" is made literal for Eunice at the end of the play when she is entrusted with the care of the Kowalski infant. To Stella's question "How is the baby?" Eunice replies "Sleeping like an angel" (404). In her maternal dealings with the women in the play, Eunice is not like the predatory mothers found in other Williams's plays such as *Suddenly Last Summer* or *The Milk Train Doesn't Stop Here Anymore*.

Consistent with her maternal instincts and consolation, Eunice is associated with food and providing sustenance to the people in her life, another sign of feminine solicitude versus male selfishness in *Streetcar*. Like Martha in St. Mark's Gospel, Eunice is busy about the business of hospitality. Exhibiting tough love for her husband, Eunice asks Stella to "tell Steve to get him a poor boy's sandwich 'cause nothing's left here" (245). The reference to the "poor boy" resonates with more meaning than just Williams's incorporating some New Orleans cuisine into the play. Steve for Eunice is a "poor boy," someone who is out of luck and who needs taking care of because of his schoolboy immaturity. Later, Eunice demonstrates the same kind of concern for Steve's meals. Upset with him for missing dinner, Eunice expresses her wifely anger justifiably through food. "Break it up down there! I made the spaghetti dish and ate it myself" (264). Stella recognizes Eunice's role as food provider when, the morning after the Poker Night, she asks Blanche, who has spent the night at Eunice's, "Eunice and you had breakfast?" (313). Most significant of all, Eunice brings grapes to Stella's for Blanche, who superciliously inquires "Are they washed?" (409). Eunice answers that she just got them from the French Market. In Williams's symbolic French Quarter, associating Eunice with a market further deepens her maternal responsibilities, her solicitude. Stanley and Steve are occupied with factories, garages, bowling alleys, and bars; Eunice supplies the balance necessary to life in *Streetcar*. She goes to the French Market as well as to the Four Deuces—food and drink, all in healthy measure.

Eunice's maternal achievements stand out in the otherwise motherless world of *Streetcar*. So many characters in the play are denied mothers and consequently suffer because of that. Mitch, for example, grieves as he watches his mother die. "She won't live long. Maybe just a few months" (353). For that reason and others, too, he is driven into Blanche's arms, with tragic results for him as well as for her. It is ironic that in a play in which family is central, Stanley does not once mention a mother (or a father); in the script he is an orphan. Stanley is thus cut off from the maternal affection that can enrich sincere relationships. Blanche, too, is portrayed as "motherless" and so without nurturing support. "All those deaths! The long parade to the graveyard! Father, mother!" (261). In such a context in which characters are motherless or where motherhood is under siege, Eunice's maternal attributes offer a significant source of trust. Representing that trust in a motherless world, Eunice is fittingly linked to Stella's baby, the most potent life force in the play. Just before *Streetcar* ends, "*Eunice descends to Stella and places the child in her arms*" (418). Therefore, thanks to Eunice, Stella at the end of *Streetcar* receives the object of her desire and her only earthly hope—the newborn child (Tischler 139). Eunice's adopted maternity here harmoniously complements Stella's natural maternity.

As her dedication to friends and caregiving demonstrates, Eunice is a key representative of feminine place in *Streetcar*. This side of the play has been overlooked or even surrendered by some feminist critics when they describe Williams's French Quarter setting. Pamela Hanks, for example, observes that "Blanche moves in a symbolic space circumscribed by the male power that imprisons her" (118). Although there is much truth in this observation, much is also missing. Space in *Streetcar* is filled with more than Stanley's male domination. There are such things as white radios, colored Chinese lanterns, Eunice's upstairs succor, and visible examples of female bonding. Eunice does offer a strong feminine alternative to Stanley's male physicality. Essential to Eunice's—and the feminine—community is a strong identification with home, both as a physical location and a metaphoric site for the cultivation of affairs of the heart. "Get yourself home here once in a while" (264), Eunice orders to her carousing husband Steve. This is advice applicable to many in *Streetcar*.

Williams seems to take pains to call our attention to Eunice's communal alternative to Stanley's control at crucial junctures of *Streetcar*. In fact, the first thing we see in *Streetcar* is not Stanley tossing a blood-stained package of meat, but Eunice and *"the colored woman taking the air on the steps of the building"* (243). Engaged in pleasant conversation and mutual respect, these two women portray the sympathetic, nonthreatening feminine community available to Blanche. In welcoming Blanche to her destination, Eunice symbolizes hospitality, concern, and friendship, all associated with a feminine sense of place. Williams emphasizes these attributes of feminine bounty through the idea of "house," "home," and "apartment." I think Adler is wrong to say that Blanche's "unmannerly curtness and her refusal to enter into the continual party that is typical of life in the Quarter immediately cost her the approval of one member of the on-stage audience, the upstairs tenant Eunice . . . " (26). To Blanche's puzzlement about where 623 Elysian Fields might be, Eunice invitingly replies: "That's where you are now" and assures Blanche that "you don't have to look no further" (246). When Blanche in amazement remarks, "This—can this be—her home?" Eunice helpfully states: "She's got the down stairs here and I got the up." Unlike Stanley, who taunts and later paralyzes Blanche over the issues of ownership, Eunice offers reassurance, assistance, and sharing. She even volunteers to give Blanche freedom of the house in order to hurry Stella home from the bowling alley. Not boundary directed, Eunice does not battle for turf but happily invites Blanche into her world, her house. Symbolically, Eunice resides above the Kowalskis; Eunice's positioning as the representative of these positive values makes her "upstairs" apartment almost a god-like, god-benevolent location. I think of the gods' space atop the Greek skene as an analogous location. Her apartment becomes the sanctuary that both DuBois sisters will look to as the play progresses. It may be a "horrible place," according to Blanche, but it becomes a safe house from Stanley's terrorism.

Eunice's cordiality and feminine solicitude are graphically conveyed through stage directions that empower her as a doorkeeper, a protector of portals. She functions in this capacity as a female guardian of place, a female counterpart of St. Julian the Hospitalier. Thus, quite literally, Eunice is associated with domestic order, peace, and protection. Her gates open and close at key moments throughout the play, but especially in scenes 1, 3, and 11. Significantly, Eunice "*can let*" Blanche "*in*" to Stella's apartment. "*She gets up and opens the downstairs door*" (248) to help, not hinder, Blanche. Appropriately enough, thanks to Williams's use of Eunice, as we saw, an audience's introduction to the Kowalski household is a feminine one. Eunice comfortingly reassures Blanche that she can find happiness there (provided that feminine values are given a chance). No idealist, Eunice realistically points out: "It's sort of messed up right now, but when it's clean it's real sweet" (8). However distraught Blanche is by the appearance of the place, she has to acknowledge Eunice's thoughtfulness. Blanche's polite but guarded acknowledgement will later be transformed into an urgent plea from the DuBois sisters to Eunice to open and close doors for them.

Terrified by a drunken Stanley's rage during the Poker Night, Blanche "*rushes into the bedroom*" and demands, "I want my sister's clothes. We'll go to that woman's upstairs" (304). Again, Eunice's role as guardian door-keeper is emphasized. "*With her arms around Stella, Blanche guides her to the outside door and upstairs*" to Eunice's and safety. Stanley's doors open to trouble and violence; Eunice's close for protection and peace. That peace, though, is short-lived. Quickly penitent, Stanley demands of Eunice, on the phone and by shouting outside to her, that he wants "my girl to come down with me!" With seasoned incredulity about male promises, Eunice shouts back: "Hah" and "*slams the door*" (306–7). For the moment Blanche and Stella are safe, until Stanley prevails upon his pregnant wife with his lamenting cries of "Stella." Although only temporarily, Eunice's apartment with its closed doors supplies a feminine place of survival until Stanley is ready to sound the all-clear with his repentant cries. Victims of male violence, the DuBois sisters are forced to leave their home; they would have nowhere to go and no one to protect them were it not for Eunice's fortified sanctuary.

Eunice is associated with a different set of portals/gates in scene 11. Seated at their poker table, the men are again, as in scene 3, ominously separated from the women in the bedroom. Eunice declares the reason for such separation: "I always did say that men are callous things with no feelings, but this does beat anything. Making pigs of yourselves" (404). Eunice's observations refer to more than the men's table manners; because of Stanley's and Mitch's brutality, the men have descended the evolutionary scale, proving Blanche's worst fears as expressed in her "Don't hang back with the apes" speech in scene 4. A clear line of separation must be drawn between Mitch, Stanley, the other poker players, and the women. Williams draws that line literally and metaphorically for the audience through this significant stage direction involving Eunice and gates: Eunice "*comes through the portiers into the bedroom*" (404) after she describes the men's behavior. Again associated with portals, Eunice and the portiers can signal the divisions between the sexes. On the male side of the curtains are the signs of male power and privilege: a messy poker table, liquor bottles, strict rules of the game, and inflamed tempers. In this instance, the bedroom is feminine because the sisters use it as a place for private conversation. But unlike earlier doors that Eunice guarded, the portiers in scene 11 offer a highly vulnerable female refuge, as they did in scene 3 when, just before his rampage, Stanley *"stalks fiercely through the portiers into the bedroom"* (302). Eunice's doors of cordiality in scene 1 and those of safety in scene 3 are now replaced with the easily parted portiers. Regardless of how vigilant and loving Eunice is, Stanley can walk back and forth between the portiers. In fact, Eunice's role as gatekeeper has been diminished because of Stanley's crime. Hence, when the Matron and the Doctor arrive, it is Eunice's unfortunate duty to meet them: "Excuse me while I see who's at the door" (411).

The portiers between the poker players and the women in the bedroom become for Blanche in scene 11 the curtain on her final, fatal stage. Through the props of the portiers, Eunice assumes the duties of Blanche's stage manager, her artistic assistant. When it is time for Blanche to meet the Doctor and the Matron, Eunice patiently answers Blanche's questions about how the lady is dressed and calms her apprehensions about passing in front of the men at the poker table on the other side of the portiers. Like a nervous actress on opening night, Blanche *"looks fearfully from one to the other and then to the portiers"* (411). Reassured by Eunice's and Stella's compliments about how nice she looks, Blanche agrees to make her appearance, which is also her final exit. *"Blanche moves fearfully to the portiers. Eunice draws them open for her. Blanche goes into the kitchen"* (413). On the other side of Eunice's portiers lies male entrapment, the consequences of Stanley's brutal act. Eunice has no choice but to participate in the pageant that marks Blanche's fatal departure. Eunice and Stella now act like ladies in waiting in Blanche's train: *"Blanche crosses quickly to the outside door. Stella and Eunice follow."*

Across the portiers, Blanche finds herself on a dangerous, unappreciative stage. Frightened, she *"rushes past him [Stanley] into the bedroom"* (414). Seeing an unprotected Blanche, *"The Matron advances on one side, Stanley on the other"* right through the portiers into the bedroom. Feminine intimacy and consolation associated with the bedroom and crystallized through Eunice's role as gatekeeper have been shattered, violated. Coming into the house from the sinister, male side of the portiers, the grim Matron, *"divested of all the softer properties of womanhood"* (415), becomes Blanche's new lady in waiting, her new gatekeeper. The Matron is an anti-Eunice, a masculinized woman. But, after Blanche's short-lived struggle, *"the Matron releases her. Blanche extends her hands toward the Doctor. He draws her up gently and supports her with his arm and leads her through the portiers"* (418). "As *if she were blind,*" Blanche goes out with him, beyond Eunice's doors of protection, but into a world promised by "the kindness of strangers." Her Doctor escort, Death as the gentleman caller, has replaced Eunice.

If Eunice has been a feminine witness and protector and an outspoken critic of Stanley's rage, how are we to respond to her advice to Stella: "You done the right thing, the only thing you could do. She couldn't stay here; there wasn't no other place for her to go" (416–17). Eunice even restrains Stella from going back into the house: "Stay with me and don't look." Has Eunice caved in and accepted Stanley's dominance? Certainly, she has been chastised for this, as Anca Vlasopolos's assessment of her indicates. But, again, such a response is not fair. Eunice is no coward, no feminine turncoat in the last few minutes of *Streetcar*. She is appalled by Stanley's victimization of Blanche, and Eunice's resiliency directs our attention to Stanley's crime. Above all, Eunice is an arch-realist. In the midst of Blanche's great *agon*, it is Eunice who pulls Stella back into everyday reality. Eunice is a survivor and wants the same for Stella. These two women are literally and symbolically outside the intensely tragic sphere that Blanche inhabits. Williams signals their being removed from such a sphere by having Stella and Eunice remain outside the house on the porch. Throughout *Streetcar*, Eunice has had to stay in the world of reality. She and Stella are unlike Blanche, who has walked between two worlds, the present and the eternal. Now, because of Stanley's crime, Blanche has been transported into the eternal world of timelessness.

In asking "What else could you do?" and counseling Stella not to believe Blanche, Eunice is indeed being the realist and reclaiming a life for Stella. Whether all feminists agree with her or not, we see the compassion, the counsel, and the caring Eunice offers her friend, a new mother who needs reassurance to go on with her life with Stanley. Ironically, Eunice represents the Realpolitik of the (male-dominated) nuclear family and expresses what's needed ("Don't look") to survive and move forward in this particular moral economy.

Moreover, in turning Blanche over to the Doctor, Eunice is passing on her responsibility, the role of the kind, nurturing stranger, to an individual who has the manners and grace Blanche needs and honors. Eunice, therefore, is very much in character in these final gestures. She is kind and supportive to Blanche, complimenting her, seeing after needs, and wishing her well. Eunice, we must remember, does not let the villain in at the gate, nor does she abandon Blanche. Eunice provides.

In light of the virtues Eunice represents, Stella is symbolically positioned during the last few minutes of *Streetcar*. She is *"crouched a few steps up on the stairs"* (418). The stairs have been associated with Eunice and feminine values throughout the play, and having Stella appear on them reasserts as it reassures us of Eunice's importance in Stella's life in the future. Even though Stanley, standing at the foot of the stairs fondling Stella, promises her a more tranquil life, that future with him is still dubious. The stairs leading up to Eunice's apartment thus bring us full circle back to the comforting realization that Eunice is never far away.

Eunice Hubbell's time for critical recognition has long been overdue. She plays a far more sensitive and important role in *Streetcar Named Desire* than either the male critics or the male characters are willing to concede. Having been marginalized by these two allied groups, Eunice has wrongly been dismissed as a comic foil and trivialized as far as the tragic effects of the play are concerned. A large part of her unfriendly critical reception has to do with her advancement of feminine values and virtues. As I have tried to show, she demands fresh attention as both an independent, authentic character and as a participant in the on-going plot involving the Kowalskis and Blanche. She symbolizes feminine friendship, feminine sense of place, and a hardy realism that triumphs amid so much pain. In fact, an essential point that surfaces in *Streetcar* is that Eunice achieves the sexual fulfillment that escapes Blanche and that may vanish in Stella's relationship with Stanley. In this light, Eunice is a pivotal character in *Streetcar*, the one who supplies the necessary balance to survive in the brutal world of the French Quarter while at the same time symbolizing the compassionate virtues that lie at the core of Williams's belief system. There are a number of Eunices in the Williams's canon: women who have been dominated and silenced by dictatorial male characters and who have been stereotyped or erased by patriarchal critics. Eunice's sisters include Aunt Nonnie and Miss Lucy in *Sweet Bird of Youth*, Big Mama in *Cat on a Hot Tin Roof*, and La Madrecida in *Camino Real*. Like Eunice, they demand to be heard, to be freed from critical neglect or stereotype. Their recognition as women, as shapers and reactors to plot and as viable, alternative voices needs to be honored. They are due and owing.[1]

NOTE

1. I am deeply grateful to Toby Zinman, William Kleb, and June Schlueter for reading earlier drafts of this essay and giving me their responses.

WORKS CITED

Adler, Thomas P. *A Streetcar Named Desire: The Moth and the Lantern.* Twayne Masterwork Studies No. 47. Boston: Twayne, 1990.

Boxill, Roger. *Tennessee Williams.* New York: St. Martin's, 1988.

Brustein, Robert. "Williams' Nebulous Nightmare." *Hudson Review* 12 (Summer 1959): 259.

Debusscher, Gilbert. "Trois images de la modernité chez Tennessee Williams: Un micro-analyse d'*Un Tramway nommé desir.*" *Journal of Dramatic Theory and Criticism* 3 (Fall 1988): 143–56.

Edwards, Ann. *Vivien Leigh: A Biography.* New York: Simon and Schuster, 1977.

Hanks, Pamela Anne. " 'Must We Acknowledge What We3 Mean?' The Viewers's Role in Filmed Versions of *A Streetcar Named Desire*." *Journal of Popular Film and Television* 14 (Fall 1986) 114–18.

Lant, Kathleen Margaret. "A Streetcar Named Misogyny." *Violence in Drama*. Cambridge: Cambridge UP, 1991. 225–38.

McLuskie, Kathleen. " 'The Emperor of Russia Was My Father': Gender and Theatrical Power." *Images of Shakespeare: Proceedings of the Third Congress of the International Shakespeare Association, 1986*. Ed. Werner Habicht, D. J. Palmer, and Roger Pringle. Newark: U of Delaware P, 1988. 174–87.

Shakespeare, William. *Othello. The Complete Works of Shakespeare*. 3rd ed. Ed. David Bevington. Glenview: Scott, Foresman, 1980.

Tischler, Nancy. *Tennessee Williams: Rebellious Puritan*. New York: Citadel P, 1961.

Vlasopolos, Anca. "Authorizing History: Victimization in *A Streetcar Named Desire*." *Theatre Journal* 38 (Oct. 1986): 322–38.

Williams, Tennessee. *A Streetcar Named Desire. The Theatre of Tennessee Williams*. 7 vols. to date. New York: New Directions, 1971. Vol. 1: 239–419.

Williamson, Marilyn L. "Doubling, Women's Anger, and Genre." *Women's Studies* 9 (1982): 107–19.

9

The White Goddess, Ethnicity, and the Politics of Desire

Lionel Kelly

To write about these terms is to engage with myth, history, and realism; like other plays that achieve the status of a contemporary classic, *A Streetcar Named Desire* has a history of its own, which derives from particular performances by those who have played its central characters, and this history has become part of the play's mythology. To approach *Streetcar* through the subject of myth is, of course, an established orthodoxy: here, I seek not to depart from that orthodoxy, but to look at it obliquely. Thus, I shall be concerned with Blanche DuBois as a version of "the white goddess."

Stanley Kowalski forms the center of my interest in the play's "realism" and its relationship with ethnicity. He is presented as an ethnic intruder in a site in which two prevalent other ethnicities, the southern white and the southern black, prevail. Both of these he seeks to subordinate, the one through an appeal to a legality that surmounts ethnic specificity, the other through a braggart appropriation of their modes of social being. At the same time, I am interested in the notion of realism as a strategy of dramatic expression, moving formally away from the accidental toward a typology of character. I shall move then from the ethnicity of the play's setting, to Kowalski, and then to Blanche.

In the opening stage direction of *Streetcar*, a scene of poverty is modified by what Williams calls its *"raffish charm,"* its *"atmosphere of decay"* attenuated by the lyricism of a *"peculiar tender blue"* sky (243). The anthropomorphized Mississippi River adds its *"warm breath"* to the *"faint redolences of bananas and coffee"* from the river warehouses. This famous evocation of a New Orleans "section" depicts a lapsarian Elysian Fields, where loss and deprivation are to be reenacted through the entry of Blanche DuBois. This raffish charm and attenuated decay are equally evoked by the persistent sound of Negro music, *"a tinny piano being played with the infatuated fluency of brown fingers."* Williams becomes more specific, equating the Blue Piano with the *"spirit of the life which goes on here,"* where "Blue," I take it, stands for "the blues," a sound of music historically and socially metonymic of the Afro-American experience of cultural and economic disempowerment, especially, if not uniquely, in the southern states. At the risk of the obvious, what "blues" music articulates here is, almost perversely, associated with "spirit," itself a word of powerful resonance for this text. This stage direction seeks to establish an ethos of communal warmth and vitality, partly through its appeal to a representation of New Orleans life both picturesque and conventional, where poverty is redeemed, by implication, through a vivid independency of spirit, and that proposition of a poor yet vital communality, which always seems to attend representations of the underprivileged, as though the world of shared sorrows is redeemed by overcrowding. It is a powerfully nostalgic idea, repeatedly inscribed in representations of the stratifications of social communities.

The sense of community here is enforced by the ensuing stage direction that gives us two women *"taking the air on the steps of the building,"* the white one named, her colored neighbor significantly unnamed. Williams, I suggest, seeks to ameliorate his unnaming of Eunice's colored neighbor by a confident appeal to New Orleans' cosmopolitanism *"where there is a relatively warm and easy intermingling of races in the old part of town."* In what follows, that assertion of racial intermingling is both documented, if loosely, and put at risk by the conflict of values and desires embodied by Blanche and Stanley. At one level, this opening stage description seeks to designate a social milieu characterized by a tolerant acceptance of racial difference, which in this context inevitably entails differences of social and economic status. But there is another level of signification that survives despite the topographical and historical accuracy of Williams's use of names, here specifically the *"Elysian Fields,"* then later *"Cemeteries,"* and the streetcar named *"Desire,"* a level that transcends the particularities of time and place because of the mythical connotations of names such as the "Elysian Fields" and the psychological imperatives of the concept of "desire." And, of course, Blanche DuBois's name merely deepens that mythological encoding, as though, against the grain of the play's dramatic realism, it is only natural to find the "white woman of the woods," the White Goddess at home in the Elysian Fields. And while the mythic implications of Blanche's name seem to enlarge the sense of distance between herself and Stanley, they also displace that locus of ethnic communality Williams is at pains to elaborate at the opening. The ethnic issue (the dramatic conflict) here, though enacted in the site of an Afro-American experience, is effectively a conflict between Blanche's appeal to an inherited aristocracy of place and status against Stanley's immigrant *arriviste* ambitions.

If Williams's opening stage direction asserts racial intermingling in this old sector of New Orleans, the "Negro Woman"—as the cast list designates her—opens the play on a note of sexual ambivalence that is proleptic of

Streetcar's concerns with desire: "... she says St. Barnabas would send out his dog to lick her and when he did she'd feel an icy cold wave all up an' down her. Well, that night when—".[1] Her narrative is then disrupted by another unnamed figure, a sailor in search of a particular bar, a stereotypical figure of the sexual predator in port and an icon of the mythological voyager (and, thus, another Blanche) buoyed by a desire that is bound to be sold short, as this text implies. Thus, disruption, severance, and failure are notions etched deep in the opening lines, despite the anonymity of the speakers at this point. What is also difficult to resist at this early moment in the play is a sense of ethnic typecasting centered in the unnamed Negro woman, whose social identity is predictably marginalized through her namelessness (in a play in which names are singularly dramatic and metaphorical, as in "Stella" and "Blanche"), yet whose sexual mores are swiftly suggested through this ambivalent narrative of sexual excitation. A certain toying with sexual promise and flirtation is foregrounded in the first two scenes of the play, and, thus, the use of the Negro woman as a received version of sexual availability, through her risque discourse, seems to fit her, paradoxically, as a prolepsis of Blanche, despite their differences of caste and "spirit." I draw attention to these issues, which are at once obvious, because of my sense of how much the dominant characters in the play are controlled by their ethnic roles.

If my insistence on the problem of the "Negro woman" looks myopic in relation to the substance of the play as a whole, I dwell on her both because her presence signalizes these ethnic issues very early in the text, and because her unnominated presence focalizes the conflict between Williams's fiction of racial intermingling and the reality of ethnic divisiveness in the world of his play. "The Mexican Woman" of scene 9 is but another version of this, and here Williams is content to rely on what is little more than a tourist view of otherness (387):

A Vendor comes around the corner. She is a blind MEXICAN WOMAN in a dark shawl, carrying bunches of those gaudy tin flowers that lower-class Mexicans display at funerals and other festive occasions.

There are other ethnicities involved, historically, realistically, in the choice of New Orleans as setting: this Orleans invokes the other one in France, the Elysian Fields invokes the Champs Elysées, as well as the Virgilian echo. But, beyond the fact that Blanche's family name is of French origin, the contribution of old Europe to the ethnic mix of New Orleans is hardly represented in this text, nor is the sense of other ethnic communities, as in the writing of Kate Chopin for example, who gives a much more densely realized expression of racial mingling. They are not here, of course, because Williams does not need them: He's content to rely on that picturesqueness I wrote of earlier, like a simple equation, black means blues, New Orleans means jazz, Mexico means cultural fetishism. And the European presence Williams calls on here is significantly other than the French, Spanish, Indian, Creole mix Chopin gives us: It is Polish, and probably a popularized version of Polish ethnic identity at that, socially encoded in the name "Polack," which is used to such dramatic effect here. Why did Williams give his intruder figure this specific ethnic identity, which has puzzled other commentators, as though Kowalski has strayed from the immigrant settlement where we should most expect to find him?

The answer, I suspect, has little to do with Williams's knowledge of immigrant patterns of location in North America, for I doubt that he had more than a conventional understanding of the history of East European migration to the United States. And in any case, Kowalski is not "at home" where he is: He is merely there, in a past that is not documented, and in relation to a future that remains a possibility, so that in his case, past and future are untenanted sites (unlike the case of Blanche), allowing full reign to the dominant present of the dramatic action. Williams, I think, wanted someone who would be markedly extraneous to the ethnic mix he had already described as mingling harmoniously in New Orleans, an ethnic mix that, in all received populist and highbrow versions of the town, emphasizes its black, Indian, and Mediterranean European racial identities. Kowalski is a Pole, I suggest, because, like Valentine Xavier in *Orpheus Descending*, he is an outsider, and thus a dangerous intruder into a community because of his desire to "take possession" and to assert his place in the local scheme of things. Xavier, it is true, is a much more passive version of this figure, who is made a sacrificial scapegoat for the failures of that community in its relations with ethnic difference. In *Streetcar* it is through Kowalski that the matter of civil rights is raised, not in the sense of racial or gender issues, but in that passage about the Napoleonic Code in scene 2 (272):

STANLEY: In the state of Louisiana we have the Napoleonic code according to which what belongs to the wife belongs to the husband and vice versa.

As I understand it, Louisiana was the only civil law state, and its civil code of 1825, revised in 1870, and still in force, is closely connected with the Napoleonic Code, presumably because of the historical dominance of French culture in the state. However, the accuracy of Stanley's invoking the code is less important than his willingness to do so, and I take it that in regard to the mutual ownership of possessions by husband and wife, the code is no different in effect from the English law upon which the laws of the early New England settlements were based. Stanley's citing of the code is proof of his interest in his "rights," like his resourcefulness in finding out the truth of Blanche's history as we read in scene 7. This hardly needs pointing out, but his sense of the rights of others is sufficiently indicted, for example, by his willingness to call his poker companion Pablo Gonzales by the epithet "greaseball." In fact, this epithet gives us a kind of descending scale of immigrant status inscribed in the text, for in an early exchange between Stella and Blanche when Blanche is reminded that Stanley is Polish, she responds with, "Oh, yes. They're something like Irish, aren't they?" and goes on "Only not so—highbrow?" (256), a comfortable joke between the sisters as this stage direction indicates: "(*They both laugh again in the same way.*)" Irish, Polish, Mexican, and beyond them, the ethnic otherness of the unnominated "Negro woman." There is a difference between the intentionally exploited racism of "Polack" and "greaseball," and what we might call the unacknowledged racism of the "Negro woman," and there will be those who would argue that both kinds are historically accurate transcriptions of the cultural mores of New Orleans in the 1940s, and are thus legitimized by the play's realism. On the other hand, it might be argued that Williams's intentional conflict between southern aristocracy (Blanche), and parvenu aggression (Kowalski), in pursuit of a newly accommodated Americanism, relegates the historical precedence of the Afro-American presence, either through indifference, or through a casual dependence on the given social determinants of place. In either case, however, through indifference or casualness, the effect is shocking in a writer of Williams's stature.

Pierre Macherey has written that "the area of shadow in or around the work is the initial moment of criticism. But we must examine the nature of this shadow: does it denote a true absence, or is it the extension of a half-presence?" (82). For Macherey, that shadow is the ur-image, that other that the work is about, what it *manifests*, but what it cannot say. And this nonsaying, or silence, is what gives the work life, a life constituted in the text by the "more or less complex opposition which structures it" (82). Yet, however we look at it, the representation of Afro-American ethnicity in *Streetcar*, even if it is merely deployed for local color, is nonetheless there, a "half-presence," displaced by the primary drama between Blanche and Kowalski, yet something in the text that we cannot ignore.

Kowalski's history is summarily sketched in a way that preserves, for Blanche, the caste distinction between officers and men, thus affirming her sense of social superiority over him, even if that sense cannot survive the brash vigor of his presence. Kowalski the migrant warrior (a master sergeant in the engineer corps) becomes the itinerant salesman, both occupations in which the notion of territorial exploration and possession are explicit. The possessive sense is particularly marked in Williams's stage direction on Kowalski's entrance (265):

Branching out from this complete and satisfying center are all the auxiliary channels of his life, such as his heartiness with men, his appreciation of rough humor, his love of good drink and food and games, his car, his radio, everything that is his, that bears his emblem of the gaudy seed-bearer.

The dominance of the possessive pronoun here underscores the presentation of Kowalski's acquisitiveness and is the countersign to what is otherwise marked as the essence of his flamboyant presence, his *"animal joy,"* the sign of his vigor in the sexual domain (which is another version of "spirit"), where his conflict with Blanche will be enacted ultimately. To write of Kowalski's *"auxiliary channels"* is to invoke a military ethos about him, and the atmosphere of the barrack room is right for much of Kowalski's time on stage, especially evident in his desire to dominate his male friends, and in his appeal to an absent "authority" who will validate his own view of things, as in the matter of Blanche's clothes and costume jewelry, which Kowalski refuses to distinguish from the real thing in what may be read as a strategic ploy (274–75):

What's this here? A solid-gold dress, I believe! And this one! What is these here? Fox-pieces! (*He blows on them.*) Genuine fox fur-pieces, a half a mile long! Where are your fox-pieces, Stella? Bushy snow-white ones, no less! Where are your white fox-pieces?

and then:

I got an acquaintance who deals in this sort of merchandise. I'll have him in here to appraise it. I'm willing to bet you there's thousands of dollars invested in this stuff here!

and:

I have an acquaintance that works in a jewelry store. I'll have him in here to make an appraisal of this. Here's your plantation, or what was left of it, here!

In this dialogue with Stella, Williams exploits a disjunction between Kowalski's idiomatic style, as in "What is these here?" and a formal idiom inherent in his use of words such as *appraise, appraisal*, and *acquaintance*, where he is reaching out for a verbal dignity equal to his legalistic imperatives, indicative of his desire to master his world, a mastery particularly elusive in relation to women's clothes and jewelry, and that he will attain only through the equivocal accomplishment of his rape of Blanche. I think the strained formalism of Kowalski's language is clearly marked whenever he invokes the legal and is quite distinct from that idiomatic style that is customarily his, and that he uses to call his wife and his male companions to order in those social contexts in which he seeks to express power over them.

Marlon Brando's dominant portrayal of Kowalski has cast a long shadow over productions of this play, both from the original stage production of 1947 and the film version of 1951, despite contemporary objections to his stage performance from Eric Bentley and Harold Clurman as too sensitive

(Boxill 90). *Sensitivity* is not a word one would apply to Kowalski's role as the text gives it. His sexual arrogance culminating in rape, his legalistic concern for his rights, and his abrasive dismissal of Blanche's social airs and graces are all manifestations of his power, or of his "spirit," to use Williams's word. In addition, he is someone for whom room must be made in the ethnic melting pot, whose claims on an American identity come with a brutal disregard for competing claims and an especial scorn for Blanche's version of social aristocracy (374).

STANLEY: I am not a Polack. People from Poland are Poles, not Polacks. But what I am is a one hundred per cent American, born and raised in the greatest country on earth and proud as hell of it, so don't ever call me a Polack.

It is instructive that Kowalski cites the rallying call of Huey Long, the Louisiana demagogue, in defense of his domestic power (371):

What do you two think you are? A pair of queens? Remember what Huey Long said—"Every Man is a King!" And I am the king around here, so don't forget it.

In the realization of these dimensions of Kowalski's character, Brando's performance is deeply imprinted on the play's history, and has become a part of the mythology of *Streetcar* in the national consciousness, which, if it does not inhibit other actors in the role, stands as the dominant expression of Kowalski's ethnic identity, which in itself stands as a powerful counter to Blanche's constrained sense of historical definition.

Of course, in terms of southern history, Blanche has a very precise sense of historical definition, particularly as that history is read in terms of family. In scene 3, for example, Blanche explains her name to Mitch (299):

BLANCHE: It's a French name. It means woods and Blanche means white, so the two together mean white woods. Like an orchard in spring. You can remember it by that.
MITCH: You're French?
BLANCHE: We are French by extraction. Our first American ancestors were French Huguenots.

Blanche DuBois, Belle Reve, Laurel: These names have been read as consonant with Williams's central preoccupation with crippled protagonists whose vitality is undermined by their commitment to a romanticized version of their own history, which is in part a romanticized version of the pre–Civil War South, and one of the most recent accounts of *Streetcar* in this tradition is in Judith J. Thompson's book on Williams, *Memory, Myth, and Symbol*, which takes a Jungian view of Williams's appeal to the collective unconscious. A book that does not feature in Thompson's references is the one that put the notion of "the White Goddess" into wide circulation at a moment contemporary with the first productions of Williams's play, Robert Graves's *The White Goddess* of 1948. As the subtitle of this book tells us, Graves is concerned with what he calls "a historical grammar of poetic myth," and his thesis (9–10) is as follows:

that the language of poetic myth anciently current in the Mediterranean and North-ern Europe was a magical language bound up with popular religious ceremonies in honour of the Moon-goddess, or Muse, some of them dating from the Old Stone Age, and that this remains the language of true poetry—"true" in the nostalgic modern sense of "the unimprovable original, not a synthetic substitute."

As far as I am aware, there is no evidence that Williams knew the book, and its publication postdates the first production of *Streetcar*; nonetheless, the contiguity of their interest in the figure of the white goddess is striking and, I think, pertinent, despite the sense of absolute difference between Williams's play and Graves's anthropology of myth. Williams said of himself in interview that "I think I write mainly from my unconscious mind," and that "we all have in our conscious and unconscious minds a great vocabulary of images, and I think all human communication is based on these images as are our dreams" (quoted in Thompson 8).

In Graves, the white goddess is the inspirer of all true poetry: Her history is immemorial, her manifestations protean, her names are various as the religions and demonologies she appears in. As he puts it (20):

I cannot think of any poet from Homer onwards who has not independently recorded his experience of her.... The reason why the hairs stand on end, the skin crawls and a shiver runs down the spine when one writes or reads a true poem is that a true poem is necessarily an invocation of the white goddess, or Muse, the Mother of All Living, the ancient power of fright and lust—the female spider or the queen-bee whose embrace is death.

I do not wish to force analogies, yet Blanche's relationship to poetry is one of death, for Allan Grey kills himself following her gaze on him after dis-covering his homosexuality (at the aptly named Moon Lake Casino), and here the idea of a perversion of generative lust issuing in death is clearly inscribed. In opposition to this, Kowalski's repudiation of Blanche's poet-icized self-mythology manifested in her cultivation of fine feelings and sen-sitivity insures him to her at the level of social manners, even as it propels him toward her in another perversion of sexual power, the rape. In Graves, the demonological manifestations of the white goddess associate her with witchcraft, among other things, and again, Blanche names herself in this form in an early exchange with Kowalski (279):

BLANCHE: I cannot imagine any witch of a woman casting a spell over you.

an unconsciously ironic prolepsis. Blanche constructs a version of her history in which she is the pursued object of desire, and in this, the name of Shep Huntleigh (shepherd and hunter, I take it, pastor and pursuer in one) assumes a totemistic significance for her. The contrast between her "beautiful dream" of herself and the reality of her condition is dramatized through the evidence of her alcoholism and nymphomania, this latter suggested by the scene with the young collector for the daily newspaper (symbolically named the *Evening Star*), and later ratified by Kowalski's discoveries about her life in Laurel. In Graves, the white goddess is a triple deity, goddess of the sky, earth, and underworld: in the underworld she was concerned with birth, procreation, and death; on earth with Spring, Summer, and Winter, and she animated trees and plants and ruled all living creatures; in the sky she was the Moon in her three phases, New Moon, Full Moon, and Waning Moon. In addition, she is for Graves the absolute embodiment of primal energies in female form (339):

But it must never be forgotten that the Triple Goddess . . . was a personification of primitive woman—woman the creatress and destructress. As the New Moon or Spring she was girl; as the Full Moon or Summer she was woman; as the Old Moon or Winter she was hag.

This is a totalizing scheme in support of Graves's thesis that the white goddess is the only source of true poetic inspiration. Not only does Williams identify Blanche with the white goddess, but also he provides a version of her history that identifies her with primitive forces, both "creatress and destructress," from girl, to woman, to "waning star." This history is given in part by Stella, who speaks nostalgically of Blanche's youthful beauty, by Kowalski in his recovery of the scandal of her more recent history in Laurel, and through what is enacted before us with Mitch and Kowalski on stage. And Williams's willingness to call on such names as Moon Lake, *Evening Star*, and Stella as appropriate modes of nomination reinforces the conjunction between Blanche and those astral bodies rightly associated with the white goddess in her shape as the Moon Goddess. Blanche's creativity is, of course, little more than illusory; for the duration of the play it is no more than the nurture of her appearance, her wardrobe of props, clothes, jewels, and makeup. However, we can read these guises as tropes of the multiform shapes assumed by the white goddess in the sexual chase, as recorded by Graves through a variety of sources, so that it is right to see Blanche's nymphomania as a thwarted mimesis of the white goddess's predatory sexuality, which has as its occasion the generation of all living things. Blanche's destructive energies are evident both in economic terms—the loss of Belle Reve— and in psychological terms in her relationship to Allan Grey, and later self-destructively to Mitch, to Kowalski, and, ultimately, to Stella.

I take it that one of the attractions of Blanche's role for any actress is that Blanche is not merely an etiolated version of the southern belle of popular romance narratives. She has a self-protective wit and an understanding of her own capacity for "performance," which she enjoys exploiting. I have already cited her Irish/Polish joke whose effectiveness is measured in shared laughter; another example of her satiric thrust comes in scene 1 (252) when she challenges Stella about the squalor of the Kowalski apartment:

BLANCHE: What are you doing in a place like this?

STELLA: Now, Blanche—

BLANCHE: Oh, I'm not going to be hypocritical, I'm going to be honestly critical about it! Never, never, never in my worst dreams could I picture—Only Poe! Only Mr. Edgar Allan Poe!—could do it justice! Out there I suppose is the ghoul-haunted woodland of Weir! (*She laughs*).

Despite the comic intent of this calling upon Poe, to name him at all is to gather in a nexus of common interest between Poe, Graves, and Williams, in which source of imaginative inspiration is located in a figure of supernatural power and beauty: the white goddess in one or another of her manifestations. Of course, Blanche is a secularized version of her, and, like one of Poe's self-immolating characters denied access to the true sources of inspiration, Blanche is a figure for whom desire has turned in upon itself in a program of willful self-destruction. Thus, her summoning of Poe's "ghoul-haunted woodland" is finally a self-irony, a picturing of groves sacred to the Goddess, now populated with ghouls, of which Allan Grey is one, and Blanche herself is soon to be another.

If desire is a streetcar leading to the underworld, it is proper to note that in this play, the underworld is not that of Virgil's dwelling place of the happy dead, but the squalor of the Kowalskis' apartment and finally, for Blanche, the doors of the asylum. The cultural assumptions that underwrite Williams's use of names in this play derive from the counterpointed resources of ethnicity and myth. In so far as *Streetcar* addresses an historical reality in the 1940s of its setting, it does so through its representation of the conflict between these resources, with Blanche's fading star erased from the scene of ethnic vitality by Kowalski's claimant American nationalism. At the same time, the myth of national union is questioned as Blanche's dream gives way not to the power of the North, but to the demands of the immigrant in the figure of Kowalski. Blanche's case may also be read as a version of that history freely inscribed in post–Civil War narrative realizations of the difficulties of unionist accommodation. Henry James's northerner, Olive Chancellor, is thus a perfect foil to Blanche DuBois. Sexually inexperienced, materially rich, disavowing the social necessity of good manners that so pointedly delineates Blanche's discomfort in the Kowalski household, in hindsight, Olive's desire for a partnership with Verena Tarrant, with all that is involved in terms of sexual ambivalence, seems an accomplished proposition despite its failure in practice. By contrast, the iterative fatigue at the heart of Blanche's self-presentation follows from a ritual of performance in which the ritual is finally more important than the desires that animate it. Verena Tarrant is not an immigrant, but she is, like Kowalski, deracinated, and like him the dubious agent of an accommodation neither James nor Williams really believed in. These two works, different in so many ways, end on the same key. Where James tells us that Verena's tears on leaving Olive for Basil are proleptic not of union, but of further severance, so the drama of warring contestants in *Streetcar* gives way to the anonymous Doctor and Matron, whose white coats are the very sign of erasure.

The last words of *Streetcar*—in a boldly imaginative stroke—call Kowalski and his male companions to another ritual performance of that game so iconic of American identity, poker, and that dealer's hand whose name is metonymic of male dominance (419):

STEVE: This game is seven-card stud.

NOTE

1. My use of this speech by the Negro Woman, and the following brief conversation with "A Sailor" uncovers a fascinating variation between the text in *The Theatre of Tennessee Williams* ([New Directions 1971]: 243–44) and that in the British editions of the play. The history of the early British editions of *Streetcar* is complex. The first British edition appears to have been that published by John Lehmann, London, 1949, and this had gone to a fourth impression by 1952. However, the *Cumulative Book Index* lists the 1949 Lehmann edition as correctly published by Secker and Warburg, and it appears that Secker and Warburg became Williams's British publishers from that time, with the paperback rights going to Penguin, in association with Secker and Warburg, somewhat later. The first Secker and Warburg edition of *A Streetcar Named Desire* was thus 1949, reprinted in 1957 and 1968, and this edition is the authority for the first Penguin edition of 1959, described as published "In Association with Secker and Warburg." The Penguin edition has been frequently reprinted and is the text most British readers of this play have used over the past thirty-odd years. It has not proved possible, so far, to discover the authority of the Secker and Warburg edition of 1949, and I do not know if they worked from a manuscript or typescript version, or from an American printing. What appears to have happened is that at some point in time the opening exchanges of the play, between the Negro Woman, a Man, and Sailor have been dropped, either by Tennessee Williams's authority, or by mistake. On the face of it, it seems to me to be an authorial revision, since these exchanges in the Secker and Warburg and Penguin editions have a degree of internal consistency of theme and vocabulary that makes them entirely consonant with the other material in scene 1, and I regard it as highly unlikely that these exchanges would have been interpolated by an over-imaginative and unnamed editor at Secker and Warburg's. I suspect that Williams revised this whole passage out of the text because the reference to St. Barnabas

makes no kind of sense, even though the topics of sexual temptation and alcoholic indulgence remain pertinent to the first scene and much else that follows. The opening fifteen lines of speech in the British editions are omitted from *The Theatre of Tennessee Williams*, vol. 1.

I imagine I am not the first British reader to be puzzled by the Negro Woman's reference to St. Barnabas. There is nothing in the standard accounts of the life and work of St. Barnabas, nor in the Acts of the Apostles, where his story is told, to associate him in any way with what is related here. According to the editors of the Variorum Spenser, St. Barnabas' Day, in the old calendar, was the day of the summer solstice, hence the use Spenser makes of him in the fifteenth stanza of the "Epithalamium": see *The Works of Edmund Spenser: A Variorum Edition, The Minor Poems Volume 2*, edited by Charles Grosvenor Osgood, Henry Gibbons Lotspeich, and assisted by Dorothy E. Mason (Baltimore: The Johns Hopkins Press 1947. 246). Until it is possible to see a manuscript or typescript of the play and to assess the authority of *The Theatre of Tennessee Williams* edition, this problem remains unsolved. One other curiosity remains. In *all* the editions I have seen, the "Negro Woman" is also named as "Colored Woman." Perhaps this distinction was unimportant to Williams in 1947?

WORKS CITED

Boxill, Roger. *Tennessee Williams*. Macmillan Modern Dramatists. New York: Macmillan, 1987.

Graves, Robert. *The White Goddess*. London: Faber and Faber, 1948.

Macherey, Pierre. *A Theory of Literary Production*. Trans. Geoffrey Wall. London: Routledge & Kegan, 1978.

Thompson, Judith J. *Tennessee Williams' Plays: Memory, Myth, and Symbol*. University of Kansas Humanistic Studies 54. New York: Peter Lang, 1987.

Williams, Tennessee. *A Streetcar Named Desire. The Theatre of Tennessee Williams*. 7 vols. to date. New York: New Directions, 1971. Vol. 1: 239–419.

10

The Myth Is the Message, or Why *Streetcar* Keeps Running

Mark Royden Winchell

Certain works of literature seem to enter the popular imagination from the moment they are published. Their appeal is not confined to language or genre; they embody stories and characters that can be transferred from one art form to another without loss of power. For this reason, such stories and characters are often known to many more people than have read the original work. No doubt, millions with little idea who George Orwell was "know" that "1984" and "Big Brother" are ominous concepts. The term *Uncle Tom* is widely used by persons who would have difficulty identifying Harriet Beecher Stowe. Dr. Jekyll and Mr. Hyde, Tarzan, Frankenstein, and Dracula haunt a culture that has largely forgotten the names of Robert Louis Stevenson, Edgar Rice Burroughs, Mary Shelley, and Bram Stoker. Recognizing that this is so is far easier than explaining why it is so.

With few exceptions, sophisticated literary critics dismiss works that have touched a mass audience. Particularly in our own century, the gap between elite and popular culture is an article of faith. As a result, the literary clerisy spends its time analyzing or deconstructing texts while the majority culture continues to enjoy songs and stories. (As Dwight Eisenhower is reputed to have said: "I may not know what's art, but I know what I like.") Of course, in times past, Shakespeare appealed to both the aristocracy and the groundlings; the serialized fiction of Dickens and Thackeray was read as avidly as soap operas are now watched; and Longfellow, prior to reading before Queen Victoria, signed autographs in the servants' quarters.

Among twentieth-century American poets, only Robert Frost bridged the gap between serious and popular literature. In the realm of fiction, the trick was turned (but only in selected novels) by Ernest Hemingway, John Steinbeck, Scott Fitzgerald, and Robert Penn Warren. In drama, where performance enables a writer to reach an audience beyond the confines of the printed page, the record is no better. Eugene O'Neill never seized the popular imagination, and Edward Albee came close only in *Who's Afraid of Virginia Woolf?* For Arthur Miller, *Death of a Salesman* enjoyed a popular and critical success neither precedented nor duplicated in his career.

The one American playwright who is a conspicuous exception to the dichotomy between "high" and "low" culture is Tennessee Williams. Williams's South, with its sexual ambivalence, self-delusion, and irrational violence, has become part of our popular mythos, the ambience of countless B-movies and television melodramas. With only slight exaggeration, Marion Magid writes (290):

> A European whose knowledge of America was gained entirely from the collected works of Tennessee Williams might garner a composite image of the U.S.: it is a tropical country whose vegetation is largely man-eating; it has an excessive annual rainfall and subsequent storms which coincide with its mating periods; it has not yet been converted to Christianity, but continues to observe the myth of the annual death and resurrection of the sun-god, for which purpose it keeps on hand a constant supply of young men to sacrifice.... [T]he sexual embrace...is as often as not followed by the direst consequences: cannibalism, castration, burning alive, madness, surgery in various forms ranging from lobotomy to hysterectomy, depending on the nature of the offending organ.

Beyond this, particular Williams plays, such as *The Glass Menagerie* and *Cat on a Hot Tin Roof*, have entered American popular culture to a degree unmatched by the work of any other critically acclaimed dramatist. Even these achievements, however, pale to insignificance in comparison to what Williams wrought in *A Streetcar Named Desire*. Surely, no play of the American theatre, perhaps no play in English since the time of Shakespeare, has won such praise from *both* the critics and the populace. When they agree on so little in the realm of literature, one wonders why the critics and the people are of a single mind on this one play.

In seeking to answer this question, I have found myself repeatedly borrowing concepts from the criticism of Leslie Fiedler. Although Fiedler's massive bibliography includes commentary on most major works of American literature (as well as many minor ones), I am not aware of his having written on *A Streetcar Named Desire*. Nevertheless, *Streetcar* seems particularly suited for a Fiedlerian treatment (if such a pompous phrase does not violate the populist spirit of Fiedler's muse). At least since his seminal essay, "Cross the Border—Close the Gap" (1969), Fiedler has tried to identify the universal sources of literary response by treating popular culture with the same reverence critics automatically extend to canonical texts. Moreover, *Streetcar* raises many of the same issues that Fiedler has long found at the heart of our storytelling tradition.

A Fiedlerian approach to *Streetcar* would identify those elements in the play that transcend the distinction between elite and popular culture. What is needed is an understanding of the play's mythopoeic power. This is something quite different from a cataloging of allusions to ancient legends, which may or may not be known to a mass audience.[1] *Streetcar* is a play that raises disturbing questions about hearth and home, sex roles, family loyalty, and the power of eros. Because this is done within the context of a drama, the aesthetic distance between audience and artifact is much less than it would be with a sociological essay or even a novel. We respond to issues of universal concern at a visceral level long before that response is articulated, or "rationalized," in the form of criticism. I suspect that *Streetcar* remains such a riveting play in the country of its origin precisely because its particular treatment of universal themes—myth as opposed to mere mythology—is deeply rooted in American culture and literature.

Fiedler has argued for more than forty years that we can pretty well divide the canon of American literature between works that view home as Heaven and those that see it as Hell. The texts celebrated in *Love and Death in the American Novel* (1960) (and, before that, in D. H. Lawrence's *Studies in Classic American Literature* [1923]) belong to the latter category. Beginning with Washington Irving's Rip Van Winkle, "The uniquely American hero/anti-hero . . . rescues no maiden, like Perseus, kills no dragon, like Saint George, discovers no treasure like Beowulf or Siegfried; he does not even manage at long last to get back to his wife, like Odysseus. He is, in fact, an anti-Odysseus who finds his identity by *running away from home*" (Fiedler, *What Was Literature?* 152). The reason for this is quite simple. At home, he is subject to a loathsome form of tyranny known as "petticoat government." The tyrant may be a henpecking wife, such as Rip's Dame Van Winkle, or a nitpicking guardian, such as Huck Finn's Miss Watson (we have endless variations of these two in TV situation comedies and the funny pages of the daily newspaper). In either case, the only escape is into the wilderness and the society of fellow males.

Against this basically misogynistic canon is a countertradition of domestic literature. From the popular women novelists whom Hawthorne dismissed as that "damned tribe of scribbling females" to the writers of today's soap operas, laureates of the domestic tradition posit a stable home life, complete with heterosexual bonding and close family ties, as the greatest human good. Even when it is thwarted by the conflicts necessary to literature and endemic to life, it is still the ideal. As antithetical as they might seem, the domestic paradigm and the misogynist tradition both agree that the woman rules the home. The only disagreement is whether she is a benevolent despot or a hideous shrew. The patriarchal insistence that the man is king of his castle is generally understood as mere male bluster.

To say the least, the Stanley Kowalski household does not conform to the matriarchal conventions of our literature. Stanley is unquestionably the king of his castle. As a traveling salesman, he enjoys the freedom of the road. As captain of his bowling team, he is at no loss for male camaraderie. These experiences, however, are not an evasion of domestic unhappiness.

Stanley's loving and *obedient* wife is always waiting for him, eager to gratify and be gratified. Even in the home, she accommodates him and his friends. Rip Van Winkle may have to meet his buddies at Nicholas Vedder's tavern, Dagwood Bumstead may have to hold his card games in the garage, but Stanley plays poker in the middle of his apartment. Only in the person of Eunice, who threatens to pour boiling water through the floorboards of the upstairs apartment, do we see even a vestige of the henpecking wife. As politically incorrect as it may be, the Kowalski household embodies a patriarchal vision of home as Heaven. There is not enough potential conflict here for either tragedy or farce. Not until Blanche enters the scene.

From the moment of her first entrance, Blanche brings with her a vision of home that varies sharply from what she encounters in Elysian Fields. Even before she utters a word, her expression of *"shocked disbelief"* speaks volumes. In first identifying Stella by her maiden name, Blanche instinctively places her sister back in her old home rather than in the one where she is "Mrs. Stanley Kowalski." Later in the scene, Blanche verbalizes her displeasure with Stella's current living arrangements, suggesting that she has somehow betrayed the memory of Belle Reve. Only a little scrutiny is required to show how problematic Blanche's air of superiority actually is.

To begin with, she has come to Elysian Fields not from Belle Reve but from Tarantula Arms. It is doubtful that accommodations there were any more aristocratic than in the French Quarter. Moreover, reliable information about Belle Reve itself is quite sparse. Clearly, the family home in Laurel has been lost on a mortgage. But how grand was it? With the exception of Stella, the closest that anyone in Elysian Fields has come to the place is a photograph of a mansion with columns. That photograph has been enough to impress Eunice and Stanley; however, Stella, who has actually lived in Belle Reve, seems unconcerned about its loss. Blanche, who at the very least is a pathological liar, remembers the place as a plantation. But there are no plantations in Laurel, Mississippi, which is in the heart of the Piney Woods. If there were even servants at Belle Reve, we hear nothing of them. In fact, Stella says that when *she* waits on Blanche, it seems more like home. There are enough hints in the play to suggest that the grandeur of Belle Reve is as suspect as the value of Blanche's rhinestone tiara and summer furs. (The supposedly hardheaded Stanley is taken in by all three.)

Even if we see Belle Reve as a latter-day Tara, it is lost in a way that Tara never was. Margaret Mitchell's image of the Old South as a matriarchal Eden had captured the public imagination by the time that *Streetcar* premiered on Broadway in 1947. In 1951, moviegoers would have been reminded of this image by the mere fact that Vivien Leigh, who had played Scarlett O'Hara on the screen, was cast as Blanche in the film version of Williams's play. In Mitchell's antebellum South, women ruled the home while men fought duels and argued over secession. These same men mortgaged the matriarchal paradise by leading the South into a war it could not win. (The region's only assets, according to Rhett Butler, were "cotton, slaves, and arrogance.") After the war, Scarlett adapted to changing circumstances to do whatever was necessary to regain Tara and hold off the carpetbaggers. This Darwinian feat, however, was beyond the capabilities of the leading men of the old order (anachronistic cavaliers such as Ashley Wilkes), who were reduced to riding in white sheets at night to prove their manhood. The only exception was the social outcast Rhett Butler.

Belle Reve is not destroyed by war or Reconstruction, but like Margaret Mitchell's South, it is victimized by a failed patriarchy. Over a period of centuries, to hear Blanche tell it, Belle Reve was lost as her "improvident grandfathers and father and uncles and brothers exchanged the land for their epic fornications" (284). (In fact, only a female cousin left enough insurance money to provide for her own burial.) Unlike Scarlett, the women of Belle Reve are incapable of filling the void left by these inadequate men. Stella escapes from this doomed home, and, except for Blanche, all the other women die. Blanche herself is denied a normal family life when she discovers her husband's homosexuality, and the guilt she experiences from driving him to suicide leads to a series of debaucheries that renders her incapable of even pursuing the modest career of a high school English teacher.

Although Blanche is less than an admirable character, she strikes some audiences as at least an object of pity when she falls into Stanley's brutish clutches. And yet, if we look at the situation objectively, Stanley's motives— if not his methods—are superior to Blanche's. His patriarchal authority is never challenged by Stella; however, Blanche does little else from the moment of her arrival at Elysian Fields. When she tells Stella in scene 1 that she will not put up in a hotel because she wants to be close to her sister, her need for companionship is apparent (not to mention her lack of funds). But this residency also gives her a strategic position from which to undermine Stanley and to entice Stella with fantasies of life among the aristocracy. Not only does she install herself as an indefinite squatter in a two-room apartment, she does everything within her power to wreck the contented home life that had existed in that apartment. One can hardly blame Stanley for fighting back.

Throughout much of the play, the conflict between Stanley and Blanche would seem to be between a crude member of the underclass and the quintessential schoolmarm. The standards of etiquette and decorum that Blanche purports to represent have been the scourge of every redblooded American male since Miss Watson tried to force Huck to mind his manners (while she was preparing to sell Nigger Jim down the river). What Mark Twain plays for farce is deadly serious in the world of *Streetcar*. Blanche is not trying to "sivilize" an urchin who is living in her home. She is trying to wreck the home she has invaded. Although never really hidden, this intention is made unmistakably clear in Blanche's speech to Stella toward the end of scene 4 (a speech that Stanley overhears). What she has just finished proposing to Stella is a kind of feminist variation on the anti-Odysseus theme. In this scenario, Stella will run away from home to join Blanche (who has already fled Laurel) in a chaste female bonding—not in the forest or on the river, but in a shop of some sort endowed by a sexually unthreatening Shep Huntleigh.

When Stanley's boorish behavior is insufficient to drive Blanche away, he discovers something that must be the realization of every rebellious schoolboy's fantasy: the schoolmarm is not what she pretends to be. As Henry Fielding observed in his preface to *Joseph Andrews*, the exposure of hypocrisy is the source of endless delight. When Stanley reveals the sordid details of Blanche's recent conduct to Stella in scene 7, it is with a kind of righteous gloating. "That girl calls *me* common!" he says (358). The only reservation that might prevent the audience from sharing Stanley's glee is the hope that a reformed Blanche will find happiness as Mitch's wife, a solution that would also remove her from the Kowalski household. Stella is convinced that this would happen if Stanley would only keep his mouth shut.

Unfortunately, all available evidence suggests otherwise. Blanche's new-found circumspection is only a ruse to lure Mitch to the altar. If there is any doubt of this, consider the end of scene 5, when Blanche's attempted seduction of the newsboy is followed immediately by the arrival of Mitch, with a bunch of roses in his hand. As Blanche's husband, Mitch would probably arrive home one afternoon to find his wife in the sack with some less hesitant newsboy (just as Blanche found her former husband in bed with a man). She sees Mitch not as a spouse to love (even in the exclusively physical way that Stella loves Stanley) but as a sexually timid benefactor, a poor girl's Shep Huntleigh. It is hardly dishonorable for Stanley to want to protect his naive friend from such a fate. In the world of male camaraderie, his bond with Mitch is just as compelling as the blood ties that unite Stella and Blanche.

If Stanley is justified in wising Mitch up about Blanche's past, he clearly crosses the line of acceptable behavior when he attacks her sexually in scene 10. And yet even this inexcusable act must be analyzed within the context of the play. There is little evidence to suggest that Stanley returned home that night with the intention of raping Blanche.[2] He is in a good mood because of the impending birth of his child and even offers to "bury the hatchet" and drink "a loving cup" with Blanche.

It is only after she speaks of casting her pearls before swine that his mood changes. This reference can't help reminding Stanley of the tirade he over-heard in scene 4. (That speech, with its Darwinian imagery, was more than a little ironic, since it is Blanche, not the atavistic Stanley, who is in danger of becoming extinct because of an inability to adapt to a changing envi-ronment.) Although he had not overheard her references to Shep Huntleigh in that earlier scene, a woman as talkative as Blanche might well have tipped her hand to him at some point during her interminable stay in the Kowalski apartment. In any event, *the audience* is reminded of Blanche's plot to "rescue" Stella by breaking up her marriage to Stanley. As Stanley has yet to lay a hand on Blanche, our sympathies must still be with him.[3]

Since the consummation of what happens between Stanley and Blanche occurs offstage, we are left to imagine the details. On the basis of what we do know, it is reasonable to assume that Stanley believes he is simply doing what Mitch was unable to do in the preceding scene: enjoy the favors of a notoriously promiscuous woman. Blanche held Mitch off by screaming "Fire," something she does not do when Stanley approaches her. When he says, "So you want some roughhouse! All right, let's have some rough-house!" his assumption is that she enjoys violent foreplay. It is possible to interpret Stanley's next statement—"We've had this date with each other from the beginning" (402)—as a confession that he has been plotting to destroy her. But it is at least as plausible that he is referring to Blanche's flirtatious advances, which began as early as scene 2.[4] Whatever happens offstage, Stanley can hardly be said to have driven Blanche insane. She may think that she is waiting for Shep Huntleigh when the Doctor and Matron come to cart her off to the insane asylum in scene 11, but she also thought that in scene 10 before Stanley even came home. If anyone drives Blanche crazy, it is Mitch by foiling her wedding plans.[5]

Despite all of these mitigating factors (which seem far more disingenuous in the postfeminist nineties than they would have in 1947), the rape so diminishes Stanley morally that we are deprived of any easy satisfaction we might have felt in his triumph over Blanche. If Williams personally empathized with Blanche more than with Stanley, the rape may be his desperate attempt to win audience sympathy for a victimized woman. But that is about all he is able to do. It is beyond even Williams's considerable art to convince us that Blanche is a genuinely tragic figure; she has too many flaws, too little stature, and almost no self-knowledge. Blanche can excite pity in the truly sensitive but only fear in the most defeated and self-loathing among us.[6]

Although critics have never been entirely comfortable with the confused feelings Williams's two antagonists evoke, some balance is necessary to maintain dramatic tension.[7] The rape creates that balance. It does not elevate Blanche to the level of tragic heroine, but it does prevent the audience from siding too enthusiastically with Stanley. Remove the rape, and *Streetcar* is reduced to a sexist melodrama, in which the gaudy seed-bearer reasserts patriarchal control over a household threatened by a hypocritical and self-serving matriarchy.[8] Of course, the circumstances of the rape are ambiguous enough that what the mass audience loses in melodrama it gains in sado-masochistic titillation.[9]

In a sense, Williams's audience can have it both ways: it can censure Stanley and pity Blanche (the "proper" moral and aesthetic response, to be sure) while guiltily enjoying his triumph over her. At least, this would seem to be true for the men in the audience. As males, we have secretly cheered the bad boy on as he proves something we have always wanted to believe, that the sententious schoolmarm is really a secret nympho. There is even a sense in which the male who has allowed himself to identify with Stanley can see *Streetcar* as having a fairy tale ending. The witch has been dispatched (if not to the hereafter, at least to the loony bin); the home is safe; and the prince and princess of Elysian Fields live happily ever after—seeing colored lights unsubdued by magic lanterns. But what of the woman spectator? In what way is she able to experience the mythic power (as opposed to merely admiring the artistry) of Williams's play? It is certainly not through a macho identification with Stanley.

One can imagine a woman who believes herself wronged by men feeling an affinity with Blanche. If we read *Streetcar* as a feminist fable, Stanley's rape of Blanche might be a paradigm for how men deal with women in a patriarchal society. (Stanley and Mitch would both seem to be purveyors of the double standard, while Stella is nothing more than a sex object and childbearer.) Not surprisingly, Sandra M. Gilbert and Susan Gubar see the play as an indictment of "the law of the phallus and the streetcar named heterosexual desire" (52). In an even more detailed feminist analysis, Anca Vlasopolos reminds us that it is not just Stanley but the entire cast of the play that expells Blanche at the end. Stanley and Mitch may have been the catalysts of Blanche's downfall, but Stella—with the encouragement of Eunice—seals her sister's fate by choosing to believe Stanley so that her marriage might be preserved. The poker buddies simply stand around in awkward, bovine acquiescence.

The problem with these interpretations is not that they are untrue but that they are inadequate. For much of her life, Blanche's difficulties stemmed from the lack of a forceful patriarchy. As we have seen, her male forebears abdicated their role as providers and saddled her with mortgage and debt. Her behavior toward her husband may have had terrible consequences, but it was not without provocation. Allan Grey wronged Blanche by marrying her, knowing that she loved him in a way that could bring her only traumatic pain when she discovered the truth about his sexual orientation. He then allowed her to believe that the fiasco of their wedding night was her fault. Finally, when she quite understandably tells him that he is disgusting (which he is), he takes the coward's way out by killing himself—apparently not caring what effect this will have on Blanche or anyone else he leaves behind. It is the absence of assertive men, not their chauvinistic presence, that has been Blanche's undoing. In fact, Blanche even admits to Stella that Stanley may be "what we need to mix with our blood now that we've lost Belle Reve" (285).

For women, the emotional power of *Streetcar* may come from an identification with Stella. Unlike Stanley and Blanche, who, depending on your perspective, are either superhuman or subhuman, Stella seems a fairly ordinary person. In purely Darwinian terms, however, she is clearly the heroine of the play. She has survived because she has successfully adapted herself to changing circumstances. (Blanche is doomed by her inability to adapt, whereas Stanley seems bent on adapting the environment to himself.) Although Blanche blames Stella for betraying Belle Reve by leaving, there is no reason to believe that she could have saved the place by staying. Unlike Lot's wife, she does not cast even a regretful glance back. Stella has no illusions about the desirability of a world in which women are worshiped but not supported. Stanley spells out the difference between these two worlds in his typically blunt manner. He reminds Stella: "When we first met, me and you, you thought I was common. How right you was, baby. I was common as dirt. You showed me the snapshot of the place with the columns. I pulled you down off them columns and how you loved it, having them colored lights going!" (377).

In pulling her "down off them columns," Stanley brings Stella into a world of male dominance. At least symbolically, it is an act of brute force, and one that Stella "loves." As Gore Vidal noted nearly forty years after the Broadway premiere of *Streetcar*: "[W]hen Tennessee produced *A Streetcar Named Desire*, he inadvertently smashed one of our society's most powerful taboos (no wonder Henry Luce loathed him): he showed the male not only sexually attractive in the flesh but as an object for something never before entirely acknowledged by the good team, the lust of women" (10). Moreover, the fact that Stanley, as a "Polack," is considered socially inferior to the DuBois sisters makes his sexual assaults on them what Fiedler calls "rape from below." For Stella, this simply adds to the fun; for Blanche, it presumably adds to the horror.

We know that Stella was "thrilled" when Stanley broke the light bulbs with her slipper on their wedding night and that she nearly goes crazy when he is away on the road. The notion that women enjoy this kind of brute sexuality has long been a commonplace in popular literature. After all, an entire genre of romance novels, which are purchased almost exclusively by women, is called "bodice rippers." In one of the most memorable scenes in the greatest romance novel of all time, *Gone With the Wind*, Rhett Butler takes Scarlett by force in what is quite literally an act of marital rape. After quoting this scene in the novel, Fiedler writes: "Finally, however, [Scarlett] *likes* it (as perhaps only a female writer would dare to confess, though there are echoes of D. H. Lawrence in the passage), likes being mastered by the dark power of the male, likes being raped" (*What Was Literature?* 208).

We have a similar phenomenon in the relationship of Stanley and Stella, except that Stella does not even put up token resistance. In the scene from *Gone With the Wind*, Rhett carries a protesting Scarlett up the staircase of their mansion. In *Streetcar*, we have a scene that is almost the mirror opposite. After Stanley has gone ape on his poker night and hit the pregnant

Stella, she and Blanche flee upstairs to Eunice's apartment. When he realizes what has happened, Stanley proceeds to scream (*with heaven-splitting violence*): "STELL-LAHHHHH." According to the stage directions:

The low-tone clarinet moans. The door upstairs opens again. Stella slips down the rickety stairs in her robe. Her eyes are glistening with tears and her hair loose around her throat and shoulders. They stare at each other. Then they come together with low, animal moans. He falls to his knees on the steps and presses his face to her belly, curving a little with maternity. Her eyes go blind with tenderness as she catches his head and raises him level with her. He snatches the screen door open and lifts her off her feet and bears her into the dark flat.

(Like Scarlett, Stella wears a look of serene contentment on the morning after.)

If there is a single scene in *Streetcar* that remains in the memory, it is this one. The film version has been endlessly replayed as a kind of touchstone in the history of the cinema. Moreover, it has been parodied and spoofed by countless impressionists and nightclub comedians. Now a permanent part of our popular culture, this scene can be said to sum up iconographically what *Streetcar* is all about. For men, it is a fantasy of complete domination; for women, one of complete submission.

Like other works that have entered the realm of popular myth, *Streetcar* loses none of its power when transferred to another medium. This fact is particularly astonishing when one considers that, in bringing this play to the screen, Williams and director Elia Kazan faced not only the normal aesthetic challenges of such an undertaking but a battle with the censors, as well. The story has been frequently told of the many lines of vulgar or suggestive dialogue that had to be bowdlerized.[10] Then, there was the insistence that any hint of Allan Grey's homosexuality be removed. Finally, the censors would allow Stanley's rape of Blanche to remain only if Stella would punish Stanley by leaving him (on the assumption that only the breakup of this home could preserve traditional family values). Nevertheless, the subversive appeal of the play manages to survive.

The sanitizing of Williams's language (which is not all that shocking when judged by today's standards) is about as effective as the bleeping of profanity on television. Adult theatregoers know how people such as Stanley Kowalski talk without having to hear the actual words. Besides, more than enough sexual energy is conveyed by Marlon Brando's body language and magnetic screen presence. The issue of Allan's homosexuality is not crucial, either. In talking about her husband's weakness, Blanche at least implies a deviancy that dare not speak its name. It is perhaps even more in character for her to withhold the sordid details from Mitch.

Finally, when Stella leaves Stanley in the movie (just after Blanche has been escorted out of the apartment by the psychiatrist and the Matron), it is not for the first time. She has left him many times before, most recently in the aftermath of the poker game. As Maurice Yacowar points out, "Stella's last speech is undercut by several ironies. She expresses her resolve to leave to the baby, not to the rather more dangerous Stanley. And she does not leave the quarter, but just goes upstairs to Eunice's apartment; and Stanley's call had been enough to bring her back from Eunice's before" (23). When the movie closes with Stanley screaming for Stella, it is difficult not to visualize her returning much as she had in that earlier unforgettable scene.

It is more than a little ironic that Tennessee Williams, the homosexual misfit, should have written such an aggressively heterosexual play. As a man who shared many of Blanche's faults (promiscuity, self-hatred, and paranoia, though never hypocrisy), he must have felt closer to her than most of his audiences do, pity being the greatest kindness that most of these strangers are willing to extend to her. Certainly, it takes a jaundiced view of home and family to present the Kowalski household as their embodiment.[11] But that is exactly what *Streetcar* does. For nearly fifty years there has been a place in the American imagination where it is always three a.m., and a man in a torn t-shirt screams for his wife with "*heaven-splitting violence.*" Despite the protests of film censors and outraged feminists, she will always slip down the rickety stairs and into his arms. This is because "there are things that happen between a man and a woman in the dark—that sort of make everything else seem unimportant" (321), and because "life has got to go on. No matter what happens" (406). As long as people continue to believe such things, *A Streetcar Named Desire* will keep running.

NOTES

1. See, for example, Thompson 25–51.

2. Bert Cardullo argues convincingly that "Williams carefully structures act 3, scene 4, so as to make the rape seem incidental, the result more of Stanley's sudden and uncontrollable drunken lust than of his calculation and deliberate cruelty" (138).

3. Harold Clurman notes that, during the original Broadway production, the audience sided with Stanley for the bulk of the play (78). Emily Mann goes even further in contending that, contrary to Williams's intentions, Stanley, at least Marbon Brando's Stanley, eventually "became a folk hero" for American audiences. See Kolin (19).

4. Roger Boxill notes that Stanley "is quite right in telling [Blanche] that she accepted the date with him a long time ago" (82). Also, a director who so chooses can accentuate Blanche's sexual attraction to Stanley and her complicity in her own ravishment. For a discussion of how John Erman did this in his television film of *Streetcar*, see Schlueter.

5. The question of when, and even whether, Blanche goes mad is controlled to some extent by the actress playing the role. For a discussion of the different inter-

pretations of Blanche's mental state in the performances of Jessica Tandy and Uta Hagen, see Bentley 88–89.

6. Blanche has had her critical defenders. Their arguments, however, tend to focus on Williams's own sympathies (Nelson 149) or on philosophical elements in the play (Tischler 138) rather than on audience reaction. I think that Roger Boxill has it about right when he says that "audiences favour Stanley, at least in the beginning, while readers favour Blanche" (80).

7. For a plausible defense of the balance that Williams has struck in his characterization of Stanley and Blanche, see Berlin.

8. Boxill makes precisely this point when he says: "If Blanche is portrayed as a neurotic and pretentious woman of whom history is well rid, and Stanley as a healthy animal whose brutishness is but a symptom of his 'acute sensitivity,' then *Streetcar* becomes a melodrama" (90).

9. According to Signi Falk, the opening night theatregoers sided with Stanley to the point that during the rape scene "waves of titillated laughter swept over the audience" (175).

10. For discussions of the film version of *Streetcar*, including the issue of censorship, see Phillips and Yacowar.

11. John Gassner says as much when he argues that "Williams . . . seems to have succumbed to a generally jaundiced view of normality by giving the impression that the common world is brutish, as if life in a poor neighborhood and Stan and Stella's sexually gratifying marriage were brutish" (377).

WORKS CITED

Berlin, Normand. "Complementarity in *A Streetcar Named Desire*." *Tennessee Williams: A Tribute*. Ed. Jac Tharpe. Jackson: UP of Mississippi, 1977. 97–103.

Boxill, Roger. *Tennessee Williams*. New York: St. Martin's, 1987.

Bentley, Eric. *In Search of Theater*. New York: Knopf, 1953.

Cardullo, Bert. "Drama of Intimacy and Tragedy of Incomprehension: *A Streetcar Named Desire* Reconsidered." *Tennessee Williams: A Tribute*. Ed. Jac Tharpe. 137–53.

Clurman, Harold. *Lies Like Truth*. New York: Macmillan, 1958.

Falk, Signi. "The Profitable World of Tennessee Williams." *Modern Drama* 1 (December 1958): 172–80.

Fiedler, Leslie. "Cross the Border—Close the Gap." *Fiedler Reader*. Briar Cliff Manor, NY: Stein & Day, 1977. 270–94.

———. *What Was Literature? Class Culture and Mass Society*. New York: Simon & Schuster, 1982.

Gassner, John. "*A Streetcar Named Desire*: A Study in Ambiguity." *Modern Drama: Essays in Criticism*. Ed. Travis Bogard and William I. Oliver. New York: Oxford UP, 1965. 374–84.

Gilbert, Sandra M. and Susan Gubar. *No Man's Land: The Place of the Woman Writer in the Twentieth Century*, I: *The War of the Words*. New Haven: Yale UP, 1988.

Kolin, Philip C., ed. "*A Streetcar Named Desire*: A Playwright's Forum." *Michigan Quarterly Review* 29 (Spring 1990): 173–203.

Magid, Marion. "The Innocence of Tennessee Williams." *Essays in the Modern Drama*. Ed. Morris Freedman. Boston: D. C. Heath, 1966. 280–93.

Nelson, Benjamin. *Tennessee Williams: The Man and His World*. New York: Obolensky, 1961.

Phillips, Gene D. *The Films of Tennessee Williams*. Philadelphia: Art Alliance, 1980.

Schlueter, June. "Imitating an Icon: John Erman's Remake of Tennessee Williams's *A Streetcar Named Desire*." *Modern Drama* 28 (March 1985): 139–47.

Thompson, Judith J. *Tennessee Williams's Plays: Memory, Myth, and Symbol*. New York: Lang, 1987.

Tischler, Nancy. *Tennessee Williams: Rebellious Puritan*. New York: Citadel, 1961.

Vidal, Gore. "Immortal Bird." *New York Review of Books* 13 (June 1985), 5–6, 8–10.

Vlasopolos, Anca. "Authorizing History: Victimization in *A Streetcar Named Desire*." *Theatre Journal* 38(Oct. 1986): 322–38. Rpt. in *Feminist Readings of Modern American Drama*. Ed. June Schlueter. Rutherford, N.J.: Fairleigh Dickinson UP, 1989. 149–70.

Williams, Tennessee. *A Streetcar Named Desire*. The Theatre of Tennessee Williams. 7 vols. to date. New York: New Directions, 1971. Vol. 1: 239–419.

Yacowar, Maurice. *Tennessee Williams and Film*. New York: Ungar, 1977.

11

The Broken World: Romanticism, Realism, Naturalism in
A Streetcar Named Desire

W. Kenneth Holditch

In 1947 Blanche DuBois first rode that rattletrap streetcar named Desire into "the broken world" of the New Orleans French Quarter, which her fictional presence transformed, along with the vehicle of her descent, into an American legend. Subsequently, numerous and varied interpretations of *A Streetcar Named Desire* have been advanced. They range from the irrelevant and irreverent, such as Mary McCarthy's gratuitously destructive summary of the plot as merely the story of a pesky in-law's visit (one wonders what response such a cavalier dismissal of rape would evoke from feminist critics had McCarthy been male), to a reading of the drama as symbolic representation of the fall of the South, to serious attempts at classifying it as a tragedy in the ancient mode. Many of these approaches are valid, in part at least, for any great work of literature is layered in terms of meaning and significance and does not offer up its full measure of truth to only one reading or analysis. Such a diversity may be as valid a touchstone as any in identifying masterpieces of literature.

A Streetcar Named Desire is, among other things, a classic study of the destruction of a Romantic protagonist committed to the ideal but living in the modern age, a broken world, a wasteland growing progressively more pragmatic and animalistic as the twentieth century advances. Blanche DuBois is the delicate last remnant of an agrarian, aristocratic order that, before its decline and eventual demise, was somehow able to balance its belief in a metaphysical and religious system with the demands of the flesh. When she finds herself stranded and desperate in the grossly realistic world of urban New Orleans and the Naturalistic order of the post–World War II years, her fate is sealed. Viewed from this angle, the dramatic portrayal of her descent into destruction may be considered a paradigm for the decline of Western civilization and the subsequent fragmentation and secularism that many authors—Henry Adams, Pound, Yeats, Eliot, Hemingway, and

Faulkner among them—have examined. However, *Streetcar* also reflects a growing awareness of authors nurtured on half a century of Realism and Naturalism that the phenomenal world is basically incompatible with ideality and that ultimately the human being committed to the transcendent dream or vision must be brought up short or even sacrificed on the altar of materialism. It is that aspect of the drama that this paper will examine.

Romanticism is innately egocentric, and if humanity is nothing more than some species evolved from lower animal forms, the Romantic's self-centered view is surely at odds with the prevailing natural order, focused as that order is on concern for the perpetuation of the race, not the individual. Such is the dilemma idealistic authors from Tennyson on have had to face, and literature offers many dramatic portrayals of Romantics trapped in a Naturalistic environment, the most significant perhaps in Emma Bovary and another striking example in Thomas Mann's *Death in Venice* where Aschenbach is destroyed by his belief that he has found the embodiment of his ideals in the flesh of a teenaged Polish boy. In *The Great Gatsby*, Nick Carroway observes that the title character, who in effect created a Platonic version of himself and Daisy, is doomed on the moment he abandons that ideal and enters the phenomenal world to kiss his beloved, a woman all too human, all too fallible. A century before F. Scott Fitzgerald, Arthur Schopenhauer had pointed out (III, 348–49) that:

> even the most passionate and dedicated lover is apt to experience an extraordinary disillusionment when he at last arrives at his goal, so that he is left wondering that "what was so longingly desired accomplishes nothing more than every other sexual satisfaction.

"Disillusionment" is the key word in this passage, as it is in the understanding of any Tennessee Williams play. Blanche's unsatisfying search for consolation and comfort in the arms of anonymous lovers effectively demonstrates Schopenhauer's theory. Like Gatsby, she cannot find in reality (among what John Donne called "dull sublunary lovers") the ideal of which she has dreamed, and, in the words of Hart Crane's "The Broken Tower" that serve as epigraph for the play, the search for the "company of love" and the holding of "each desperate choice" tarnishes, even destroys the original vision.

Among those literary works that deal with the plight of the Romantic in an alien setting, two novels, Kate Chopin's *The Awakening* and William Faulkner's *The Wild Palms*, are pertinent to a study of *A Streetcar Named Desire*. Both portray heroines who, like Blanche, move inevitably along paths toward destruction and have other remarkable parallels that underscore the similar views of the human experience. In the novels as in the play, New Orleans, or some area of it, functions as a catalyst effecting radical changes in characters' lives, though the city's influence is less pronounced in *The Wild Palms* than in the others. This is not to suggest any influence of Chopin and Faulkner on the playwright—indeed, that seems unlikely, since it is doubtful if Williams had read *The Awakening* in the 1940s and the influence of Faulkner upon him lay in other directions—but a preliminary examination of the novels will help elucidate the dilemma Blanche faces in *Streetcar* and one truth about the human condition with which Williams's greatest drama is concerned.

The identification of the city of New Orleans with romance and mystery is as old as the first literature written about the old French city, but it is a place also associated with decadence and corruption, with sins of the flesh, glamorous perhaps on the surface but underneath as unsettling to the outsider as the abundance of insects and rodents that infest its old buildings and streets, warehouses, and wharves. Thus, Bourbon Street, outward symbol of that sensuous and sensual lifestyle, is, in reality, Walker Percy writes, "as lewd and joyless a place as Dante's Second Circle of Hell, lewd with that special sad voyeur lewdness which marks the less felicitous encounters between Latin permissiveness and Anglo-Saxon sex morality"(16). Nineteenth-century literature contains frequent tales of young men corrupted by the city's pleasures and excesses, and Justin Kaplan states that by the time of Walt Whitman's arrival in 1848, it already had the reputation of being the "wickedest city in Christendom" (139). In the twentieth century, the fascination the city exerted continued to elicit ambivalent and ambiguous responses from writers. Eudora Welty, for example, has a character describe it in "The Purple Hat" as "the birthplace of ready-made victims" (224).

To some extent, this equation of the city with both romance and decadence is a product of the fiction writers who have for two centuries spun a web of the imagination around it until finally, in the words of Cleanth Brooks, "New Orleans has become a city of the mind, and is therefore immortal." That fictional representation, however, is rooted in substantial fact, for in truth, the place is more romantic than perhaps any other American city due to several factors: the aura of history in the French Quarter and environs and in the Garden District; its Old World charm, fading rapidly now in the strong glare of "Progress," but still much in evidence; a way of life that is much more Latin than American, Mediterranean than southern, Catholic permissive than Calvinist prohibitive. As Walker Percy describes that unique foreignness, "It is as if Marseilles had been plucked up off the Midi, monkeyed with by Robert Moses and Hugh Hefner, and set down off John O'Groats in Scotland" (12). Juxtaposed to the Romantic, however, there is also the decadence evident in day-to-day life, from widespread corruption in government to the almost pagan tolerance of the luxurious and sensual lifestyle practiced by a large percentage of its residents and indulged in by many tourists, some in search of just such freedom and license.

That Williams was aware of the city's paradoxical nature is clear not only from the text of *Streetcar* but also from his personal comments. Although professing to have been shocked by his first encounter with the French Quarter in 1938, he admitted to having found in that exotic milieu "a kind of freedom I had always needed. And the shock of it against the Puritanism of my nature has given me a subject, a theme, which I have never ceased exploiting" (quoted in Tischler 61). His initial stage directions in *Streetcar* include comments on the "*raffish charm*" and "*a kind of lyricism*" that "*gracefully attenuates the atmosphere of decay*" (243) in the Faubourg Marigny, an area adjacent to and much like the Quarter. That description identifies the paradox of a place both poetic and appealing on the one hand, decadent and repellent on the other, a paradox present in the two novels as well.

It should be pointed out that it is not New Orleans alone where Naturalistic forces have exerted themselves, for at Belle Reve, Blanche has encountered death and the destruction of her dreams. The deterministic elements are, of course, within the individual, not in the place, or not in the place alone. The symbolism of the city is extremely complex, for New Orleans represents here not only the Naturalistic truth of the human condition, but Romance and Desire and the denial of Death, whereas Belle Reve, the "ideal world," has succumbed to lust and death, underscoring the idea that in a biological universe, Romance is either impossible or of limited duration.

Written at the end of the nineteenth century, *The Awakening* concisely capsules what was happening to literature during that crucial period when the Romanticism of the past was giving way to a growing democratic impulse here and abroad and to a concomitant desire on the part of readers and writers for fiction reflecting the world in which they lived. The subsequent Realistic movement in turn spawned Literary Naturalism, which drew on recent scientific discoveries and changing political, sociological, and psychological attitudes. Kate Chopin's protagonist, Edna Pontellier, a Romantic idealist nurtured on French novels, Emerson, and Whitman, dreams first of an ethereal love—with a famous dramatic actor, a cavalry officer, a handsome young Creole—and later of one idealized but not devoid of passion, one that transcends the demands of being wife and mother. Freed from domestic and social bondage, she finds that the modern world, perhaps any phenomenal world, will not accommodate her dream. She awakens to discover a real world in which Platonic girlhood infatuations and meetings of the soul give way to sexual desires and congress between flesh and flesh.

Emile Zola in "The Experimental Novel," a prime document of Literary Naturalism, posits an ideal method of plotting a novel, placing a protagonist in an unfamiliar environment and observing the results (9). This is exactly the pattern of *The Awakening*, for Edna's belated entry into sensual maturity is occasioned, among other elements, by the atmosphere of Grand Isle and the French Quarter and the clash of her own southern Protestant background—"sound old Presbyterian Kentucky stock" (948)—with the easy-going attitude of New Orleanians. The local matrons' jokes about sexual matters and flirtation with young, unmarried Robert Lebrun shock Edna. Adele Ratignolle, a typical "wife-mother" content to spend her life in single-minded devotion to husband and children, recognizes the difference between Edna and the Creole culture and warns Robert to be careful about his attentions, for "she is not one of us; she is not like us" and may misinterpret his flirtation (900).

As it did for young Thomas Lanier Williams, the shock of this easy-going, sensual lifestyle against "the Puritanism" of her character effects a remarkable change in Edna. She undergoes a series of "awakenings," beginning with a realization that her life as merely wife and mother stifles her individuality and culminating in the depressing recognition of several inescapable facts: that Romantic love is evanescent, especially when it finds embodiment in the flesh of a particular person; that though humans may yearn to be more than dust, may conceive of themselves as "a little lower than the angels," the predominant fact of existence is their animal nature, the purpose for that existence to perpetuate the species.

Gradually, awakened from her fantasies of Platonic love to the reality of fleshly passion—that is, having moved beyond the Romantic phase into the Realistic phase, in which she is briefly involved in a purely physical affair with the rakish Alcee Arobin—she still clings to the notion of an idyllic life. As time passes, she is disillusioned by the perception that her sexual desire for Robert will be superseded by other "love." Circumscribed by social and religious training, Robert insists on marriage as a component of their union, not realizing how far beyond mere convention Edna, controlled now by her physical nature, has moved. "Instinct had prompted her to put away her husband's bounty in casting off her alllegiance" (963), and having foresworn her duties to one union, she has no intention of accepting the bondage of another, believing now that marriage is "one of the most lamentable spectacles on earth" (948). Edna proposes that they love one another and "be everything to each other" (993), and Robert, denied the formal relationship, flees. His departure, combined with another traumatic experience, pushes Edna out of the Realistic phase into acceptance of a purely Naturalistic view of the universe.

The second psychological trauma results from the birth of Adele's baby. Although Edna has borne children, she is not the "mother-woman" and is repelled by the process as witnessed from a new perspective (994):

Her own like experiences seemed far away, unreal, and only half remembered. She recalled faintly an ecstasy of pain, the heavy odor of chloroform, a stupor which had deadened sensation, and an awakening to find a new life to which she had given being, added to the great unnumbered multitude of souls that come and go.

This "scene of torture" effects in her an "inward agony" and "a flaming, outspoken revolt against the ways of Nature" (955). Her later discussion with Dr. Mandelet reveals that the experience has "awakened" her to yet another level of consciousness, not yet fully expressible, in which she recognizes that "nobody has any right—except children, perhaps—and even then, it seems to me—or it did seem—" (995).

Dr. Mandelet, the character most sensitive to Edna's plight, responds (996) that

> youth is given up to illusions. It seems to be a provision of nature; a decoy to secure mothers for the race. And Nature takes no account of moral consequences, of arbitrary conditions which we create, and which we feel obliged to maintain at any cost.

The physician's advanced scientific view, diametrically opposed to the prevalent nineteenth-century Romantic version of nature and to the earlier idealistic inclinations of the protagonist, represents succinctly the attitudes of Darwin, Spencer, Schopenhauer, and the Literary Naturalists. His opinion and Edna's final, disheartening "awakening" are similar to the devastating realization of the correspondent in Stephen Crane's "The Open Boat" that "nature does not regard him as important" and "feels that she would not maim the universe by disposing of him..." (902).

Faced with such stark truth, Edna's options narrow to three: she can reassume the identity of "Pontellier's wife"; she can live according to her instincts, a "fallen woman" outcast from a condemning society; or she can escape through death. She recognizes clearly her own powerful physical drives: "To-day it is Arobin; tomorrow it will be some one else" (999). She does not care for what people say nor for her husband, but she now perceives the full implication of her earlier remark to Adele that "she would give up the unessential, but she would never sacrifice herself for her children" (999). Mere existence is "unessential," but her individuality is vital, and living within the confines of her society, meeting its expectations for the mother-woman, she cannot be "herself." Faced with such a tragic paradox, Edna, a Romantic imprisoned in a Naturalistic universe, chooses physical death rather than disgrace or "spiritual death."

Learning to swim symbolized for Edna her first "awakening" and the assertion of individuality, and it is to the sea, a giant personification of Nature, that she returns. Even in her last moment, the thoughts of the Romantic who has faced reality and found in its visage awful Naturalistic truths return to sentimental visions, "the blue-grass meadow that she had traversed when a little child, believing that it had no beginning and no end," the voices of her father, sister, and the cavalry officer who was the object of her childhood infatuation (114).

Faulkner originally called *The Wild Palms*, his 1936 contrapuntal novel, *If I Forget Thee, Jerusalem*, but it was first published as *The Wild Palms*,[1] a title that underscores the battle between Romanticism and Naturalism that forms the basis of the tragedy of Charlotte Rittenmeyer and Harry Wilbourne. A study in behaviorism, Harry, like Edna, fits Zola's pattern of the protagonist set down in an alien environment. An unimaginative young man from Oklahoma interning at a New Orleans hospital, he follows a dull routine without much pleasure, seemingly without desire. On his twenty-seventh birthday, he awakens to look down the length of his body and with uncharacteristic insight sees it as symbolizing his existence, "as if his life were to lie passively on his back as though he floated effortless and without volition upon an un-returning stream" (516–17). (At this point, his name is decidedly ironic, since he is not "Will-born" but the victim of forces over which he has no control.) That evening he is coaxed by a friend into attending a Bohemian party in the French Quarter at which he meets Charlotte, a married woman with two daughters. Almost immediately they fall in love, an emotion new and puzzling for him but instinctively understood by her. His discovery of a lost wallet filled with money enables them to flee the "Respectability" and "Security" that the Romantic Charlotte believes to be destructive of true love. A few months later, the more pragmatic Harry begins to want to "take the illicit love and make it respectable," but Charlotte resists (551):

Listen: it's got to be all honeymoon, always. Forever and ever, until one of us dies. It can't be anything else. Either heaven, or hell: no comfortable safe peaceful purgatory between for you and me to wait until good behavior or forebearance or shame or repentance overtakes us.

Her options—heaven or hell—bring to mind John Crowe Ransom's "The Equilibrists," lovers whose predicament it is to have come *between* them the very honor that, ironically, exists *among* even thieves.

Charlotte professes belief in a love that never dies but rather leaves those who prove unworthy of it. Ironically, she uses a nature image to describe love: "It's like the ocean: if you're no good, if you begin to make a bad smell in it, it just spews you up somewhere to die . . ." (551). Her unplanned pregnancy shocks her, for she had thought that "when people loved, hard, really loved each other, they didn't have children, the seed got burned up in the love, the passion" (634). As in *The Awakening*, children are the embodiment of Naturalistic reality that brings an end to Romance, which for Charlotte involves only two people. Having abandoned her daughters, Charlotte is unwilling to bear again because children hurt "too damned much." She refers here not to the pain of childbirth observed by Edna in *The Awakening* but to the suffering one's obligations to offspring inflict on the parent. She believes that with a baby between them as constant physical reminder of their true positions in Nature, love, or her Romantic concept of it, would vanish. She wants to retain the relationship for which they have fought and suffered. She urges Harry to perform an abortion to save the ideals, to prevent their sinking into a respectable life.

Harry, transformed by Charlotte from his passive, volitionless state into a man who is "Will-born," briefly accepts her ideals; he comes to depend upon love with "boundless faith" that it will provide for all needs. His faith, however, is short-lived, and he later states, in "Waste Land" language reminiscent of Ezra Pound, that there is no place in the contemporary world for love (587–88):

We have eliminated it . . . we have got rid of love at last just as we got rid of Christ. We have radio in the place of God's voice. . . . If Jesus returned today we would have to crucify him quick in our own defense to justify and preserve the civilization we have worked and suffered and died shrieking and cursing in rage and impotence and terror for two thousand years to create and perfect in man's own image; if Venus returned she would be a soiled man in a subway lavatory with a palm full of French postcards.

Faced with this appalling vision of an unidealistic universe, he thinks of "the old incorrigible earthly corruption" and of the irony that only through "physical striving" can human flesh "try to capture what little it is ever to know of love" (646, 698). The paradox—that the ideal must find its expression in the real (and, although he does not here express it, is therefore doomed)—is similar to that expressed by William Butler Yeats's Crazy Jane who tells the bishop that "Love has pitched his mansion in/ The place of excrement . . . " (295). In the isolated Michigan cabin to which Charlotte and Harry retreat in a desperate doomed attempt to keep love alive, there is no calendar, and when he tries to create one from memory based on Charlotte's menstrual cycle, he is amused to be employing "Nature the unmathematical, the overfecund, the prime disorderly and illogical and patternless spendthrift, to prove his mathematical problem for him . . . " (572). Implicit in his action is the idea that nature, specifically that part involved with procreation of the species, exerts continual control over human life.

Yet another victim of the inevitable battle between Romance and the "broken world" of Naturalism, Charlotte dies as a result of the abortion beside the Gulf in which Edna Pontellier drowned herself. Naturalistic forces, again in the form of a child, this one unborn, have first tarnished and then destroyed the Romantic's dream of ideal love. Convicted of murder, Harry refuses an opportunity offered by Charlotte's husband to escape through suicide. He chooses life—"*Between grief and nothing, I will take grief*" (715)—because one of many ironies of the Romantic's dilemma is that after the ideal and the dream are frustrated, "there's got to be the old meat, the old frail, eradicable meat for memory to titillate" (709). The Romantic dream can live only as long as the flesh endures, inescapably part of nature.

When Blanche DuBois arrives in New Orleans, she has already been evicted from her Romantic dream of life, her Platonic vision of the ideal love relationship, exemplified by Belle Reve—not, perhaps, what Belle Reve ever was, but Blanche's fantasy version of the Mississippi plantation. The fantasy that has sustained Blanche in the past is shared, in varying degrees, by her sister Stella and even by Stanley, that brutal resident and representative of a Naturalistic universe, who, despite the fact that he typically associates the fabled plantation house with money and other material possessions, does speak of "the place with the columns" (377) with some degree of fascination, even admiration.

Blanche has not yet fully accepted the loss of that dream, for which she had "stayed and fought" and "bled" and "almost died" (260), and she encloses herself in an aura of illusion fragile as the paper lantern with which she suppresses the harsh light of reality. These illusions are, in a sense, decadent ideals employed in a self-protective or self-serving way, a fact she acknowledges in her remark to Stanley that "after all, a woman's charm is fifty percent illusion." She does, however, follow that admission by insisting that "when a thing is important, I tell the truth . . ." (281). Even her name she romanticizes, telling Mitch that it is French for "white woods. Like an orchard in Spring!" (299), a comparison that suggests A. E. Housman's "Loveliest of Trees" and hints at the parallels between the play and Chekhov's *The Cherry Orchard*. On the other hand, in the Naturalistic world, "white woods" may evoke either blooming fruit trees or a decayed forest, and numerous writers, including Poe in "The Narrative of Arthur Gordon Pym" and Melville in *Moby Dick*, have made much of the terrifying associations of whiteness.

Already damaged by the loss of Belle Reve and the harsh realities of disease and death, Blanche's Romanticism is reduced in some moments to nothing more than sentimentality, for example, in her choice of songs to sing: "Paper Moon," which affirms that belief can make fantasy real; and "From the land of the sky blue water/ They brought a captive maid!" (270), in which the Indian girl, a stylized version of the Noble Savage, is removed from an idyllic realm (sky-like) and held prisoner in a harshly realistic world. When Mitch shows Blanche the inscription on his cigarette case, "And if God choose,/ I shall but love thee better after death!" (297), she remarks, "It sounds like a romance." (It is, of course, no romance, because whatever the idealistic poet's God may *choose*, the outcome will be determined by what nature blindly *wills*.) When Mitch tells her that the girl is dead, her response is exaggeratedly sympathetic, imparting an ironic tone to her statement that "sorrow makes for sincerity, I think" (298).

Again, as in *The Awakening* and *Wild Palms*, the situation in *Streetcar* matches Zola's archetypal plot. In all three, the protagonists are Romantics thrust into Naturalistic settings strongly charged with sexual energy. The stage directions state that when Blanche arrives, her face wears an expression "*of shocked disbelief*" and her "*appearance is incongruous to this setting*" (245). She questions why her sister is in "this horrible place" and, in hyperbolic language typical of her Romanticism, insists that even in her "worst dreams" she could not have pictured it. "Only Poe! Only Mr. Edgar Allan Poe!—could do it justice! Out there I suppose is the ghoul-haunted woodland at Weir!" (252). Stella, who has been pulled down into the real world by her relationship with Stanley, replies to this rhetorical question with a humorously mundane non sequitur underscoring the conflict between ideal and real: "No, honey, those are the L & N tracks" (252). The allusion to Poe's "Ulalume" is significant, since the poem details the persona's trip, in the company of Psyche, into the woodland of Weir where he encounters the reality of the death of his beloved. The struggle between Psyche, the soul, and Astarte, "the sinfully scintillant planet," named for the goddess of love and fertility (the flesh), represents, yet again, the battle between ideal and real. The juxtaposition of Blanche's reference to dreams with her mention of Poe is appropriate, since the poet professed to believe that confinement in flesh was what separated human beings from the ideal. Further, he wrote much of dreaming, most notably one poem in which occurs the refrain "*All* that we see or seem/ Is but a dream within a dream" (97).

For Blanche, reality is symbolized by three intolerable elements: "I can't stand a naked light bulb, any more than I can a rude remark or a vulgar action" (300). New Orleans represents for her the grossest elements of a world she has tried to avoid. When she complains about the Kowalskis' living conditions, Stella replies, "New Orleans isn't like other cities" (252), and Mitch's response to Blanche's "I'm not properly dressed" is "That don't make no difference in the Quarter" (308). From the time of her arrival, she sets out to transform the New Orleans milieu, placing a paper lantern over the harsh light, putting new covers on the furniture, adjusting an unsatisfactory environment to her own needs. "I've done so much with this place since I've been here," she tells Mitch (382). Just before the rape, Stanley complains that she has spread powder and perfume throughout the apartment, put up the paper lantern, "and lo and behold the place has turned into Egypt and you are the Queen of the Nile!" (398). In the final scene, he returns to this motif as a final gratuitous attack on her.

Blanche also remolds people to fit her dream, a process that contributes to her unrealistic approach to life, for example, her inability to accept the physicality of her husband Allan. In New Orleans, she sets out to convert those around her: the newspaper boy becomes a "young Prince out of the Arabian Nights," the somewhat clumsy and socially inept Mitch her Rosenkavalier, a Samson, and "a natural gentleman, one of the very few that are left in the world." (In the last passage, the word *natural* must be taken as ironic, since in the Naturalistic sphere, there are no "gentlemen" in the sense in which she uses that word.) Alone in the apartment with Mitch, she refuses to switch on the light so that they can pretend to be Bohemians in "a little artists' cafe on the Left Bank in Paris!" She lights a candle and announces, "*Je suis la Dame aux Camellias! Vous etes Armand!*" (339, 344, 349).

Reality, however, is not to be denied for long, and all her painful losses— deaths of numerous relatives, her part in Allan's suicide, financial collapse, her own ostracism from the community—return to haunt her, as in the almost surreal scene in which the Mexican woman in the street is selling "flores para los muertos" and Blanche, mutters to herself, "Crumble and fade and—regrets—recriminations.... 'If you'd done this, it wouldn't've cost me that!' " The woman offers "corones para los muertos" and Blanche responds with "Legacies! Huh.... And other things such as bloodstained pillow-slips." She has been extremely close to death, she says, and since "the opposite is desire" (388–89), she lost herself in sexual indiscretions in Laurel.

Blanche's five-month stay in the Kowalski apartment on Elysian Fields can be charted as a steady decline from the transcendent poetic vision that was part (though certainly not all) of her past through a destructive descent during which she is forced by the animalistic Stanley, aided consciously or unconsciously by Stella and Mitch, to face first reality and then the brutal facts of a Naturalistic world. She hopes at one point to find in Mitch "a cleft in the rock" of this alien world, but Stanley prevents that. Every action of Stanley's in relation to her is violent: the touch of his hands fouls Allan's love letters; he forces her to relive the loss of Belle Reve; he investigates her past in Laurel and discovers the sordid liaisons to which she has stooped in her attempt to ease the pain of her husband's death; and his birthday gift to her is a ticket to return her to the scene of her disgrace. Each act forces Blanche to acknowledge more and more of reality and brings her further down into the depths of the broken world. The descent culminates in the indignity of her rape—a kind of symbolic death, which occurs, iron- ically, on her birthday—and the subsequent mental collapse.

Stanley is anything but a dreamer. "A different species" as Stella describes him in Naturalistic terms, he is characterized in an understatement by Blanche as "a little bit on the primitive side" and "not the type that goes for jasmine perfume..." (279, 285). His ideals are limited to the fleshly, his vision centered in his own body, specifically in the sexual organs. Stage directions portray him as the breeder in Naturalistic terms that exemplify the driving will Schopenhauer identifies as the abiding motivation behind human action:

Animal joy in his being is implicit in all his movements and attitudes. Since earliest manhood the center of his life has been pleasure with women, the giving and taking of it, not with weak indulgence, dependently, but with the power and pride of a richly feathered male bird among hens.

The sexual drive, the playwright continues, constitutes Stanley's "*complete and satisfying center*" from which radiate all other aspects of his life, including love of food, drink, games, and his automobile, everything "*that bears his emblem of the gaudy seed-bearer.*"

The passage brings to mind Schopenhauer's definition of the sexual impulse as the "desire of desires" and "the focus of the will, its concentration and highest expression" (III, 380), as does Blanche's later diatribe when Stella suggests that she saw Stanley "at his worst" in the violent finale of the poker game (319):

On the contrary, I saw him at his best! What such a man has to offer is animal force and he gave a wonderful exhibition of that! But the only way to live with such a man is to—go to bed with him! And that's your job—not mine!

That drive determines his aggressive behavior with men and his attitude toward women, whom he classifies sexually and crudely just as any male of a lower species presumably sees the female merely as physical mate.

One of the earlier titles of the play was, significantly, "The Poker Night," and that event, portrayed in scene 3 (and restaged in scene 11), opens with a Naturalistic description of Stanley and his friends in their bright colors recalling the "*richly feathered male bird*" simile of scene 1. They are "*men at the peak of their physical manhood, as coarse and direct and powerful as the primary colors*" (286). Blanche's subsequent description of the scene underscores the Naturalistic elements inherent in it (323):

Night falls and the other apes gather! There in the front of the cave, all grunting like him, and swilling and gnawing and hulking! His poker night!—you call it—this party of apes! Somebody growls—some creature snatches at something—the fight is on! *God*!

Stanley represents the "New Man," opposed to or ignorant of the transcendent; he has pulled Stella (the star) down from the columns (the sky) to live in the sensual, sexual, broken world; even his scoffing at astrology may be interpreted broadly as representing total involvement with the earthly and earthy. His persistent jibes about Blanche's noble and regal airs—he calls her "Dame Blanche," "Her Majesty," and "visiting royalty"—are juxtaposed to his own espousal of the Populist doctrine of Huey Long ("Every man a king"), which he understands about as well as any of that demagogue's followers probably did. Thus, he aligns himself with the leveling process of modern "Democracy," which is, by its very nature, un-Romantic, however much the nineteenth-century poets, Wordsworth and Whitman for example, may have protested that they spoke for and to the masses.

Schopenhauer identifies self-preservation and propagation of the species as the two strongest human urges (I, 425), and Stanley is the perfect representation of this philosophical principle. After the rape and just prior to Blanche's being removed to the state mental institution, Stanley verbalizes his philosophy of life: "Luck is believing you're lucky.... To hold front position in this rat-race you've got to believe you are lucky" (403). The animal imagery and the sentiment, aside from the notion of luck, are Naturalistic, reflecting his belief in the survival of the fittest and his unconscious acknowledgement, in unlettered terms, of Schopenhauer's primacy of the will. Stanley's destruction of Blanche results from his determination to protect the status quo, in which he is the Populist King, from any usurpation by female royalty, as well as to protect his cave from another invading animal.

If Stanley's being is totally centered in his sexuality, the much more complex Blanche is ambivalent and exists on two levels; she is at once the Romantic and the passionate female, and the inevitable conflict between the two elements leads to her defeat. When she insists (396) that

Physical beauty is passing. A transitory possession. But beauty of the mind and richness of the spirit and tenderness of the heart—and I have all of those things— aren't taken away, but grow!

there seems little doubt that she does indeed believe in such an ideal. Yet when confessing to Mitch her indiscreet behavior with the soldiers and the young student and in other exchanges, she does admit the importance of sexuality and seems to recognize the Naturalistic implications of sexual attraction. She repulsed Mitch's advances, she tells Stella, because "men don't want anything they get too easy. But on the other hand men lose interest quickly. Especially when the girl is over—thirty" (334). When she apologizes for her inability to be amusing on their evening out, Mitch asks why she even tried "if you don't feel like it," and she replies, "I was just obeying the law of nature" that "the lady must entertain the gentleman— or no dice!" (341). The law involved is, of course, that will to mate and procreate to which Schopenhauer attaches such importance. Stella's defense of her devotion to Stanley reflects that same law: "There are things that happen between a man and a woman in the dark—that sort of make everything else seem—unimportant." Blanche responds, "What you are talking about is brutal desire—just Desire!—the name of that rattle-trap streetcar..." and Stella asks, "Haven't you ever ridden on that streetcar?" Blanche's reply is, of course, to be read in two ways, and surely that is her intention: "It brought me here" (321). The physical cannot be denied, but sexuality is insufficient for the idealist, and for Blanche, nothing makes the "higher nature" of the human being "unimportant." Although she has left behind the ruins of a beautiful dream world in which gentlemen protected ladies, in which proper dress and good manners constituted a veritable courtly dance with each participant knowing his or her place, she is unprepared to cope with a man who reduces all females to their lowest common denominator, and certainly unwilling to confuse sexuality with love.

It is ironic for the idealist that, as Robert Frost observes, "Earth's the right place for love," and Blanche has sought in sensuality an escape from the guilt associated with Allan's death and an end to her painful loneliness. She has left the spiritual realm to enter "the broken world" (or, in Puritan terms, the fallen world) Hart Crane describes in "The Broken Tower," which supplies the epigraph for *Streetcar*.

Williams's favorite poem was John Keats's "Ode to a Nightingale" in which the persona yearns to be free of the Naturalistic world, "where youth grows old and spectre-thin and dies," and to move into the ideal realm of the fabled bird. In the ode, the escape is transitory or unfulfilling, as with much of Hart Crane's poetry, where the symbols—Royal Palm, Air Plant, and bridge, for example—are only temporary means of escape from what Williams called in *Night of the Iguana* "The earth's obscene corrupting love" (371). Stanley dwells permanently in this "broken world" without recognizing its deficiencies or yearning for anything beyond hit own masculine pleasures. Young, virile, and very much in charge, totally "caught in such sensual music," as William Butler Yeats termed it, he cannot perceive that his world is no place for aging men (or women), nor can he conceive of a day when he will be aging (or old) and no longer "cock of the walk."

The contrast between the two views is verbalized in the argument between Stella and Stanley over Blanche's clothes and jewels: "The Kowalskis and Duboises have different notions," he says, and his wife answers, "Indeed they have, thank heavens!" and later comments, "Blanche and I grew up under very different circumstances than you did" (275, 358). Blanche knows as well something that Stanley can never perceive, since he will never comprehend the full implication of having raped his sister-in-law. Belle Reve has been lost not because of Blanche's flightiness or incompetence—or not alone because of that—but because of the power of fleshly appetites. Our "grandfathers and father and uncles and brothers exchanged the land for their epic fornications," Blanche admits. "The four-letter word deprived us of our plantation..." (284). Here the idealistic Romantic in a Naturalistic universe recognizes an awesome paradox of human nature—as Yeats describes it, a soul clothed in tattered mortal dress, symbolized by Blanche's faded finery. She is, indeed, two people, Romantic idealist and passionate female, one who creates a false front of illusion, another who can assert, "I didn't lie in my heart..." (387). Unable to separate them and suppress the idealism of her nature, *unfit* to survive if you will, she is destroyed.

For her, Stanley is "*bestial*" (322), and in one of her long arias, she acknowledges the Naturalistic reality of his world in which she has been forced to dwell:

He acts like an animal, has an animal's habits! Eats like one, moves like one, talks like one! There's even something—sub-human—something not quite to the stage of humanity yet! Yes, something—ape-like about him, like one of those pictures I've seen in anthropological studies. Thousands and thousands of years have passed him right by, and there he is—Stanley Kowalski—survivor of the stone age! Bearing the raw meat home from the kill in the jungle! And you—*you* here—*waiting* for him! Maybe he'll strike you or maybe grunt and kiss you! That is, if kisses have been discovered yet!

The ape comparison is part of an elaborate system of symbols in *Streetcar* that indicates the Naturalistic nature of the environment. Stanley is a Capricorn, the goat, and Stella compares him to a pig in his eating habits. In addition, there are repeated references to birds and to predatory cats, wildcats, tigers, sharks, and to bulls, sheep, birds, chickens, rats, moths, butterflies, and spiders.

Carried away by her own metaphor—there is much of the poet in Blanche as in most of Williams's protagonists—she spins out an elaborate conceit that stresses the Naturalistic nature of Stanley and his friends. At this point, Blanche has been forced by a convergence of circumstances and environment to face the reality of humanity's animal nature in a biological universe, a nature of which even she partakes, and she acknowledges this, for her, painful fact in the conclusion of the aria (323):

Maybe we are a long way from being made in God's image, . . . but there has been *some* progress since then! Such things as art—as poetry and music—such kinds of new light have come into the world since then! In some kinds of people some tenderer feelings have had some little beginning! That we have got to make *grow*! And *cling* to, and hold as our flag! In this dark march toward whatever it is we're approaching. . . . Don't—don't hang back with the brutes!

In *Summer and Smoke,* Alma voices a similar view of the evolutionary process when she quotes Oscar Wilde's aphorism "All of us are in the gutter, but some of us are looking at the stars" (197).

Although Blanche may find some consolation in this limited optimism, she acknowledges on two occasions the deficiencies of her life-view. When she admits that "I never was hard or self-sufficient enough" (332), she reveals her understanding of the Naturalistic principle of "the survival of the fittest." The other admission is associated, as in *The Awakening* and *The Wild Palms,* with the birth of a baby. Discovering that Stella is pregnant, Blanche reacts "*dreamily*" and comments to her sister that perhaps Stanley is "what we need to mix with our blood now that we've lost Belle Reve" (285). Later she informs Mitch that "if it weren't for Stella about to have a baby, I wouldn't be able to endure things here" (350) and idealizes the child's future in the hope that "candles are going to glow in his life" and that "his eyes are going to be like candles, like two blue candles lighted in a white cake" (373–74).

After the traumas of Stanley's cruelty at the party and Stella's first labor pains, Mitch, having been apprised by Stanley of Blanche's reputation in Laurel, confronts her, demanding to know why the room is unlighted. She replies, "I like it dark. The dark is comforting to me" (383). He insists that he has "never had a real good look at you"—and surely the word *real* is of special significance here—and tears from the light bulb the Chinese paper lantern that represents the thin tissue of ideals and illusions by which she has lived, "So I can take a look at you good and plain!" When Blanche comments that he doesn't mean to be "insulting," Mitch significantly answers, "No, just realistic." What follows is one of the most famous passages in *Streetcar*, what might be termed Blanche's credo, her avowal of Romanticism (385):

I don't want realism. I want magic! Yes, yes, magic! I try to give that to people. I misrepresent things to them. I don't tell truth. I tell what *ought* to be truth. And if that is sinful, then let me be damned for it!

Mitch's response to this painful baring of her tortured soul is to turn upon her the "naked light bulb" that Blanche detests, scattering her illusions like fog dispersed by sunlight.

Until the end, she retains her sense of humor, a last protective coloration against annihilation, and she responds to Mitch's question about the Flamingo Hotel by calling it "The Tarantula Arms," but in the lines that follow, she faces and acknowledges the reality of what her life had become in Laurel: "Yes, I had many intimacies with strangers. After the death of Allan— intimacies with strangers was all I seemed able to fill my empty heart with" (386). She explains these casual couplings as the result of panic, the panic itself a product of her need to survive. With her beloved husband dead because of her unkindness and Belle Reve having slipped piece by piece through her fingers, she fled for solace, ironically, to the Elysian Fields, the one place where her dreams and visions were certain to be destroyed. Mitch seemed to offer protection against the brutality of the new world in which she found herself, and she was willing to compromise with her concept of the ideal mate, the young, sensitive, intelligent lover, in order to achieve salvation; but reality in the form of her past intruded again (387):

I thanked God for you, because you seemed to be gentle—a cleft in the rock of the world that I could hide in! But I guess I was asking, hoping—too much! Kiefaber, Stanley and Shaw have tied an old tin can to the tail of the kite.

In the stage directions in the final scene of the play, Blanche hears the Matron's greeting echoed "*beyond the walls, as if reverberated through a canyon of rock"* (405). Here the rock, which metaphorically represented a sanctuary in her earlier statement, is converted into a simile for a vast and terrifying place.

The vicious final clash between Blanche and Stanley is inevitable, as indicated by her earlier recognition that he "is my executioner" and by Stanley's affirmation, just prior to raping her, that their encounter has been inevitable from "the beginning" (351, 402). The final triumph of the Naturalistic view of life is acted out in no uncertain terms in the rape. This scene is a capsule version of the movement in the play from the Ideal to the Naturalistic view of human existence. Blanche's Romanticism is reduced by this point to falsehoods and fantasies, her powerful imagination now employed in the creation of lies to preserve herself in an animalistic environment. She lies to Stanley about having rejected Mitch when he supposedly returned to apologize because they are incompatible and "deliberate cruelty is not forgivable." Then she adds, ironically, "We have to be realistic about such things" (397). Her illusions of a "white knight" who will rescue her from this trap, these "desperate circumstances" (400) is reminiscent of the plight of the Indian maiden about whom she sang earlier.

Already the clash between Romanticism on the one hand, Realism and Naturalism on the other has begun to unsettle her sanity. Layer by layer, Stanley, charged with the assurance of his own male potency due to the imminent birth of his child, strips away Blanche's ideals, forcing her one final, fatal time to face what is real. Enraged by her romanticizing, he counters her story that Mitch apologized, that she refused him, and that Shep Huntleigh awaits her with the accusation that "there isn't a goddam thing but imagination! . . . And lies and conceit and tricks" (398). In a reversal of his earlier insistence that her clothes and jewels were expensive, he insists that she "take a look at yourself in that worn-out Mardi Gras outfit, rented for fifty cents from some rag-picker! And with the crazy crown on!" (398). His powerful physical presence, intruding into the next-to-last sanctuary of illusion to which she flees (insanity being her final sanctuary), and the threat of his sexuality that charges the scene force Blanche into confrontation with the Naturalistic truth of life.

That truth is symbolized impressionistically by shadows, *"grotesque and menacing,"* by *"inhuman voices like cries in a jungle,"* by *"the roar of an approaching locomotive,"* and by the encounter outside the window on Elysian Fields between prostitute, drunkard, and policeman (399–400). As Stanley moves toward her, his tongue protruding from his mouth, she retreats until, cornered in the bedroom, she makes a last desperate attempt to prevent her violation. Her resistance intensifies—even satisfies—Stanley's male aggressiveness, and the animalistic nature of the violent mating is underscored by his calling her "Tiger" and saying that she and he (the Naturalistic man) have "had this date" (the inevitable destructive encounter of two opposing life views) "from the beginning" (402). It is interesting that he will not tolerate the passionate and physical elements that are part of Blanche's past any more than he can understand or accept her idealism, though he expects and enjoys the sensual in Stella.

The conclusion of the play is a reflection of the earlier gathering of the "apes" with, the stage directions state, the same "*raw, lurid*" atmosphere "*of the disastrous poker night*" (403). At various points in this scene, Impressionistic devices highlight the Naturalistic message: drums sound, "*lurid reflections appear*," and again the "*cries and noises of the jungle*" (404) are heard, presumably only by Blanche, now fully aware of the awful facts of life. A stage direction describes her standing with a "*mirror in her hand and a look of sorrowful perplexity as though all human experience shows on her face*" (407). Stanley has won, his puissance and his reign assured by his grossly Naturalistic action against Blanche. Not satisfied with having destroyed her idealism, in effect having brutally dragged her down off the columns, he performs one more gratuitous and devastating act by tearing the paper lantern from the bulb and holding it toward her. "*She cries out as if the lantern was herself*" (406).

Despite her mental collapse, Blanche still clings to fragments of her belief in, or at least hope for, something beyond, that progress of mankind up from the apes, a belief expressed in her enduring ability to depend "on the kindness of strangers" and her poetic observation that "those cathedral bells—they're the only clean thing in the Quarter" (400, 408). The tower of the cathedral seems here to echo Hart Crane's "Broken Tower" from which the persona fell into the broken world more than to suggest any orthodoxly religious idea. With Blanche's new knowledge has come a sense of approaching death (the end of desire). "I can smell the sea air," she says, and then goes on to identify the ocean with the end of life: "And when I die, I'm going to die on the sea" (400). The passage parallels the death of Charlotte beside the Gulf of Mexico and the suicide of Edna Pontellier, as all three protagonists return to the sea, the birthplace of life in a Naturalistic world.

The final statement of Naturalistic philosophy in *Streetcar* comes from Eunice, when she responds to Stella's remark that she cannot believe Blanche's story and remain with Stanley: "Don't ever believe it. Life has got to go on. No matter what happens, you've got to keep on going" (406). The philosophy is dramatized, in the very last action of the play in which Stella "*sobs with inhuman abandon*," Stanley kneels by her and "*his fingers find the opening of her blouse*" (409). The concluding line of the play— "This game is seven-card stud" (409)—translates in terms of Schopenhauer's views into "life is about procreation and belongs to the breeders."

In *The Awakening, The Wild Palms,* and *A Streetcar Named Desire,* Romance is frustrated by the harsh reality of economics, social convention, religion, and the biological reality of birth and death, all those hereditary and environmental forces with which the Naturalistic writers from Zola to

Dreiser were concerned, even obsessed. Viewed in relation to Literary Naturalism, *Streetcar* represents perhaps the plight of any Romantic in the real world, the plight not only of fictional characters such as Emma Bovary and Aschenbach, but also of Romantic poets from Keats to Hart Crane, the plight of the poet-playwright Tennessee Williams as well as of his most famous creation, Blanche DuBois. What are the implications of this passage from Romance to Reality? When he wrote *Streetcar*, the playwright seemed to have believed that the modern world is antagonistic to the ideal as to the dreamer, a tenet he continued to espouse in varying degrees for the rest of his life. Yet there is no doubt that he believed that the human being, while accepting the limitations of the physical, must cling to some vestige of hope in something beyond the Naturalistic world represented by Stanley, must "look at the stars," must not "hold back with the brutes." Later, that message is reiterated and even intensified in such plays as *Camino Real*, which is structured on the contrast between two streets, one that is merely real, and the other, the one for which Don Quixote and Casanova and Kilroy continue to search and struggle, that is "real," the way of gold. One must, Williams's Lord Byron insists, "*Make voyages!—Attempt them!*— there's nothing else . . ." (508). Tentative as it may be, something of that hope is hinted at in one of Blanche's last lines in *Streetcar* as she passes Stanley and the other poker players, who symbolize the broken world to which she has descended: "I'm only passing through" (413).

NOTE

1. The Library of America edition, the text I have cited here, reinstates Faulkner's original title with the previously published title in brackets: *If I Forget Thee, Jerusalem [The Wild Palms]*.

WORKS CITED

Brooks, Cleanth. "New Orleans in Literature." Lecture in Jambalaya Series. New Orleans, La. May 1977.

Chopin, Kate. *The Awakening. The Complete Works of Kate Chopin*. Vol. II. Baton Rouge: LSU P, 1969.

Crane, Stephen. *Stephen Crane: Prose and Poetry*. New York: The Library of America, 1984.

Faulkner, William. *If I Forget Thee, Jerusalem [The Wild Palms]. Novels 1936–1940*. New York: The Library of America, 1990.

Fitzgerald, F. Scott. *The Great Gatsby*. New York: Scribners, 1925.

Kaplan, Justin. *Walt Whitman: A Life*. New York: Simon and Schuster, 1980.

McCarthy, Mary. *Theater Chronicles 1937–1962*. New York: Farrar, Strauss, 1963.

Percy, Walker. "New Orleans, Mon Amour." *Signposts in a Strange Land*. New York: Farrar, Straus and Giroux, 1991.

Poe, Edgar Allan. *Poetry and Tales*. New York: The Library of America, 1984.

Schopenhauer, Arthur. *The World as Will and Idea*. Trans. R. B. Haldane and J. Kemp. London: Trubner, 1883. 3 vols.

Tischler, Nancy M. *Tennessee Williams: The Rebellious Puritan*. New York: Citadel, 1961.

Welty, Eudora. *The Collected Stories of Eudora Welty*. New York: Harcourt Brace Jovanovich, 1980.

Williams, Tennessee. *Camino Real*. *The Theatre of Tennessee Williams*. 7 vols. to date. New York: New Directions, 1971. Vol. 2: 417–591.

———. *Night of the Iguana*. *The Theatre of Tennessee Williams*. 7 vols. to date. New York: New Directions, 1971. Vol. 4: 247–376.

———. *A Streetcar Named Desire*. *The Theatre of Tennessee Williams*. 7 vols. to date. New York: New Directions, 1971. Vol. 1: 239–419.

———. *Summer and Smoke*. *The Theatre of Tennessee Williams*. 7 vols. to date. New York: New Directions, 1971. Vol. 2: 113–256.

Yeats, William Butler. *The Collected Poems of W. B. Yeats*. London: Macmillan, 1955.

Zola, Emile. *The Experimental Novel and Other Essays*. New York: Cassell, 1983.

12

Birth and Death in
A Streetcar Named Desire

Bert Cardullo

Images of birth and death, of rebirth and death-in-life abound in *A Streetcar Named Desire*, but they are most prominent in several scenes whose juxtaposition reveals meaning that less formalistic considerations of the play often overlook. Tennessee Williams counterpoints these scenes to suggest that Stanley's and Blanche's pasts and futures were not and will not be so different, and, thus, that they are less villain and victim, as Marxist and feminist critics like to contend, than mutual victims of desire—hence the title of the play, whose streetcar bears both this man of the street and this plantation-belle-become-street-walker to their respective dooms. A close reading of scenes 5, 7, 9, 10, and 11 will support my thesis, and it is just such close reading, I would argue, that tends to be absent from sociopolitical essays using *Streetcar* as one more piece of evidence in their continuing indictment of materialist, misogynous American society.

Sandra M. Gilbert and Susan Gubar, for example, simplistically assert that *Streetcar* "dramatizes the dynamics of the battering of women" (50), that Stanley "represents in his brutishness the phallic origin of the male species" (51), and that the drama's homosexual author "brilliantly indict[s] ... the streetcar named heterosexual desire" (52). But can this play really be reduced to a diatribe against heterosexual desire—Blanche's as well as Stanley's—as opposed to homosexual desire? Aren't Gilbert and Gubar guilty here of the intentional fallacy as well as their own peculiar brand of sexism? And if *Streetcar* is an indictment of anything, isn't it an indictment of *excessive* desire instead of desire itself? Of emotional violence against human beings—Blanche's against her young husband, Allan Grey, Stanley's against Blanche, hers against him—in addition to physical violence against women? As I have argued elsewhere (Cardullo 149), Stanley is no mere phallic brute intent on subjugating the opposite sex, no mere violent defender of the patriarchal social order, despite assertions to the contrary by Anca

Vlasopolos and Pamela Anne Hanks[1] as well as Gilbert and Gubar: before Blanche's arrival, he and Stella enjoyed, through compromise, an intimate, happy marriage, and in this could be said to have achieved a degree of civilization, of humanity, unequaled by the DuBoises of Belle Reve; before Blanche's arrival, Stanley also enjoyed the best of friendships with Mitch, who in some ways is as sensitive and in need of understanding as Blanche. Elia Kazan understood Stanley Kowalski's character in the original production of *Streetcar* and therefore cast the appealing Marlon Brando in the role (in contrast with the gruff Anthony Quinn, who played Stanley opposite Uta Hagen's Blanche during the last days of the play's Broadway premiere), about whose performance Irwin Shaw wrote(35):

He is so amusing in a direct, almost childlike way in the beginning, and we have been so conditioned by the modern doctrine that what is natural is good, that we admire him and sympathize with him. Then, bit by bit, with a full account of what his good points really are, we come dimly to see that he is...brutish, destructive in his healthy egotism, dangerous, immoral, surviving.

Marxist critics offer a reading of *Streetcar* as superficial as that of the feminists when they analyze, not the play Williams wrote, but the one they wish he had written. Thus, Yuri Zubkov can ask, "What is the social conflict? What kinds of social forces do Stanley and his friends on the one hand and Blanche on the other personify?" He gives the following answer (61):

When it comes to Blanche, the situation is clear: first, owner of a patrimonial estate, then a teacher, and, at the same time half a whore, half a priestess of love. But who are Stanley, Mitch, Pablo, Steve? They are laborers...They are separate individuals but none of them knows anything except poker, bars, and fights. And they are made to personify the American working class.

Clearly Stanley, Mitch, Pablo, and Steve are not the laborers Zubkov had envisioned. M. Koreneva, for her part, accepts the brutality of these four men and sees "connections between [it] and the fundamental laws of American society." But she faults Williams for not exploring those connections, for not analyzing the socioeconomic causes of his male characters' brutality (24):

What phenomena are responsible for the use of violence and its continuing rule in [the United States]? Why have violence and ruthlessness become the social norms? It is absolutely useless to try to find in [Williams's play] any answers to these important questions.

By contrast, Soviet critic Vitaly Vulf commends Williams for revealing social causes beneath the cover of psychological conflicts; he sees Blanche's downfall as the result, less of her sexual dissoluteness and hypersensitivity, than of the death of the Southern aristocracy and the rise of the common man (68). In Vulf's view, Blanche is the product of one evil system—the feudalism of the old South—and the victim of another—the capitalism of the rejuvenated Union.

American critics have seen a similar social transition in *Streetcar*, but they usually put a positive spin on it, as does Jacob H. Adler in this excerpt from "Tennessee Williams' South: The Culture and the Power": "Blanche has in her something of a genuine culture and beauty which Stella has abandoned and which Stanley cannot see; and, as with the aristocrats in *The Cherry Orchard*, we must regret its passing, even as we recognize the decadence and futility and even degradation which make its passing both necessary and inevitable" (42). Harry Taylor is one of those American Marxists who put a negative spin on the social transition in *Streetcar*, albeit a spin whose negativity is confused, since he seems to champion the patrician Blanche at the expense of the plebeian (if patriotically capitalistic) Stanley (52; 54–55):

The characters [Williams] hates or fears or despises always win; while those to whom his sympathy is drawn inevitably go down. In such a context there can be no conflict, . . . no future except for evil. . . . Great drama cannot emerge out of flight and hysteria, but arises from genuine conflict, an element that can only be generated by the writer's conviction that the battle is vital and that the means to wage it exist. Williams will write greatly only if he can re-examine reality and . . . recognize . . . that the forces of good in this world are adult and possess both the will and the power to change our environment. . . . Surely the absence of the socio-historic periphery in the author's mind weakens his attack, . . . depriving it of the aura of larger reality and of moral conviction.

My problem with Taylor's reading, as with the readings of Adler, the Russian Marxists, and the feminists, is that it ignores the *human* element in the play, the struggle between Blanche and Stanley as human beings, as individuals, instead of as social symbols or gender representatives. They are human beings *first*, and it is as complex beings that Tennessee Williams presents them to us, not as victor-victim, oppressor-oppressed, or working man-decadent woman. *Streetcar* is not reducible to a sociological or political tract, a mere reflection of its critics' theoretical biases, and I hope to prove this by a detailed examination of selected scenes from the play. My method is formalistic, which is to say that it depends on formal considerations and organic connections within the work of art itself, not on a theoretical framework imposed on the art object from without. Such theoretical frameworks, in my opinion, often substitute their own visions for those of the artwork. How are they able to do this? By ignoring the text, by eschewing close analysis—a consideration of as many elements as possible in a scene's makeup—for selective perusal—a consideration of only those elements that support the critic's ideological bent. I must stress this point, for the reading of *Streetcar* that follows gains what authority it possesses from its thoroughness, not from any ideological conviction behind it. I unabashedly declare that I have no ideological axe to grind—unless one considers humanism an ideology—and that the only theory that resides in my interpretation of *Streetcar* is that the play's the thing, not the theory; that the playwright is king, not the critic; that art and the artist are meant to be served, not supplanted. I suffer, then, from what could be called the aesthetic bias: the compulsion to treat works of art as *works of art*, as alternative worlds to our own that are at once coherent and mysterious, compelling and cathartic, humane and cruel—in a word, inviolable.

Let me begin my investigation of birth-and-death imagery in the play, and by extension of the fates of Blanche and Stanley, with scene 7, throughout much of which Williams interweaves Blanche's singing of "It's Only a Paper Moon" in the bathroom while Stanley reveals her lurid past to Stella in the kitchen. Of course, this juxtaposition is immediately comic: the gruff Stanley complains to the quiet Stella about all the lies Blanche has been telling, while Blanche herself sings "blithely" of love, according to Williams's stage direction (360), and thoroughly enjoys her bath. Stanley and Blanche are so different, it seems, that their presence together on the same stage is funny, and it is even funnier here since Blanche is oblivious to Stanley's revelations about her past and, later, his need to use his own bathroom. But Williams is trying to do more in this scene than create a comic juxtaposition.[2] The content of the song Blanche sings is as important to an interpretation of the scene as the fact that she is singing blithely. Blanche sings verses from "It's Only a Paper Moon," and it is no accident that Williams chooses this song for her to sing. It is Blanche's birthday, and a birthday supper is planned at Stanley and Stella's apartment, to which Mitch is invited. (It is September 15, and Blanche and Mitch have been dating for some time.) Blanche is singing on one level of her hope that Mitch will believe in her, that he will love and marry her. The world that Blanche has created for Mitch *is* "make-believe" and "phony" (360): she has lied to him about her past, painting a portrait of herself as an old-fashioned girl with high ideals and strict morals. But Blanche suggests that this world would not be make-believe if Mitch believed in and married her. Then she would truly become what she has pretended she is: a proper, loving, faithful woman. Blanche thus hopes to celebrate the day of her birth as the day of her rebirth through union with Mitch. She bathes in this scene—as she does many other times during her stay with the Kowalskis—not only to cool off from the heat, but also in a sense to cleanse or purify herself of her sexual indiscretions, to be reborn. After her bath in scene 2, she says to Stanley, "Here I am, all freshly bathed and scented, and feeling like a brand new human being!" (276)

The comedy in scene 7 is undercut by our knowledge that, even as Blanche sings her love song, Stanley is telling Stella, as he has already told Mitch, of the "phony" image Blanche has been presenting all summer. Stanley has made sure that Mitch will not be coming over for supper, and Stanley will soon give Blanche her only birthday present: a bus ticket back to the real world, in Laurel, that she has been trying to deny since arriving in New Orleans. Without Mitch's love, Blanche's world will become a kind of "honky-tonk parade," a "melody played in a penny arcade" (361): during the rape scene (scene 10) we hear the "*Blue Piano*," drums, and a "*hot trumpet*" (401–2); and as Blanche is being led away to an insane asylum in scene 11, we hear "*the swelling music of the 'Blue Piano' and the muted trumpet*" (419). Without Mitch's love, Blanche's world will become "make-believe" and "phony" in another sense: She will lose her mind and believe that the Doctor who has come to get her is her old beau Shep Huntleigh, with whom she will embark shortly on a Caribbean cruise.

At the end of scene 8, after the birthday supper unattended by Mitch, Stella's labor pains begin and Stanley rushes her to the hospital: the imminent birth of their child has thus substituted for Blanche's failed rebirth.[3] Then, in scene 9, Mitch appears and confronts Blanche about her past, armed with the truth that Stanley has provided him. During this confrontation, "*a blind Mexican woman in a dark shawl, carrying bunches of those gaudy tin flowers that lower-class Mexicans display at funerals and other festive occasions*" (387), comes up to the door of the Kowalski apartment trying to sell some of her "flowers for the dead." Little attention has been paid by critics to the role of the Mexican Woman Vendor in scene 9, since it seems fairly obvious that she is meant to be a kind of death figure with whom Blanche comes face to face as she is beginning to experience the spiritual death—paradoxically, on her birthday—that will lead to her commitment to an asylum. The Mexican Woman becomes a visual symbol of Blanche's fate, then. But Williams's choice of a *blind Mexican* woman to sell "flowers for the dead"—and gaudy tin flowers at that—and his movement of her onto and off the stage greatly enhance the power and richness of this symbol.

The Mexican Woman is not simply a symbol of the death or doom that awaits Blanche. Williams uses his Vendor not only to ordain the future, but also to recapitulate the past. She becomes, in her blindness, a symbol of all the deaths at Belle Reve that helped to deplete Blanche's finances and break her will. (Blanche told us in scene 1 that "the Grim Reaper had put up his tent on our doorstep!" [262].) The blind Mexican Woman finds her way to Blanche's doorstep in scene 9; she seems to stalk Blanche, even as death blindly stalked the DuBois family at Belle Reve. The moment Blanche slams the door on the Mexican Woman, she begins talking to an uncomprehending Mitch about all the death that plagued Belle Reve, as if the Mexican Woman herself had suggested the topic for conversation. The "flowers for the dead" that the Mexican Woman sells are themselves symbolic of all the deaths at

Belle Reve that helped to drive the DuBois family into bankruptcy—a symbolism that is underlined by the juxtaposition of the Mexican Woman's calls with Blanche's evocation of the dying that surrounded her (388–89):

MEXICAN WOMAN [*she turns away and starts to move down the street*] Flores para los muertos.

[*The polka tune fades in.*]

BLANCHE [*as if to herself*]: Crumble and fade and—regrets—recriminations... "If you'd done this, it wouldn't've cost me that!"

MEXICAN WOMAN: Corones para los muertos. Corones...

BLANCHE: Legacies! Huh.... And other things such as bloodstained pillow-slips— "Her linen needs changing"—"Yes, Mother. But couldn't we get a colored girl to do it?" No, we couldn't of course. Everything gone but the—

MEXICAN WOMAN: Flores.

BLANCHE: Death—I used to sit here and she used to sit over there and death was as close as you are.... We didn't dare even admit we had ever heard of it!

Williams has the Mexican Woman offer "flowers for the dead" to Blanche partly because, were Blanche to die now, she could afford no better flowers for her own funeral. But the flowers are also symbolic, in their gaudy tinniness and their display at "festive occasions" as well as at funerals, of all the cheap, good times that Blanche enjoyed with strangers, young soldiers, high school boys. They are symbolic of the desire that finally lost Blanche her job at the high school in Laurel, and also of the larger desire that seems always to have characterized and divided the DuBois family, from the "epic fornications" (284) of the men to Stella's elemental lust for Stanley. Once Blanche slams the door on the Mexican Woman, she speaks not only of all the death at Belle Reve, but also of all the desire she cultivated in order to forget death; again, the Mexican Woman, with her "*gaudy tin flowers*," has provided Blanche with her cue and continues to cue her as she chronicles the slaking of her desire (389):

MEXICAN WOMAN: Flores para los muertos, flores—flores...

BLANCHE: The opposite is desire. So do you wonder? How could you possibly wonder! Not far from Belle Reve, before we had lost Belle Reve, was a camp where they trained young soldiers. On Saturday nights they would go in town to get drunk—

MEXICAN WOMAN [*softly*]: Corones...

BLANCHE: —and on the way back they would stagger onto my lawn and call— "Blanche! Blanche!"—the deaf old lady remaining suspected nothing. But sometimes I slipped outside to answer their calls.... Later the paddy-wagon would gather them up like daisies... the long way home...

[*The Mexican Woman turns slowly and drifts back off with her soft mournful cries....*]

So Williams has summarized, through the symbol of the Mexican Woman, the forces behind the play's tragedy: the desire of the DuBois men that squandered away the family fortune and deprived the family of love; the sickness and dying that finally bankrupted the family; and the desire that Blanche used to escape death and achieve intimacy with others, however fleeting. When Blanche finishes speaking of death and desire in scene 9, she is confronted with a Mitch who wants what he has "been missing all summer" (389). She is confronted, in other words, with yet another reminder of her past, a man who wants a cheap, good time. The cheap, good time that Stanley has at Blanche's expense in scene 10 is, of course, what seals her doom. Her desire will have led to her spiritual death, even as the illicit desire of her forebears led ultimately to the death of the DuBois line and the loss of Belle Reve.

It is entirely appropriate that a Mexican woman of the lower class becomes the cumulative symbol of death and desire in *Streetcar*. The Mexican Woman speaks a foreign language and repeats one sentence over and over again ("Flores [or 'corones'] para los muertos" [388]); Blanche taught English and is highly articulate. The Mexican Woman is poor, and from a poor foreign country; Blanche's family was once wealthy, and Blanche is proud of her Southern aristocratic heritage. The Mexican Woman, probably old and wearing a dark shawl, is anything but sexually attractive; Blanche once prided herself on her ability to attract men with her good looks and nice clothes. The Mexican Woman represents all that Blanche once thought she was above, and all that she has now become: a foreigner of sorts in New Orleans without a penny, whose language is not understood by Stanley and goes unheeded by Stella; a woman whose heavy makeup and costume jewelry can no longer hide her ravaged looks; a silent woman by the end of the play who does not heed Stella's desperate cries and who "allows [the Doctor] to lead her [out of the Kowalski apartment] *as if she were blind*" (418; emphasis mine).

Williams is careful not to have the Mexican Woman appear suddenly at Blanche's door and disappear just as quickly. We hear the Mexican Woman coming in the background, we hear her calls, and we hear her calls as she turns from the apartment and drifts offstage. Since she is blind, obviously she moves slowly. The effect of the Mexican Woman's movement, combined with her calls, is haunting. It is to make us feel that Blanche is haunted by her past—by the death and desire that the Mexican Woman and her tin flowers represent—that her past can never leave her; and it is to make us feel that her past will inevitably determine, indeed has already determined, her future. The Mexican Woman, in her walk up to and on from the Kowalski apartment, seems to walk out of the past and into the future, into an oblivion that Blanche herself will soon know.

Blanche leaves for an insane asylum at the end of scene 11, and Stanley remains behind with Stella: his way of life thus appears to have won out over his sister-in-law's. But it is not that simple. Life for the Kowalskis will never be the same after Blanche's departure, and Williams provides plenty of evidence for this conclusion in the final scene of the play—evidence that, once again, has hitherto been ignored by critics. If the Mexican Woman of scene 9 is *Streetcar*'s symbol of death, desire, and the past, then the newborn child of scene 11 is the play's symbol of life, maternity, and the future—for Stella, but not for Stanley. Stella's absence from scenes 9 and 10 while she is giving birth, coupled with her reappearance onstage in scene 11, serves to distance her in our minds from her husband and to prefigure her relationship with him beyond the perimeters of the play. That Stella does not once speak to Stanley in the last scene of *Streetcar* (even when addressed by him one time) is indicative of the essential silence that will permeate the rest of their lives together. That she comments, in the acting edition of the play, on the ache she feels when she is not in the same room with her baby (while Stanley, significantly, never refers to the son he so celebrated before Blanche in scene 10) and says nothing of having missed Stanley while she was away in the hospital (in scene 1 she tells Blanche, "I can hardly stand it when he is away for a night" [259]) is significative of the role her son will now play in providing her with the opportunity for self-fulfillment (however limited) implicitly denied her from the start by her husband (95; added dialogue is signified by italics in this excerpt from scene 11):

STELLA. (*Above armchair, as EUNICE enters, crosses around STELLA to backless chair in D. R. corner.*) How's my baby? *Is he demanding his supper?*

EUNICE. (*Putting bowl of grapes on backless chair, backing L. a few steps.*) Sleepin' like a little angel. Brought you some grapes.

STELLA. (*Moving downstage at L. of EUNICE. Leaving slip on back of armchair.*) *Bless him. I just ache when I'm not in the same room with him.*

EUNICE. *You better leave him right there till you know what gets settled.* Where is she?

STELLA. Bathing.

It was the imminent birth of the child that decided that Stanley and Stella's strained bond would be momentarily strengthened (scene 8), that Stanley would prevail over Stella in his efforts to expel Blanche from his home. And, ironically, it is the child's final presence that signifies the crippling of their marital bond.[4] It is not by chance that, as Stanley goes to placate his wife on the stairs at the end of the play, the child, whom Eunice has placed in Stella's arms, stands between them. Even as he kneels here, so too did Stanley kneel on these stairs in intimacy with Stella, his face pressed to her belly, at the end of scene 3.

The child itself, by remaining unnamed and unspoken of as someone with a psychological life of his own, by being kept offstage until after Blanche's exit, and by being born on the same day as Blanche, comes to function as an almost pure symbol not only of all the children Stella will bear in her steady retreat from Stanley, but of the result of things, the ironic and abrupt end of his benign domination of her. It is Stanley's lust after Stella—the epitome of this domination and crux of their relationship—that frees her, finally and ironically, to direct her attentions away from him and toward the son born of his lust. The delayed introduction of the child, whose absence from the plot up to this point lends its now unique presence the urgency of allegorical simplicity, thus sets the final moments of the play off as the anticipated, yet anticlimactic, culmination of Stanley and Stella's relationship. At her birthday supper, Blanche had wished that "candles [would] glow in [Stella's baby's] life and . . . that his eyes [would] be like candles, like two blue candles lighted in a white cake!" (373–74) And now, at the hour of her spiritual death, this baby is borne onstage in a pale blue blanket, to win Stella away from Stanley where she, Blanche, could not.

Right before Stella accepts the baby from Eunice, she yells "Blanche! Blanche, Blanche!" as her sister *walks on without turning, followed by the Doctor and the Matron* (418). Earlier in scene 11, Stella had declared to Eunice, "I couldn't believe [Blanche's] story and go on living with Stanley" (405). Blanche's story, of course, is that Stanley raped her while Stella was in the hospital giving birth, and Stella's crying out her name three times, then sobbing *with inhuman abandon* (419), suggests her anguish over the decision to believe Stanley's version of events instead of her sister's. In her heart, we might say, Stella knows what really happened, and that knowledge will color her behavior toward her husband for the rest of her life. What really happened is what probably happened on a number of occasions before Stanley ever met his wife or Blanche: his forcing himself, in a drunken lust, on a woman whose resistance he regarded as dutifully affected, whose "no" he interpreted as really meaning "yes." Such lines of Stanley's as "I never met a woman that didn't know if she was good-looking or not without being told, and some of them give themselves credit for more than they've got" (278), "[To interest me a woman would have to] lay . . . her cards on the table" (279), "Oh! So you want some roughhouse!" (402) and "We've had this date with each other from the beginning!" (402) are those of a man used to having his way with the opposite sex, a man whom Williams describes as follows (264–65):

Since earliest manhood the center of his life has been pleasure with women, the giving and taking of it, not with weak indulgence, dependently, but with the power and pride of a richly feathered male bird among hens. . . . He sizes women up at a glance, with sexual classifications, crude images flashing into his mind and determining the way he smiles at them.

Stanley may even have resorted to force to get Stella, who thought he was "common" upon meeting him for the first time but who "loved it," in his words, when she got pulled down from the grandiose columns of her Southern aristocratic past (377). In other words, just as Blanche's "intimacies with strangers" (386) after her young husband's suicide culminated in her seduction of a seventeen-year-old schoolboy and the consequent loss of her teaching post (which forced her to seek refuge with her sister in New Orleans), so too do Stanley's liberties with women culminate in his rape of Blanche and the consequent loss of his genuinely intimate relationship with Stella.

Stanley's marriage to Stella can be viewed as his attempt to "be good" and settle down, even as Blanche's courtship of Mitch can be seen as her attempt to be respectable and attract a proper husband. Stanley strays from the path of righteousness when he rapes Blanche: his incontinent past catches up with him, we might say, and in the process he returns her to her own past as a seductress. The moral difference between Stanley and Blanche, however, is that she successfully resists the lure of her incontinent past throughout *Streetcar*—in her dealings with Mitch, with the newsboy, and with Stanley himself, to whom she is clearly attracted early in the play and with whom she might have committed adultery were it not for her ill-fated attraction to his best friend. I want to concentrate here on "the newsboy scene," which comes at the end of scene 5 and which, understandably, has received far less attention than Blanche's romantic scenes with Mitch. It is fairly obvious that we are to see in the newsboy scene a confluence of past and present. We are reminded by Blanche's amorous response to the Young Man of her similar response to the high school boy in Laurel that caused her to be fired from her teaching position. And we see Blanche resist the temptation to seduce the Young Man—a reminder of her resolution to behave herself in New Orleans so that she can find a mate, find the safe harbor that has for so long eluded her.

What is less obvious, and what seems to me the scene's poignancy, is its evocation of Blanche's own lost innocence as well as her imagination and depth of feeling, an innocence or purity suggested by her very name, which identifies her with the achromatic color white as opposed to Stanley's primary colors (*The Primary Colors* was the title of the first draft of *Streetcar*), and by her astrological sign, Virgo. We may see Blanche in the negative light of seductress here, but we should also see her in a positive light, as one who recognizes her own lost innocence (not accidentally, in the figure of a young man who recalls Allan Grey) and responds to it effusively. This is one way of explaining her turning to a seventeen-year-old boy for an affair in Laurel after her many "intimacies" with men at the Hotel Flamingo: in turning to a boy, she was attempting to return to her own youth when, with Allan, she "made the discovery—love. All at once and much, much too completely" (354). So the Young Man in scene 5 can be looked at as a symbol of innocence, as a symbol of Blanche's own onetime innocence that was corrupted by others—a corruption that is visually recapitulated in the play by Blanche's arrival in New Orleans wearing *"a white suit with a fluffy bodice, necklace and earrings of pearl, white gloves and hat"* (245), and her appearance on the night she is raped in *"a somewhat soiled and crumpled white satin evening gown"* (391). As Stella tells Stanley, "You didn't know Blanche as a girl. Nobody, nobody, was tender and trusting as she was. But people like you abused her, and forced her to change" (376). To underline the theme of innocence revisited in the newsboy scene, Williams has it rain before the Young Man's entrance. The rain, like the water in Blanche's frequent baths, becomes a cleanser, a purifier, and thus one more instance of what Leonard Quirino has called Blanche's addiction to water.[5]

Blanche lets the Young Man leave the apartment finally, his innocence intact (except for a kiss), as, it could be said, she would have liked her own innocence left intact. Fittingly, Mitch appears for his date with Blanche right after the Young Man's exit. Mitch may be Blanche's hope at this point for a secure and happy future, but he will become, with the help of Stanley, another of the men who abused Blanche and caused her to relinquish not only her hold on innocence but also on sanity. At the start of the newsboy scene, there was a chance of more rain (the stage direction reads, *"There is a little glimmer of lightning about the building"* [336]), which Blanche would not have minded, since she likes the insulation and the time for reflection that the rain provides. She says to the Young Man, "Don't you just love these long rainy afternoons in New Orleans when an hour isn't just an hour—but a little piece of eternity dropped into your hands...?" (337–38). By the end of scene 5, the weather has cleared up and the trusting Blanche goes out into it, unsuspecting, with the credulous Mitch.

Blanche loses Mitch to Stanley's thorough investigation of her "recent history" (364), but Stanley loses his best friend as well, the man with whom he served in the "Two-forty-first Engineers" (365) during World War II, and with whom he now works in the same plant and bowls on the same team. Mitch speaks to Stanley only once during scene 11, at the start after the latter wins a poker hand and boasts of his luck, to which Mitch responds, "You...you...you....Brag...brag...bull...bull" (404). Blanche comes out of the bathroom shortly thereafter, and it is to Blanche that Mitch does his responding for the rest of the play, in the process revealing his guilt, sorrow, anger, and disappointment:

At the sound of Blanche's voice Mitch's arm supporting his cards has sagged and his gaze is dissolved into space. Stanley slaps him on the shoulder. (407)
[Blanche] crosses quickly to outside door.... The poker players stand awkwardly at the table—all except Mitch, who remains seated, looking down at the table. (413)
Blanche stops just inside the door. Mitch keeps staring down at his hands on the table, but the other men look at her curiously. (414)
Mitch has started toward the bedroom [after Blanche]. Stanley crosses to block him. Stanley pushes him aside. Mitch lunges and strikes at Stanley. Stanley pushes Mitch back. Mitch collapses at the table, sobbing. (417)

Mitch weeps at Blanche's departure, as does Stella, who speaks for Mitch as well as for herself when she laments, "What have I done to my sister? Oh, God, what have I done to my sister?" (416). Blanche is all alone at the end of *Streetcar*, but, in a sense, so is Stanley, who has used force to alienate Mitch even further and whose way of comforting his distressed wife is to fondle her breasts (the stage direction reads, "*his fingers find the opening of her blouse*" [419]. Stella at least has her baby to turn to and Mitch his sick mother; Stanley has nothing except those appetites—for sex, for violence, and for alcohol, all of which we see him indulge during scene 11[6]— that will finally lead to his self-consumption.

Stanley's desire has victimized him, even as Blanche's has victimized her. Since they are mutual victims of desire, it could be said that a part of Stanley leaves the Kowalski apartment with Blanche, while a part of Blanche stays behind with Stanley. As Normand Berlin has written (99),

Desire or sexual impulse...is common to both Blanche and Stanley and provides one measure of their similarity and difference. They share other measures as well. They compete for the possession of Stella, for the affections of Mitch; they share the bottle of whisky; they dress and undress in the view of others; they both wish to occupy the bathroom.

At the end of the play, Stanley may have the bathroom all to himself, but Blanche will remain the invisible barrier to his ever again achieving true intimacy with Stella and Mitch. At the end of the play, Blanche may have found temporary substitutes for Mitch and Stella in the Doctor and the Matron, but Stanley will remain the invisible barrier to her ever cleansing her mind and body of their impurities. Desire will have led, then, to a kind of living death for both Blanche and her brother-in-law.

NOTES

1. Vlasopolos's thesis is that "the hidden determinism ultimately uncovered by Williams's play has less to do with the history of the South as we now have it than with gender-determined exclusion from the larger historical discourse" (325). Hanks maintains that *Streetcar* depicts "a patriarchal social order based on a conquer-conquered, aggressor-victim, dominance-submission, subject-object, self-other dichotomy inherently inimical to woman's selfhood" (119).

2. For a discussion of the comic aspect of Williams's work—an aspect often neglected by critics—see Charles B. Brooks. "Williams' Comedy," *Tennessee Williams: A Tribute*. Ed. Jac Tharpe. (Jackson: UP of Mississippi, 1977). 720–35; and John M. Roderick, "From 'Tarantula Arms' to 'Della Robbia Blue': The Tennessee Williams Tragicomic Transit Authority." *Tennessee Williams: A Tribute*. 116–25. See also Brooks's "The Comic Tennessee Williams," *The Quarterly Journal of Speech* 44 (Oct. 1958): 275–81, in which he calls Williams "an essentially comic playwright" whose "greatest power and appeal derive from a comic vision which he seems unwilling to trust fully" (275).

3. Henry I. Schvey argues, somewhat differently than I do, that "Stella's baby, born at approximately the same time as Blanche's violation by Stanley in the previous scene, is associated with Blanche in the final moment of the play.... Williams clearly suggests an identification between the tragic fall of one and the birth of the other. [He suggests] that Blanche's symbolic death has ultimately resulted in new life.... Thus Blanche's fall is actually part of a process which goes beyond death and hints at something like heroic transcendence,... [at] spiritual purification through suffering" (109). Schvey believes that this process of transcendence or purification is augmented by Blanche's changing in the final scene from a red satin robe (406)—which she had used to flirt with Stanley in scene 2 (276) and Mitch in scene 3 (297–302)—into a blue outfit. "It's Della Robbia blue," says Blanche, "The blue of the robe in the old Madonna pictures" (409), and thus a blue that associates her with both the Virgin in Renaissance art and the Kowalskis' baby boy, whom Eunice brings onstage swathed in a "pale blue blanket" (418).

4. At the expense of what I believe to be convincing evidence in the play, Alan Ehrlich argues the opposite in "A Study of Dramatic Space in *A Streetcar Named Desire* and *Desire Under the Elms*" (136):

Blanche is escorted out by the doctor. Precisely *after* this action is completed, the child appears. The household was too crowded for a sister-in-law, as she is an outsider to the established order, the marriage; but for a son there is plenty of room. Blanche has overstayed her welcome but Baby Kowalski is accepted with open arms. "Eunice descends to Stella and places the child in her arms.... Stella accepts the child..." (418). The displacement is successful; the family is unified once more.... Williams has found the perfect gesture to reinforce the dramatic space and environment he created. The established environment, the happy marriage, could not be shaken by a sister-in-law; only a child could be incorporated into it.

5. We hear of that addiction again in scenes 10 and 11. At the start of scene 10, Blanche fantasizes about "taking a swim, a moonlight swim at the old rock-quarry" (391), and a little later she invents the story that Shep Huntleigh has invited her to cruise the Caribbean on a yacht. In scene 11, Blanche looks forward to living out her life at sea: "I can smell the sea air. The rest of my time I'm going to spend on the sea. And when I die, I'm going to die on the sea.... And I'll be buried at sea sewn up in a clean white sack and dropped overboard..."(410).

Quirino writes (81) that

Throughout the play, Blanche's addiction to water and to the baths ... seems to be connected with the geography and function of the Elysian Fields [the street where Blanche gets off the trolley named Desire to find Stanley and Stella's apartment, and which "runs between the L & N tracks and the river" (243; emphasis mine)]. In myth, the dead who entered the Elysian Fields [Elysium, the paradise of the happy dead for the Greek poets] were made to drink of the water of the river Lethe to forget all traces of their mortal past. And in Book VI of the *Aeneid*, Vergil depicts Lethe as a kind of watery purgatory where the dead are cleansed of all taint of memory and desire before they can be considered fit for reincarnation. In his adaptation of the concept of Elysian Fields for *Streetcar*, Williams, until the very end when he allows her the refuge of madness, denies the memory-haunted Blanche the full powers of the river Lethe.

6. Evidently, the men eat and drink at the poker table in the last scene, since Eunice complains that they are "making pigs of [them]selves" (404), and since Williams describes the atmosphere in the kitchen, where Stanley, Pablo, Steve, and Mitch play cards, as *"the same raw, lurid one of the disastrous poker night"* (403) in scene 3.

WORKS CITED

Adler, Jacob H. "Tennessee Williams' South: The Culture and the Power." *Tennessee Williams: A Tribute*. Ed. Jac Tharpe. Jackson: UP of Mississippi, 1977. 30–52.

Berlin, Normand. "Complementarity in *A Streetcar Named Desire*." *Tennessee Williams: A Tribute*. Ed. Jac Tharpe. Jackson: UP of Mississippi, 1977. 97–103.

Cardullo, Bert. "Drama of Intimacy and Tragedy of Incomprehension: *A Streetcar Named Desire* Reconsidered." *Tennessee Williams: A Tribute*. Ed. Jac Tharpe. Jackson: UP of Mississippi, 1977. 137–53.

Ehrlich, Alan. "A Streetcar Named Desire Under the Elms: A Study of Dramatic Space in *A Streetcar Named Desire* and *Desire Under the Elms*." *Tennessee Williams: A Tribute*. Ed. Jac Tharpe. Jackson: UP of Mississippi, 1977. 126–36.

Gilbert, Sandra M., and Susan Gubar. *No Man's Land: The Place of the Woman Writer in the Twentieth Century*. 2 vols. New Haven: Yale UP, 1988. Vol. 1: *The War of the Words*.

Hanks, Pamela Anne. "The Viewer's Role in Filmed Versions of *A Streetcar Named Desire*." *Journal of Popular Film and Television* 14 (Fall 1986): 114–22.

Koreneva, M. "Passions for Tennessee Williams." *Theatre* [Soviet Union] 8 (1971). Cited in Irene Shaland, *Tennessee Williams on the Soviet Stage* (Lanham, MD.: UP of America, 1987) 18.

Quirino, Leonard. "The Cards Indicate a Voyage on *A Streetcar Named Desire*." *Tennessee Williams: A Tribute*. Ed. Jac Tharpe. Jackson: UP of Mississippi, 1977. 77–96.

Schvey, Henry I. "Madonna at the Poker Night: Pictorial Elements in Tennessee Williams's *A Streetcar Named Desire*." *Modern Critical Interpretations: Tennessee Williams's "A Streetcar Named Desire"*. Ed. Harold Bloom. New York: Chelsea House, 1988. 103–9.

Shaw, Irwin. "Theater: Masterpiece." Review of Elia Kazan's production of *A Streetcar Named Desire* at the Ethel Barrymore Theater, New York, 1947. *The New Republic* 22 Dec. 1947: 34–5.

Taylor, Harry. "The Dilemma of Tennessee Williams." *Masses and Mainstream* 1 (April 1948): 51–5.

Vlasopolos, Anca. "Authorizing History: Victimization in *A Streetcar Named Desire*." *Theatre Journal* 38 (Oct. 1986): 322–38.

Vulf, Vitaly. "The Tragic Symbolism of Tennessee Williams." *Theatre* [Soviet Union] 12 (1971). Cited in Irene Shaland, *Tennessee Williams on the Soviet Stage*. (Lanham, MD.: UP of America, 1987). 18.

Williams, Tennessee. *A Streetcar Named Desire. The Theatre of Tennessee Williams*. 7 vols. to date. New York: New Directions, 1971. Vol. 1: 239–419.

———. *A Streetcar Named Desire* (acting edition). New York: Dramatists' Play Service, 1953.

Zubkov, Yuri. "Even in Defiance of the Play." Review of A. Goncharov's production of *A Streetcar Named Desire* at the Mayakovsky Theatre, Moscow, 1971. *Soviet Culture*. Quoted in Vitaly Vulf, "The Tragic Symbolism of Tennessee Williams," *Theatre* [Soviet Union] 12 (1971). Cited by Irene Shaland, *Tennessee Williams on the Soviet Stage* (Lanham, MD.: UP of America, 1987). 17–18.

Madame Zhang Lu Yen and Lu Yi in the Chinese premiere of *A Streetcar Named Desire*, October 21, 1988. Photo courtesy of the Tianjin People's Art Theatre and Photographer Qiu Guo Hai.

13

A *Streetcar Named Desire*: The Political and Historical Subtext

Robert Bray

"In bourgeois society . . . the past dominates the present; in Communist society, the present dominates the past."

Marx and Engels, *The Communist Manifesto*

For at least the last decade, new historicists, feminists, and Marxists have been reassessing American playwrights. When such readers examine the political and sociocultural context of American drama, however, Tennessee Williams has until very recently escaped scrutiny. Miller, O'Neill, Odets, Shepard, and, more recently, the polemical new left theater of the last decade have received perhaps a disproportionate share of critical attention. Marxist critics have been particularly neglectful of Williams's drama. Although Williams remains relatively overlooked in terms of a study of his political sympathies, one can readily determine, from his essays, prefaces, and interviews, as well as from his plays, that his view of history and society consists of a complex matrix of sometimes paradoxical elements unquestionably worth exploring.

His preface to *A Streetcar Named Desire*, "On a Streetcar Named Success," strongly questions the American capitalistic ethos and our rabid pursuit of the material, what Williams calls an "American plan of Olympus" (8). In the production notes for *The Glass Menagerie*, Williams castigates the American propensity to neutralize and standardize the human spirit into anonymity. *The Night of the Iguana*, reveals Williams's disgust with a society that allows peasants to rummage through dung hills for protein. It is therefore particularly appropriate that *Streetcar*, with its political subtext of old order versus new order, determinism, decadence, power, and oppression, should come under careful sociocultural scrutiny. Considering that a number of Williams's plays have enjoyed performances in mainland China, in the pre-Gorbachev Soviet Union, Poland, and Czechoslovakia, we as

American critics must wonder why the political subtext of his plays have not been more thoroughly investigated.

In earlier studies of *Streetcar*, some American critics commented tangentially on sociocultural overtones in *Streetcar* by viewing Blanche as a representative of a particular class. For example, Robert Emmet Jones sees Blanche as "of interest mainly from a sociological standpoint" (219). Blanche is a "social fossil" whose demise signals "the defeat of a culture ... " (219). On the other hand, Marxist critic Harry Taylor believes that *Streetcar* suffers from Williams's lack of social conviction. Blanche would have been a more tragic figure if the conflict between her and Stanley had arisen from "genuine conflict" rather than "savage" and "almost animal" confrontations (99). He hastily and rather unfortunately concludes that "the absence of the socio-historic periphery in the author's mind weakens his attack even on personal drama ... " (99). Later sociocultural studies comment on Stanley's working-class status and his relationship to the old order, frequently with contrasting viewpoints. Kenneth Bernard describes Stanley as "the mercantile man destroying once and for all the plantation culture of the Old South that is a threat to his supremacy" (340). Leonard Berkman, on the other hand, finds that, other hand, unlike Arthur Miller's work, "*A Streetcar Named Desire* is an inspired refutation of the linking of modern American drama with the common man" (249). Robert Brustein observes that "with Stanley, Williams wrought significant changes in the proletarian hero" (9–10). But rather than adulating the underclass and its predicament in the fashion of vulgar Marxism, it should be noted that Williams created Stanley "more as a product than as a producer ... " historical change, a significant difference most critics fail to acknowledge. Most recently, Anca Vlasopolos combines historiography with feminism to conclude that "the hidden determinism ultimately uncovered by Williams' play has less to do with the history of the South as we now have it than with gender-determined exclusion from the larger historical discourse" (325).

As this review of scholarship demonstrates, some of the readers' conclusions are contradictory, and major questions remain unanswered. For example, to what extent should the political and historical subtexts inform a reading of the play? Is *Streetcar* similar to other literature that, according to Louis Althusser and Frederic Jameson, should involve basic contradictions of a society (Ryan 203)? Perhaps most basically, what is the relationship between the oppressors and the oppressed, power and destiny, desire and economy, and how do Williams's characters exhibit these relationships in their dramatic struggles?

Soviet critics have attempted answers to the above questions, but considerable disagreement exists there among theatre practitioners and literary critics also. According to Carl R. Proffer, editor of *Soviet Criticism of American Literature in the Sixties*, Williams and other prominent American writers "were virtually unknown to Russian readers until the sixties" (xiii). However, at the end of the 1940s, the Soviet literary weekly *Litera-*

turnaya Gazeta described *A Streetcar Named Desire* as a play about capitalism and spiritual decay "run into absurdity" (quoted in Shaland 2). Irene Shaland's important study, *Tennessee Williams on the Soviet Stage*, chronicles the staging of Williams's plays from *Orpheus Descending* in 1961 to *Cat on a Hot Tin Roof* in 1983 in Russia and provides especially interesting insights into specific productions and critical reception in general. For example, she discovers that in 1967, a translation of ten of Williams's plays appeared in the Soviet Union and "at once became a bibliographical rarity" (5). Nevertheless, Soviet readers were often confused by Williams's themes and characters, and Soviet critics regard Williams "as a prophet who is misunderstood in his native land" (6). Williams's first major Soviet translator and Marxist critic Vitaly Vulf sees Williams's, drama as "a simple denunciation of capitalistic 'consumer society' guilty of destroying spirit, souls, and destinies" (Shaland 6). Vulf, oriented toward a vulgar Marxist, and therefore reductionist, reading of Williams's plays, finds that "the playwright clearly leads the audience to think of the crisis of bourgeois civilization" (6).

The first Soviet performance of *Streetcar* was in Moscow in 1971 by director Andrei Goncharov. Apparently avoiding an overtly political approach to the play, Goncharov instead insisted on seeing it as "the downfall and ruin of fragile beauty and its incompatibility with the vulgar and cruel world" (quoted in Shaland 11). As other Russian directors did with American plays, Goncharov also took considerable liberties with the plot. For example, he directed Mitch, at the end of the play, to rescue Blanche from the Matron and Doctor, and carry her "away up a short flight of stairs leading to a road that rushed upwards" (quoted in Shaland 19). Some critics, such as Vitaly Vulf, objected to this mutilation. According to Vulf, "the happy ending destroys the sense of the work. The director wants to show that Mitch is on a higher level than Stanley. *But*, in America, cruelty and violence are victorious" (67). Obviously, Kazan was not the only (film) director who offered happy endings to *Streetcar*.

Although Goncharov avoided the play's political subtext, such was not the case with many Soviet reviewers. According to Shaland, one critic, Yuri Zubkov, "felt offended" (17) and asked "What is the social conflict? What kinds of social focuses do Stanley and his friends, on the one hand, and Blanche, on the other, personify?" (17). Vitaly Vulf also questioned the lack of social content/relevance. According to Shaland, although Vulf wished to avoid being labeled a "vulgar-sociological" critic, he "saw *Streetcar* as a play about moral insolvency of human personality in a capitalistic society" (18). Blanche's loneliness, according to Vulf, was a result of "social conditions," not her "sexual dissoluteness" (18). Another Soviet critic, Maya Koreneva (quoted in Shaland 18), offered a similar interpretation:

For Williams, the connections between this brutality and the fundamental laws of American society are indisputable. But what phenomena are responsible for the use of violence and its continuing rule in that country? Why have violence and ruthlessness become the social norms? It is absolutely useless to try to find in Williams any answers to these important questions.

Koreneva also slights Williams in the 1976 *20th Century American Literature: a Soviet View* when writing that "all major American playwrights, with the exception of Tennessee Williams, employ . . . diversity of dramatic forms" (Koreneva 151). This brief dismissal is the only mention of Tennessee Williams throughout the 528-page critical volume.

Recent interviews with several Russian academics have offered me additional (and more favorable) interpretations of Williams's drama. During September–October, 1991, East Tennessee State University hosted a group of Russian educators and journalists, providing me with an excellent opportunity to discuss their reactions to Russian productions of Williams's drama. Two of these guests, a professor and a journalist from Moscow, had seen, among other Williams's plays, the 1971 Goncharov production. Interestingly enough, neither had thought much about *Streetcar* in terms of its political context. The journalist, Anatoly Yarochevsky, said that "Tennessee Williams's drama is of the heart. His plays speak to a universal audience because we can all understand the difficulties that beset his characters." According to Yarochevsky, the sociocultural significance of the passing of the old order was easily recognizable in the Goncharov production, and we discussed at length parallel themes and responses in Williams and Chekhov. "Both Williams and Chekhov write about how a way of life has vanished. Williams's characters, however, seem to exhibit a greater sense of psychological loss," Yarochevsky observed. It should be noted that if Soviet authorities who sanctioned this production intended *Streetcar* to be a didactic history lesson, the effect was not achieved, at least on Yarochevsky and his colleague, who prefers not to have her name mentioned.

The Soviet Union was the first, but not the only, Marxist country to produce *Streetcar*. The play premiered in Poland in December 1957 at both Torun and Wroclaw (Kolin). And in October of 1988, the play premiered in China at the Tianjiu People's Art Theater with a British director and performances by Chinese actors and actresses. As Philip Kolin and Sherry Shao interestingly note, English director Mike Alfreds saw the play as, among other things, a political allegory and believed that from "the vantage point of history and economy, *Streetcar* explored the difference between these mighty opposites [Blanche and Stanley] in terms of grace and vulgarity, the civilized and the uncivilized, the flesh and the spirit. The actress who played Blanche, Madame Zhang Lu Yen, was sensitive toward Blanche's predicament but saw her as "useless to society" (26). On the other hand, although Madame Yen found Stanley's behavior objectionable, he and his comrades "nonetheless were pushing society ahead" (26).

Seven years before this production, critic Zuo Yi combined a Marxist interpretation with observations about Williams's most persistent leitmotif, the victimization of time (quoted in Kolin and Shao 21):

They [Williams' characters] were victims of time. From Williams' point of view, the human being and the world were hostile to each other. The reason why men committed crimes was because the world itself was not perfect. When Williams exposed their sufferings using his sharp pen, to some extent he reflected the capitalist American society in which the middle and low class people were placed in situations which made them lonely and powerless. Actually, America was not a country in which every one had equal opportunities. It was a country in which the strongest existed and the weakest perished.

Similarly, Beijing critic Ma Lan observed that "Williams' play tells people that it is not a simple thing to say goodbye to the past. Burying oneself in recalling the past is an indication of the weakness and passiveness in humanity" (quoted in Kolin and Shao 27). Lan and Yi's observations about Blanche's being a temporal misfit echo findings of Williams's critics on our own continent[1] and especially call to mind Frederic Jameson's notion of the repression of history.

In *The Political Unconscious*, Frederic Jameson writes that history "is *not* a text, for it is fundamentally non-narrative and non-representational" (82). History, rather, "is what hurts, it is what refuses desire . . . " (102). In an astute analysis of Jameson's *The Political Unconscious*, William C. Dowling further states that for Jameson, history is a nightmare "that must be repressed as a condition of psychological survival not only by the master but also by the slave, not only by the bourgeoisie but also by the proletariate" (118). Blanche's failure to survive, at least in the domain of sanity, results in large part from her inability to deny her history. Blanche's history is composed of some things she loves to remember, such as her myriad beaux, but things she would also love to forget. Nightmares of the past are not confined only to her recent history, a fact some readers have overlooked. Her entire existence consists of a series of disappointments, from the suicide of her husband, to the loss of Belle Reve, to her aberrant sexual behavior and consequent expulsion from Laurel. Of course, her attempted repression of her activities in Laurel, her denial of time's inexorable march forward, and her inability to satisfy her desire are all inextricably tied to her mythic sense of southern history and her own personal past. To underscore the futility of Blanche's escaping her past, Williams's stage directions, which call for the haunting gun shots and polka music, expressionistically remind her (and the audience) of just how impossible her repression becomes.

Although Blanche has been sexually profligate in her recent past, not all of her desire is sexual. Marxists contend that sexual urges represent far less in terms of desire than Freudians would have us believe. As Dowling writes (32),

Freudian theory, despite what Freud may have believed, has as its true object not sexual desire but Desire itself, the primal energy that gives form not only to individual lives but to human society in all its manifestations.

The streetcar that Blanche rides does head toward sexual gratification, but also toward a sense of belonging to and merely surviving in a society to which she is temporally unsuited. Rejected by Stanley, Stella, and finally Mitch, Blanche's desire ultimately becomes delusional. In scene 9, she tells Mitch, "I don't want realism. I want magic!" (385). This desire for magic leads her to the phone call to Shep Huntleigh, who, she believes, could offer her sympathy and economic security. Unfortunately, he, too, is a beautiful dream.

As I indicated earlier, Williams has often been compared to Chekhov, his favorite playwright, and some studies have mentioned specific parallels between *The Cherry Orchard* and *A Streetcar Named Desire*.[2] Both authors demonstrate a profound sense of loss through the transformation of entitlement. As is the case in some of Chekhov's drama, Williams's view of history is revealed through his writings, and particularly through this play; and it is no secret that Williams, like Faulkner, was not entirely content with the South's shifting from an agrarian to an industrial society. Williams venerated the southern past because it represented order. As C.W.E. Bigsby writes, "The ordered nature of [southern] society in turn suggested a cosmic order and purpose" (46). One must be careful, however, to avoid the facile notion that Williams myopically defends the old order and its representative, Blanche; for although his poetic sentiment surely lies with his heroine, Williams's own realistic perception of Stanley as a survivor and progenitor of a new order forces us to accept on an intellectual level what Blanche might otherwise lead us to believe on an emotional or empathetic level.

Raymond Williams has written that "we can see drama, not only as a social art, but as a major and practical index of change and creator of consciousness" (273). *Streetcar* illustrates precisely those changes that were taking place in the once-agrarian South and makes us conscious, perhaps more than any single piece of literature, of the futility of romanticizing and clinging to those days of cavaliers and cotton fields. One of the most prominent vestiges of the South—the plantation—is reduced in this play to a blood-stained curse, whose white columns are replaced by "colored lamps" (373), and whose belongings have been confined to Blanche's acknowledgment that "everything I own is in that trunk" (281). This reduction of property value that so devastates Blanche becomes very significant in Marxist terms as well.

In *Writing Marxist History*, R. S. Neale argues that "property relations grant powers of control and decision making..." (xvii). An analysis of prospective property rights reveals a great deal about the relative power of Stanley and Blanche. First of all, it is Stanley's property that Blanche invades.

Blanche arrives at the Kowalski flat immediately after Stanley has delivered the blood-stained meat package, an act symbolizing his territorial control. As Kazan's "Notebook" indicates, Blanche, in desperate search of sanctuary, instead finds one more place in which she will be "excluded" as a virtual pariah (scenes 1–3) (365). Williams's stage directions reveal that Blanche first appears *"incongruous to this setting"* (245) and establish her as an intruder. Blanche's shock when she arrives at the Kowalskis' results from her juxtaposing fabricated memories of Belle Reve with the conditions of the neighborhood and shabby flat. The image of the beautiful dream serves as Blanche's singular referent for condemning Stella's present lifestyle. Blanche never fully appreciates Stella's viable, exuberant (albeit occasionally tumultuous) life since she has abandoned the family home. According to Vitaly Vulf, "Blanche is lost in Stanley's modern world and doomed to fail. Her sensitivity makes her unwelcome in the home of the 'average man' " (61). Blanche's losing the estate results in her progressively parasitic attachment to the Kowalski household as she ironically becomes more and more dependent on that which she so vehemently disdains. This dependency guarantees Stanley's leverage in the power-property equation because, sadly for Blanche, she must confess that Belle Reve, for all practical purposes, has been reduced to mortgage statements. As Raymond Selden observes, in the postwar period, state-and corporate-managed economic systems "brought to its fullest development that tendency which Marxists call 'reification' (this refers to the reduction of value to commodity value and the domination of the human world by a world of objects)" (39). This "reification" is precisely what has become of Blanche and her possessions. Like many ladies of the Old South, Blanche has been economically dependent on a patriarchy that ill-prepared its daughters for the world of commerce. Whereas the mortgages of her ancestors have left Blanche *divested*, Stanley is *invested* with the Belle Reve papers, which include the graveyard, to which all DuBois family members save Blanche and Stella have "retreated."

The most interesting point about the power-property equation thus occurs when Stanley and Blanche are discussing the foreclosure of Belle Reve. Blanche says that Belle Reve had to be "sacrificed" (270). Stanley, however, sees Belle Reve only in terms of its present liquidation value and is entirely insensitive to the "epic fornications" (284) the DuBois family has countenanced in relinquishing the property. Although Belle Reve does appear to be "lost," exactly what constitutes Belle Reve remains ambiguous, as does the process by which it has been lost. Stella says that "it had to be—sacrificed or something" (270). The dissolute DuBois ancestors have deprived Blanche and Stella of the plantation, "till finally all that was left . . . was the house itself and about twenty acres of ground, including a graveyard, to which now all but Stella and I have retreated" (284). Apparently, this last piece of property and the house itself are what have been mortgaged off, but it is unclear in every situation in which Belle Reve is mentioned whether the house itself, or just the land, has been lost. As though it takes a man, in the masculine legal world, to understand foreclosures, Stanley is left to determine exactly what has become of Belle Reve.

Significant, also, is Stanley's crude, though adequate, understanding of Louisiana's Napoleonic Code, which, in this case, empowers the husband equally through sanctity of property rights. Blanche's bitter admission of the appropriateness of the Belle Reve papers passing into Stanley's "capable hands" (284) should make persistant DuBois sympathizers wonder whether Williams took such a nihilistic view of this property transfer. Regardless of whether the papers include the house or not, what becomes symbolically important is the final merging of the moribund DuBois bloodline with that of the vibrant, vital Kowalskis. In contemporary Marxist terms, this transfer reflects historical development as well. Dowling explains that for Marx a key to understanding societal development lay in "the way the economic determined the particular system of social relations that characterizes each stage of historical development: the relations constituting the capitalist system in which we now live, the feudal system of social relations preceding capitalism, the ancient or slaveholding societies out of which feudalism developed, and so on" (46). This transfer of the Belle Reve papers into Stanley's "capable hands" thus signifies an evolving social system changing from one mode of production to another. Here, the mode of production (which, in Marxist theory, always considers property relations) symbolically evolves from postbellum agrarian to postwar urban-mechanistic because of the nature of the transfer. Stanley, who rents his property on Elysian Fields, is now "entitled" to Belle Reve, in whatever form the DuBois family has bequeathed it.

The play also raises questions about oppression and power outside of the Blanche-Stanley relationship. Indeed, minor players also function as oppressors, further exacerbating Blanche's subjugation. Consider, for example, the role of the poker players. First of all, ostensibly they form a very common lot, rather unexceptional, including Mitch. Nevertheless, these working class card players are essential to Stanley's dominance as king of the "apes." At first glance, they exist as part of the we-other relationship envisioned by Stella and Blanche. These are "the boys" (289), the rebellious louts who, from the women's point of view, invade the Kowalski apartment and contribute to the disruption of the family. A closer look, however, proves otherwise. In fact, the poker players preserve the order of the flat and ensure Stanley's dominance. They keep Stanley from seriously hurting Stella, which would result, perhaps, in legal charges and more certainly in her having a miscarriage. Had Stanley been allowed to assault his wife, unrestrained by the poker players, the ending of the play surely would have been different. As it is, they physically restrain Stanley, paradoxically allowing him continual repression of both Blanche and Stella, thus guaranteeing his dominance. These poker players can overcome Stanley only as a mob, and in scene 11, he is back in control, with Mitch calling him a "bull" (404).

Similarly, the Doctor and Matron, who come in at the play's end, are agents of oppression who implement Stanley's plan to remove Blanche from the Kowalski flat. Even Eunice unwittingly contributes to Stanley's dominance by offering Stella shelter from Stanley's occasional temper storms and thus perpetuating the cyclical violence of the Kowalski household.

Mitch, clearly an effete foil to the bestial Stanley, illustrates the ultimate dependency of the working class existence, although he, too, acts as one of Blanche's oppressors. Even though he seems "superior to the others," according to Blanche, because he has "a sort of sensitive look" (292), his bland existence exhibits none of the exuberance and determination of Stanley's. Working in the spare parts department at Stanley's factory, Mitch himself is a sort of spare part, one of those rather flat, super-ordinary Williams creations who, like Jim O'Connor in *The Glass Menagerie*, compensates for his insecurity with a somewhat pathetic attempt at machismo. Both Jim and Mitch call attention to their respective physical prowess, Jim with his "shadow" on the wall, and Mitch with his sweat. But as Stella tells Blanche, "Stanley's the only one of his crowd that's likely to get anywhere" (292). Mitch, like O'Connor, believes that the factory will afford him opportunities leading to advancement, but his unquestioning complacence will guarantee him only dependency on the bourgeoise system and exclusion from property.

If Stanley is the "author" of Blanche's history, as Professor Vlasopolos believes, then Mitch is history's messenger, confronting Blanche in her vulnerable condition with his knowledge of her promiscuity and fraudulent "innocence." Mitch, clearly out of control in the presence of Stanley, becomes another of Blanche's oppressors who denies her future by propelling her toward her tragic end. Viewed in terms of the other characters' actions and motives, then, Blanche may be seen as the ultimate outsider, positioned outside of time, social order, and place. Furthermore, the society that she represents, southern plantation, gives way to the mechanistic grit and grind of the factory, and her psychological death at the play's end must be seen as a victory for the oppressors and the new order that they represent. In this play, at least, the proletariat becomes the ruling class.

Thus, since economic and class conflict serve as the basis for much of Marxist ideology, and for *Streetcar*'s conflicts as well, Williams, it would appear, infused his play with ideological considerations. Frederic Jameson, in *The Political Unconscious*, argues that society should be seen as a dynamic, synchronic system of mutually antagonistic cultural levels (92–97). Williams delves into at least two of these cultural levels in *Streetcar*, and an examination of each culture and what it represents further demonstrates the appropriateness of employing a Marxist perspective to the play. In fact, one of the most basic evolutionary tenets of Marxist-Hegelian ideology—thesis, antithesis, synthesis—can be seen as being symbolized by the three major characters of the play, Blanche, Stanley, and Stella.

As mentioned above, when Blanche first arrives at the Kowalski flat, her initial reaction demonstrates shock and disapprobation. Never mind if Belle Reve, as Blanche romanticizes it, ever really existed at all; it is still her single, dominant referent. More than any other symbol, the plantation remains fixed as the essence of old southern culture. The first collision of the mutually antagonistic cultural levels, then, is one involving opposing settings. The Elysian Fields setting area is described as *"an easy intermingling of races in the old part of town"* (243) that especially contrasts with the rigid stratification of the postbellum plantation society.

The next contrast of cultural levels exists, of course, with the characters themselves. Virtually everything that Stanley represents (save his sexuality) disgusts Blanche, and vice versa. Blanche hates the flat. Stanley resents her presence in it. Blanche is French Huguenot; Stanley is Polish. Stanley has recently returned from serving his country in the war. Ironically, Blanche has been serving the army with less noble distinctions. With the Napoleonic Code and his various "acquaintances" (274), Stanley has the law on his side. According to Stanley, Blanche has been living outside the law. Blanche has charm and a cultivated facility with language. Stanley is boorish and inarticulate. Blanche has a chest of furs, costume jewelry, and gaudy dresses. Reminiscent of Yank in O'Neill's *The Hairy Ape*, Stanley disdains this finery and reacts violently to Blanche's possessions, hurling the furs to the daybed. This partial list of contrasting character traits illustrates the basis for antagonism between the two characters and might also make a reader more understanding, if not sympathetic, toward Stanley's resentment. As Stanley reminds his wife, "Who do you think you are? A pair of queens? Remember what Huey Long said—'Every man is a king!' And I am the king around here, so don't forget it" (371).

Stanley's invoking Long's credo here is significant to Stanley's self-concept and sense of economic worth. Long's populist position appealed most urgently to the downtrodden agrarian populace, both blacks and whites, who felt left out of the controlling economic and political system. Long's wording was carefully, indeed brilliantly chosen, for if the Kingfish could make a common man feel like a "king," Huey was guaranteed a huge block vote. Stanley's rudimentary understanding of politics suggests his belief in the quasisocialist system that Long was advocating, with the closest thing the South has ever had to a viable national socialist candidate. Stanley's disgust over Blanche's aristocratic pretensions, his reference to her as "Her Majesty," and "visiting Royalty" (361), thus uphold his veneration of Long's populist ideals and phraseology.

Viewed from a Marxist perspective, then, Blanche and Stanley do offer a rather convenient contrast of opposites. Although Blanche's generation of the DuBois family were not slave holders, part of her psyche remains tied to the glory days of the antebellum past. Blanche and her immediate ancestors, those "epic fornicators," represent the transition from a southern plantation existence into the new South, where the mode of production changes from rural-agrarian to urban-mechanistic. A Marxist view of history argues that the slave-holding classes must evolve into a feudalistic relationship, which would later be replaced by a bourgeois society, with the bourgeoisie and the proletariat emerging as the opposing classes. This bourgeoisie, who owned the modes of production, would exploit the proletariat until a revolution occurred. This dialectical relationship is represented through contrasting character elements in *Streetcar*, and Williams does seem to be conscious of at least an abstract notion of Marxist dialectics in first choosing such obvious class opposites in Blanche and Stanley and then determining who would prevail in the struggle. If these two characters can represent thesis-antithesis respectively, then it seems logical to consider Stella the synthesis of these two opposing forces.

Stella's *weltbild*, her optimism, and her pragmatic adaptability contrast so forcefully with Blanche's staid fixation on the past that one wonders how they could have come from the same family. The meeting of the two sisters in scene 1 illustrates how Stella has flourished physically since she's left Belle Reve: Blanche appears "exhausted" (254), but Stella is "as plump as a little partridge!" (254). Blanche, on the other hand, says, "I weigh what I weighed the summer you left Belle Reve. The summer Dad died and you left us ..." (255). When Stella departed, Blanche moans, "*All* the burden descended on *my* shoulders." Stella replies, "The best I could do was make my own living, Blanche" (260). Blanche badgers her sister relentlessly, hoping that she will accept some responsibility for the family misfortune in general and Blanche's own physical and mental deterioration in particular. "But you are the one that abandoned Belle Reve, not I! I stayed and fought for it, bled for it, almost died for it!" (260). Belle Reve, the beautiful dream that Blanche maintains, is precisely what Stella abandons to get on with her life.

When Stella meets Stanley, who strips her from the "columns" (377) of Belle Reve and shows her the "colored lights" (373), a dynamic variable is introduced into Stella's life, forcing her to make changes beyond merely abandoning her past. The image of the proletarian Stanley pulling Stella "down off them columns" (377) signifies his furious contempt for that very powerful symbol of landed aristocracy, the Greek revival columns. In this manner, Stella is cheapened (to Stanley's liking) by "colored lights" (377). This arrangement has been to Stella's liking also, because not only does Stanley indicate their relative compatibility—"wasn't we happy together, wasn't it all okay 'till she showed here" (377)—but also Stella herself repudiates Blanche's notion of loyalty to and love of the beautiful dream (320):

BLANCHE: I take it for granted that you still have sufficient memory of Belle Reve to find this place and these poker players impossible to live with.

STELLA: Well, you're taking entirely too much for granted.

Clearly, the Kowalski flat hardly resembles conjugal utopia, but Stella has learned that happiness is a relative term and accepts her imperfect relationship with her husband. In doing so, she abandons not only the beautiful dream, but all its cloying, romantic vestiges. Stella does agree with Stanley's pronouncement that "the Kowalskis and the DuBoises have different notions" (275), and while she may be offended occasionally by her coarse spouse, clearly she is willing to sacrifice her refined sensibilities to the pleasure and vitality that he offers.

Stella's decision not to believe her sister's story about the rape is just as much a decision about choosing a lifestyle. She can believe Blanche and leave her husband, or remain with Stanley and be guaranteed relative economic and familial security in the future. The choice that she makes places her among Williams's survivors, those like Serafina and Maggie, who may lack a poetic imagination or illusory sensibilities, but who are pragmatic enough to fathom the necessity of carrying on.

The progeny of this relationship serves as additional evidence that Stanley, both literally and symbolically, has maintained and fortified his dominance. This son, who inherits Stanley's name and lineage, will further dilute the DuBois bloodline, resulting in Stella's even more tertiary family connection to Belle Reve. The baby also suggests that the family will stay together, that the synthetic Stella has adapted to Stanley's world. As Vitaly Vulf comments, "As Stella adapts she sees Stanley as the norm. Out of people like her arises moral relativism"(67). Chances are good that the baby will also carry on the masculine, working class values of Stanley with a much greater sense of his father's morality than with that of his Aunt Blanche.

In *Modern Tragedy*, Raymond Williams quotes George Lukács as saying that the tragic hero is "the individual whose personal passions center upon the content of the collision [between forces]" (35). Lukács has written convincingly on modern drama, and some of his comments, such as the one above, seem particularly apropos of *Streetcar*. Elsewhere, in "The Sociology of Modern Drama," Lukács argues that in modern drama, "The stage has turned into the point of intersection for pairs of worlds distinct in time; the realm of drama is one where 'past' and 'future,' 'no longer' and 'not yet,' come together in a single moment" (148). Although it would be tendentious to argue that such a "single moment" occurs in *Streetcar*, the entire play seems permeated with these "pairs of worlds," particularly Blanche's and Stanley's. Another interesting observation by Lukács also seems to inform a Marxist reading of *Streetcar*: "from the past is born the future, which struggles free of the old and of all that stands in opposition. The end of each tragedy sees the collapse of an entire world" (148). This observation on modern drama captures in particular the political thrust of *Streetcar*, the clash between the old order and the emerging urban South, between Stanley's power and his taking over Blanche's property, as illustrated earlier. Accordingly, *Streetcar* should be considered in terms of its Marxist subtext, for, again according to Lukács, "Most modern dramas are historical, [and] history is meant as a substitute for mythology...injecting a new pathos" (166). Since the mythological dimensions of Williams's drama have been convincingly explored,[3] perhaps future interpretations of his work will consider more thoroughly another aspect: his concern with dramatic conflict as reflecting the political and historical forces at work in the changing South in which he lived for a great deal of his life.

NOTES

1. See, for example, Thomas Porter's *Myth and Modern American Drama*; Joseph K. Davis's, "The American South as Mediating Image in the Plays of Tennessee Williams" in *American Drama and Theatre in the Twentieth Century*; and Robert Bray's "The Burden of the Past in the Plays of Tennessee Williams" in *The Many Forms of Drama*.

2. See, for example, Thomas P. Adler's "The Checkhovian Matrix." in *A Streetcar Named Desire: The Moth and the Lantern*.

3. Most thoroughly by Judith M. Thompson in her full-length study, *Tennessee Williams' Plays: Memory, Myth, and Symbol*.

WORKS CITED

Adler, Thomas P. *A Streetcar Named Desire: The Moth and the Lantern*. Twayne Masterwork Studies No. 47. Boston: Twayne Publishers, 1990.

Berkman, Leonard. "The Tragic Downfall of Blanche DuBois." *Modern Drama* 10 (Dec. 1967). Reprinted in *Modern Critical Interpretations of A Streetcar Named Desire*. Ed. Harold Bloom. New York: Chelsea House, 1988. 33–40.

Bernard, Kenneth. "The Mercantile Mr. Kowalski." *Discourse: A Review of the Liberal Arts* 7 (Summer 1964): 337–40.

Bigsby, C.W.E. "Tennessee Williams: Streetcar to Glory." *The Forties: Fiction, Prose, Drama*. Ed. Warren French, 1969. Reprinted in *Modern Critical Interpretations of A Streetcar Named Desire*. Ed. Harold Bloom. New York: Chelsea House, 1988. 41–48.

Bray, Robert. "The Burden of the Past in the Plays of Tennessee Williams." *The Many Forms of Drama* (5). Ed. Karelisa V. Hartigan. London: UP of America, 1985.

Brustein, Robert. "America's New Culture Hero: Feelings Without Words." *Commentary* 25 (February 1958). Reprinted in *Modern Critical Interpretations of a Streetcar Named Desire*. Ed. Harold Bloom. New York: Chelsea House, 1988. 7–16.

Davis, Joseph K. "The American South as Mediating Image in the Plays of Tennessee Williams." *American Drama and Theater in the Twentieth Century*. Gottingen: Vandenhoeck and Rupreet, 1975.

Dowling, William C. *Jameson, Althusser, Marx: An Introduction to* The Political Unconscious. Ithaca: Cornell UP, 1984.

Jameson, Frederic. *The Politically Unconscious: Narrative as a Socially Symbolic Act*. Ithaca: Cornell UP, 1981.

Jones, Robert Emmet. "Tennessee Williams' Early Heroines." *Modern Drama* 2 (1959): 211–19.

Kazan, Elia. "Notebook for *A Streetcar Named Desire*." In *Directors on Directing: A Source Book of the Modern Theater*. Ed. Toby Cole and Helen Krich Chinoy. Indianapolis: Dobbs-Merrill, 1976. 364–79.

Kolin, Philip C. "The First Polish Productions of *A Streetcar Named Desire*." *Theater History Studies* 12 (1992): 67–88.

Kolin, Philip C., and Sherry Shao. "The First *Streetcar* in Mainland China." *Tennessee Williams Literary Journal* 2 (Winter 1990–91): 19–31.

Koreneva, Maya. "Eugene O'Neill and the Traditions of American Drama." *20th Century American Literature: A Soviet View*. Trans. Progress Publishers. Moscow: Progress Publishers, 1976.

Lukács, Georg. "The Sociology of Modern Drama." Trans. Lee Baxandall. *Tulane Drama Review* 9 (Summer 1965): 146–70.

Neale, R. S. *Writing Marxist History*. New York: Basil Blackwell, Incorporated, 1985.

Porter, Thomas. *Myth and Modern American Drama*. Detroit: Wayne State UP, 1969.

Proffer, Carl R., ed. and trans. *Soviet Criticism of American Literature in the Sixties: An Anthology*. Ann Arbor, MI.: Ardis Publishers, 1972.

Ryan, Michael. "Political Criticisms." *Contemporary Literary Theory*. Ed. by C. Douglas Atkins and Laura Morrow. Amherst, MA.: The U of Massachusetts P, 1989. 200–14.

Selden, Raman, *A Reader's Guide to Contemporary Literary Theory*. Lexington, KY.: The UP of Kentucky, 1985.

Shaland, Irene. *Tennessee Williams on the Soviet Stage*. Lanham, MD: UP of America, 1987.

Taylor, Harry. "The Dilemma of Tennessee Williams." *Two Modern American Tragedies*. Ed. John D. Hurrell. New York: Charles Scribner's Sons, 1961.

Thompson, Judith M. *Tennessee Williams' Plays: Memory, Myth, and Symbol*. University of Kansas Humanistic Studies 54. New York: Peter Lang, 1987.

Vlasopolos, Anca. "Authorizing History: Victimization in *A Streetcar Named Desire*." *Theater Journal* 38 (Oct. 1986): 322–38.

Vulf, Vitaly. "Tragicheskaya Simvolika Tennessi Vilyams." *Teatr*, no. 12 (1971). Unpublished Translation by Kisa Harwell.

Williams, Raymond. *The Long Revolution*. London: Chatto and Windus, 1961.

———. *Modern Tragedy*. Stanford, CA: Stanford UP, 1966.

Williams, Tennessee. "On A Streetcar Named Success." *New York Times*. November 30, 1947.

————. *A Streetcar Named Desire. The Theatre of Tennessee Williams*. 7 vols. to date. New York: New Directions, 1971. Vol. 1: 239–419.

Yarochevsky, Anatoly. Soviet Journalist. Personal interview. 19 Sept. 1991.

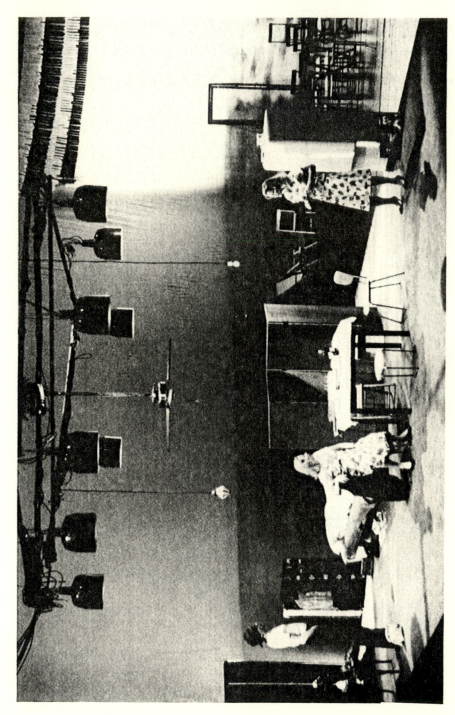

Markus Boysen as Stanley, Christiane Lemm as Stella, and Verena Buss as Blanche. Düsseldorfer Schauspielhaus production 1988. Copyright Lore Bermbach.

14

The Cultural Context of *A Streetcar Named Desire* in Germany

Jürgen C. Wolter

The transplantation of an American play to a German stage entails the intricate process of linguistic translation and cultural interpretation required by any cultural transfer. An adequate rendition of the American text into German not only has to solve questions of idiom and style but also has to take into account the differences in the cultural and sociohistorical backgrounds of the American playwright and the German theatregoer. The problem is deepened because the cultural context of the target audience is in a constant state of transformation.

The strong dependence of interpretation on context is exemplified by the changes in the reception of *Streetcar* in Germany, which were primarily caused by changes in the political, economic, cultural, intellectual, and ideological context. In the 1950s, *Streetcar* created a sensation because it opened completely new avenues of experience to a people who had been starved physically and intellectually. Its ubiquity on the German stage of the 1950s made the play part of the standard German repertoire but also caused a feeling of saturation, so that in the 1960s it was performed much less frequently; furthermore, in the context of the political crises and moral uncertainties of the 1960s, the play was considered to be of little relevance. In the following decades, directors used all possible means to counteract the feeling of jadedness in the theatregoing public and reverse the decline in its attractiveness. Hence, in the 1970s they resorted to spectacular casting to ensure a box office success, and in the 1980s they emphasized its universal relevance and frequently underlined their postmodern reinterpretation by experimenting with the stage setting. As one might expect, the flexibility of the reception in the Federal Republic of Germany contrasts strikingly with the rigidity of the Marxist point of view adopted by critics in the German Democratic Republic. Because of their Marxist ideological premises, they necessarily condemned a "retrospective" and "decadent" author whose life and work represented "the decaying bourgeois society" (Friedrich 175, 179, 159). They rejected his work because he did not write agitprop drama and was not interested in the struggle of the classes and the masses, but instead focused on the eternal truths of the human heart.

Thus, the transfer of a drama from one culture to another is never completed with the publication of the translated text, but is under constant revision according to the changes in the context of the target culture. I intend to analyze in greater detail the major determinants of the theatrical reception of *Streetcar* in Germany and demonstrate how far inadequacies of the translation and a lack of the necessary background knowledge has influenced its interpretation. I also will outline the changes in the cultural context that were responsible for the continuous process of reinterpretation from the 1950s to the 1980s. My findings are based on almost 300 reviews of 84 productions.

THE TRANSLATION AND ITS IMPLICATIONS FOR THE INTERPRETATION

The Glass Menagerie and *Streetcar* were among the American plays that had been selected for translation into German between 1945 and 1951 by the Information Control Division (ICD) of the Office of Military Government for Germany (U.S.) (OMGUS).[1] The task of the drama translation unit of ICD was to contribute to the reeducation of the German people by making available plays that promoted democratic and antimilitaristic ideas or reflected American culture (Gehring 61–73; Lange 276–92). Berthold Viertel translated *Streetcar* in 1949 for the reeducation program of ICD; as *Endstation Sehnsucht*, it premiered in Zürich in November 1949 and in Pforzheim in March 1950.

Viertel (1885–1953), an Austrian writer and director, seems to have been the ideal translator for a Williams play. As a poet, Viertel could be expected to have an ear for Williams's language and as a playwright and director he knew about the conventions of the stage. Furthermore, he had lived in Hollywood and New York as a script writer and director (1928–1932, 1939–1947) (Pfäfflin 31, 36). He used the stage version that was supplied by Williams's agent, who referred to it as the "final version"[2] (Viertel, "Tragödie"). According to Zuber ("Translation" 65–66), it differs from the reading edition published by New Directions mainly in that it lacks the interpretation aids given in the stage directions, such as: the Blue Piano *"expresses the spirit of the life which goes on here"* (243), or "...*they come together with low, animal moans*" (307). In her comparison of the different versions of the play, Zuber comes to the conclusion that Viertel's source was "possibly a precursor of the Acting Edition" (Zuber, "Problems of Propriety" 98). Viertel translated the play in less than a month and virtually without the help of a dictionary, "trying to meet the demand to translate as many plays as possible in as short a time as possible" (Zuber, "Problems of Propriety" 100). In 1949, this translation was made available to German theatres by ICD as a mimeographed typescript, and in 1954 it was published by Fischer. For his Berlin production (May 1950), the setting of which was praised for its resemblance to that of New York, although he had not seen the play in America, Viertel's stage designer, Ita Maximowna, however, acknowledged Jo Mielziner's influence. Viertel made several improvements and corrected mistakes that had slipped in. However, he never took the time to submit this revised version to Fischer (Zuber, "Problems of Propriety" 100–1). Since Viertel's translation remains the only published German translation of the play, the text still used in Germany today is the unrevised version, written in great haste for the democratic reeducation program of OMGUS.[3]

The differences between the American and German receptions of the play are partly due to inaccuracies and mistakes in Viertel's translation; others result from cuts and additions made by Viertel, and still others from the fact that Viertel's text did not give the aids to interpretation that the New Directions edition provides.

Only rarely have reviewers drawn attention to the many obvious mistakes in Viertel's translation. Most outspoken were Melvin J. Lasky and Eberhard Quadflieg, who deplored that, during his stays in America, Viertel had not learned enough English, but had lost the feeling for his mother language. Quadflieg even found the text "unintelligible gibberish" and welcomed the changes made for the production in Aachen (March 1955). One could compile a long list of mistakes in the translation; a few typical examples, however, must suffice here.

In some cases, Viertel followed the original too closely, without considering the harm this did to the German text. When Blanche, for instance, pretends to search for the liquor bottles, she exclaims: "Oh, I spy, I spy!" (251), meaning that she has just caught sight of them. In his translation: "Oh, ich spioniere! Ich spioniere!" (16), Viertel uses the German verb "spionieren" which, although etymologically related to the English verb "to spy," has only the restricted meaning of watching secretly for hostile purposes. The clumsiness of some phrases resulting from such inaccuracies of the translation may account for the many inappropriate responses from the audience, which frequently irritated reviewers.

Sometimes mistakes in the translation have a significant influence on the interpretation of the characters. For example, Blanche's expectations and aspirations expressed in "I brought some nice clothes to meet all your lovely friends in" (256), are rendered by Viertel as "Ich habe *dir* ein paar hübsche Kleider mitgebracht, damit *du mit mir* vor deinen distinguierten Freunden Staat machen kannst." (20) Retranslated, this would read: "I brought *you* some pretty clothes so that *with me you* can impress your distinguished friends" (emphasis added). Such a translation misrepresents Blanche's intentions, since her social pretensions are transferred to her sister, and, consequently, has far-reaching implications for our view of Stella. Similarly inadequate is the translation of Blanche's inquiry about the character of Stanley's friends: "Heterogeneous—types?" (257) is given as: "Interessante Typen, was?" (20). The German rendition which, retranslated, would read "Interesting types, right?" completely neglects the implications as to Blanche's higher education (Blanche's "heterogeneous types" is contrasted with Stella's "mixed lot"), and it disregards the sexual connotations of "heterogeneous" for Blanche who, after a tragic marriage to a homosexual, fled into indiscriminate heterosexual affairs.

Although some reviewers found it ingenious, many recognized that Viertel's German title *Endstation Sehnsucht* biased the interpretation of the play. They criticized the choice of *Sehnsucht* as inadequate because it reduced the ambiguity of the English word *desire* to the single meaning of "longing" in a rather Platonic way without the sexual connotations. Viertel's German title suggests that the central theme of the play is Blanche's longing for understanding; it suppresses the idea of the sexual desires of Blanche, Stanley and, last, but not least, Stella. Furthermore, *Endstation* (i.e., last stop, final destination) connotes the structural principle of cause and effect and its inevitability, referring to Blanche's final commitment to the asylum as the logical end of a series of unavoidable events. This emphasis on sequentiality in the German title caused many reviewers to interpret it as a direct reference to the asylum, as "a clinical demonstration of a case of progressive hysteria ending in insanity or a final phase of a spiritual collapse" (Frenz and Weisstein 260).

Further crucial causes of misunderstanding resulted from Viertel's treatment of American terminology. For example, in the scene the Poker Night, he deleted many poker terms since he either did not know poker jargon or (justifiably) took it for granted that German audiences of the 1950s (and later) would not understand it. So he replaced the talk about "wild" cards by a meaningless inquiry about the time, which, of course, destroys the net of overtones, which, as Philip Kolin showed ("Why Stanley and His Friends"), are connected with "wild" and "one-eyed jacks." As Paul G. Buchloh (59) also pointed out, in a German context (especially in that of the 1950s), poker players would almost automatically be associated with the upper classes or prosperous playboys who could afford gambling.

Furthermore, Viertel made several cuts that have had a tremendous impact on the interpretation of the play. For example, in the last scene, he eliminated the episode in which Eunice places the baby in Stella's arms, because he was afraid of the latent "sentimentalism" of the gesture (Viertel, "Bornierte Analyse"). Obviously, he did not see that the cut had far-reaching consequences for the interpretation of Stanley's and Stella's future marital life and Stanley's complicity in the crime.

Finally, several elements of the *mise-en-scène*, which Viertel added in his stage directions, also show that he approached Williams's text not so much as a conscientious translator but more as a creative director with the production in mind. For example, in the first scene when Eunice shows Blanche the apartment, Viertel introduces a broom as a referent to the careless disorder of Stella's household. He thus utilizes the imagery behind the proverb "a new broom sweeps clean" and ironically foreshadows the profound changes Blanche will work in her sister's life. However, that, in his stage directions, he asks for Eunice, of all persons, to tidy up the room, is less convincing.

THE IMPLICATIONS OF CULTURAL INCOMPREHENSION

A significant factor determining the reception of *Streetcar* in Germany is the play's regional context, that is, its deep roots in the culture of the American South. Many elements that belong to the everyday experience or common knowledge of an American audience in the South are used by Williams for both their topical and symbolic allusiveness. Since Germans lack a thorough knowledge of the regional background of the play—as did many Americans in the New Haven and New York audiences—there is an uncertainty whether an element of the play is used for its symbolic connotations or for its evocative qualities of local color authenticity.

Where German theatregoers do not comprehend the topical significance of some of Williams's phrases, they may only grasp its symbolic overtones. For instance, if they are not conversant with the topography of New Orleans or Mississippi, they will misunderstand names like "Desire," "Cemeteries," "Elysian Fields," "Garden District," "Laurel" to be fictitious, used solely for symbolic purposes. A similar misunderstanding based on a lack of knowledge about the region concerns the climate of the South. Since most productions could not convincingly evoke the heat and humidity of New Orleans, as time and again German reviewers have criticized, and since the climate of the Deep South is very different from anything within the average experience of a northern European, many members of the audience who have not visited the subtropics will take Stanley's urge to get rid of his shirt as a symbol of his preoccupation with sexuality, instead of a simple response to regional humidity. This confusion about the referential qualities of given facts explains why some German critics complained that Williams's symbolism was too insistent, obtrusive, and unequivocal. Not understanding the topical context, Rudolf Stobbe faulted Williams for using "a symbolic code which cannot be deciphered in this crudely naturalistic play." Two studies in 1974 provided valuable background knowledge: Jürgen Koepsel's meticulously phenomenological study of the functions of the South in Williams's plays, and Oppel's investigation of local references in *Streetcar* (" 'Every Man' ").

In contrast, although reviewers praised *Streetcar*'s local color elements (e.g., the blues) for their topical authenticity, they did not see that they were also used for their symbolic qualities. In their survey of the play's German reception in the 1950s, Horst Frenz and Ulrich Weisstein concluded that *Streetcar* "was found to be void of genuine symbols" (270). Some reviewers were disappointed that Williams, after the convincing and innovative symbolism of *The Glass Menagerie*, had returned to the traditional naturalism of Ibsen, Hauptmann, and Sudermann, which he had simply updated by incorporating much psychoanalytic material. The Swiss paper *Der Bund*, for example, complained that the naturalistic description of milieu and the vulgar language were not used for a philosophic message and artistic symbolism, but simply for superficial sensationalism ("Endstation Sehnsucht"). Because of their failure to understand the symbolic quality of some of the dramatic elements, a number of reviewers regarded the offstage sounds and music as extraneous, melodramatically sensational accompaniments devised by the director. For example, Heinz Ohff criticized the polka Blanche subconsciously hears at the end of scene 1 as a cheap melodramatic device, a kind of *"deus ex machina"* (a view shared by Kaiser).

The confusion about *Streetcar's* realism and symbolism led R. Wicke to a most egregious misunderstanding. He thought the Coburg production far too realistic. Keeping Williams's memory play *The Glass Menagerie* in mind, he saw *Streetcar* as a dream play and hence asked for stylized rather than naturalistic modern dress, for less realistic background music, and for an emphasis on the imaginary in the episode with the Young Man, whom he regarded as an epiphany from Blanche's past.

Depending on whether they emphasized the topical or the symbolic allusiveness, reviewers regarded the play as a sociological or a psychological study and then found fault with the productions if the play's social or psychological potential was not fully realized. Those who approached *Streetcar* from a sociological point of view demanded that the production strive after authenticity of milieu. Time and again, they criticized a German production for its lack of southern local color, especially if they felt that the atmosphere of heat and humidity was not naturalistically realized. However, most early German responses saw *Streetcar* as a psychological case study (Jauslin 65), and, consequently, many protested that psychoanalysis should be confined to the doctor's consulting office (Anders). Many reviewers thought that the relevance of the play's psychopathology extended from that of an individual case to that of mankind in general and considered *Streetcar* a play about the universal human affliction, "everyday realities" or "basic psychic and erotic situations" (Schueddekopf).

A flagrant misunderstanding caused by a lack of knowledge about the play's regional context concerns its local setting: Since many reviewers were not too well informed about the class structure of urban centers in the United States in general and the social topography of New Orleans in particular, they thought that the play was set in the slums, in a nonwhite neighborhood, or in some proletarian suburb of New Orleans.[4]

In general, German audiences are not familiar with the play's literary context and thus have not readily understood the allusions to Poe's "Ulalume"; neither do they see the symbolic significance of Blanche teaching Hawthorne (with his preoccupation with sin), Whitman (with his homosexuality and uncompromising individualism), or Poe (with his insane narrators who profess sanity but have a distorted view of reality), nor do they relate Blanche's name (with its connotations of whiteness and blankness) to Melville's concept of indefiniteness as exemplified by the whiteness of the whale.

Finally, linguistic problems account for potential cultural misunderstandings. Many of Williams's words come from American slang, which is not understood by the German theatregoer; examples are "meat" (244) with its sexual overtones—sometimes it is even used with reference to the female sexual organs (Wentworth and Flexner 335)—and "lamb" (251, 339), used by Blanche when she addresses Stella and the Young Man, with the secondary meaning of one who is "easily fooled, tricked, or cheated" (Wentworth and Flexner 312). Much more significant, however, is a profound difference in the linguistic stratification of society in America and Germany. In general, the sociolects used by Blanche or Stanley and his friends cannot be captured in a German translation, because here differences in idiom and pronunciation are more regional than social. For instance, Mitch's question: "Anyone want a shot?" and Stanley's reply: "Yeah. Me." (287) are rendered by Viertel (43) as "Will jemand noch etwas trinken?" and "Jawohl, ich!" (i.e.; "Does anyone want another drink?" and "Yes, I"). Thus, in German productions, the inevitable leveling of social differences with regard to language was frequently compensated by pronounced class-related behavior (or rather by what was regarded as such). Sometimes, actors seem to have unduly exaggerated this so that their acting came close to ridicule and caricature. For instance, some poker players degenerated into drunken ruffians spilling beer and devastating the props, not even sparing the members of the audience in front. In the case of Blanche, an overemphasis on her aristocratic pretensions was suggested by Viertel's awkward translation that, for example, rendered "Honey, you open the door while I take a last look at the sky" (342) as "Mein Lieber, wollen Sie nicht so gut sein aufzusperren, während ich einen letzten Blick auf das Firmament werfe?" (89) ("My dear, would you please be so kind as to unlock the door while I take a last look at the firmament?"). The overcompensation also accounts for the fact that, as many reviewers resentfully noted, German audiences frequently started to giggle or even laugh outright at the most inappropriate moments. In Rheydt, members of the audience even shouted "cheers" whenever Blanche helped herself to another drink (h. "Begierden—ausgelacht").[5]

THE 1950s: THE POSTWAR PSYCHE

When *Endstation Sehnsucht* premiered in Pforzheim in March 1950, German theatregoers were still suffering from the destruction of Nazi Germany.

They had been isolated from the international exchange of ideas for a decade, viewed the United States through the eyes of wartime or postwar propaganda, and for years had been allowed only very restricted access to American literary and dramatic culture, subject to the approval of the ICD branch of OMGUS. Consequently, many went to see American plays mainly out of curiosity. Their overriding nonliterary purpose was to extract information about the United States, about its democratic system, and about the lifestyle of a nation of admirable wealth whose cities and self-confidence had not been devastated by two world wars.

Because of this common tendency to search for traces of what they thought to be typical of the American national identity, a number of early reviewers regarded Blanche's social and moral decadence as a reflection of the typical problems of the American South; similarly, Stanley was interpreted as the epitome of the jungle laws prevailing in American society. For many, the play treated a "specifically American problem" (Be.).

Many compared what they saw on the stage with the situation in Germany or with their own conceptions of America. According to Willy H. Thiem, the first German responses to Streetcar emphasized the cultural differences and consequently thought the play "too American" in its "tone of glorious morbidity," which was only "a literary expression of exhibitionist methods to shock and bluff" (35–36). Fritz André Kracht, a German director and translator of American plays, also stressed the impact of cultural differences on the German reception. He explained the "tremendous success" of Williams, Miller, and O'Neill after the war by their "shock value"—they presented an image of the United States radically different from the paradise of reeducation propaganda—and by their exoticism—they "used settings completely foreign, strange, exciting and colorful beyond anything the German audience had ever seen" (14).

Counteracting this search for national typicalities, others emphasized the universality of Streetcar by pointing out similarities between American and German existentialist attitudes, despite the differences in the way of life of the two nations. The reviewer of Der Mittag (A.S.V.) emphasized the poetic allegory of the play and saw it as a modern Everyman, and CRS of the Basler Nachrichten concurred that fundamentally nothing but "extremely ordinary incidents" happen in Streetcar."

In the early 1960s, Hans Joachim Schaefer reconciled these conflicting views of the advocates of Streetcar's universal significance and the searchers for national typicalities: although the "consecration of everyday life" (320) and the reduction of the complexities of human existence to a chain of impressive dramatic images taken from everyday experience is, in his view, a typical feature of modern American drama, he finds that American playwrights treat the same issue as their European counterparts: "the struggle for the dignity of the human being which is threatened by the inhuman forces of our age" (320).

Since Germans were still facing the ruins not only of their homes but also of everything they had worked for, they saw Blanche's fate in the light of the futility of human endeavor and the questionableness of human existence (Dobson 31). Quite a few members of the audience will have sympathized with a character like Blanche who was destroyed because she failed to cope with harsh realities. The reviewer of the *Badische Neueste Nachrichten* thought it "an interesting symptom of our time" that after the collapse of 1945, German theatregoers had become addicted to a kind of literature that documented "inner bankruptcy" (G., "Endstation Sehnsucht"). In contrast, Hermann Missenharter of the *Stuttgarter Nachrichten* thought that the success that the play enjoyed throughout the Federal Republic testified to the consolidation of the nation's mental health: he argued that only a psychologically sound audience could stand such a display of "hysteria, schizophrenia and brutality."

In their state of demoralization and disillusionment after the war, many Germans preferred positive and encouraging plays to the "blackest pessimism" of Williams's drama or any existentialist philosophy (Frenz, "Amerikanische Dramatiker" 80). They criticized Williams for his preoccupation "with values that negate and destroy the dignity of man, with situations and characters that disgust and sicken" (Frenz and Gaither 117). On behalf of a group of young students, H. Drösemeyer demanded cheerful plays "which not only present the disease of our time, anxiety, but also overcome it." This quest for moral encouragement, of course, accounts for the success of Thornton Wilder's *The Skin of Our Teeth* in postwar Germany—according to Lange (742–46), there were ninety-eight performances of it in the first ten months after the German premier in Darmstadt on March 31, 1946—but also for the fact that German producers predominantly selected "comedy and light drama" from the collection of American plays in German translation provided by OMGUS (Frenz and Gaither 111).

As a letter to the editor of the Bremen *Weser-Kurier* confirmed, many Germans of the 1950s believed that Americans solved all problems with technology and that their national economy was an unending success story ("Diskussionen"). For that writer, and certainly for a majority of Germans, *Streetcar* presented a new image of the American citizen who, as they now noticed, shared their anxiety, their sense of desolation, their lack of orientation, their feeling of being in danger. For some reviewers, the play was "the parable of our existence" (Montijo) because it dealt with human conditions that were very actual and present for German audiences of the 1950s. Consequently, Werner Fiedler, on the occasion of the Berlin premiere (1950), wondered whether it would have the same success as in other cities and countries since nowhere had people experienced physical and psychic devastation so acutely and painfully as in Berlin. Willibald Omansen of the *Bochumer Anzeiger* even pointed out that Blanche was "a sister of those very young girls whom we met homeless and uprooted on the big railway stations after the war, dirty, painted, saucy, with a shadow of their innocence in their faces." Finally, Klaus Wagner, in *Theater heute*, suggested that those Germans who had been victims of the loss of the eastern parts of Germany to Poland—almost 8 million Germans had been expelled from these territories—and who held deep-seated prejudices against the Poles saw Stanley as representing everything negative in their biased image of the "Polack."

The importance of the economic situation of an audience for their interpretation of a play is strikingly elucidated by the very first episode of *Streetcar*. In 1950, a German audience, still very much aware of the years of starvation they had just passed through, would have interpreted Stanley's throwing the meat package at Stella as a reference to the comparative wealth of the American working classes. They would not have interpreted it as a negative image of Stanley's unscrupulous violence and lasciviousness. For most Germans of the 1950s, economic problems were paramount, and reviewers of American plays concluded that, in contrast to Europeans, for Americans psychological and social problems were of greater importance (Frenz and Gaither 116).

Many reviewers placed *Streetcar* in the context of the European literary tradition and considered it a late descendant of dramatic naturalism, which proved that American drama had finally shed its "notorious optimism" (Dr. K.) and outgrown its moonshine happy endings. For some, postwar American drama was a rehash of the realistic disillusionment that had triumphed in Europe decades before. The names of Ibsen, Strindberg, Hauptmann, and Wedekind were most frequently brought up in this context. The Detmold production (November 1951) even reminded the reviewer of the *Lippische Landeszeitung* (H.G.P.) of the old, shallow naturalism of the 1890s. He regretted that Williams had not pursued the new naturalism represented by Hemingway, Steinbeck, and Thomas Wolfe. Many who used the historical approach agreed that the subject of *Streetcar* was anything but new for the European stage—the fate of the fallen woman. Gerhard Sanden concluded that *Streetcar's* distinctive quality was not its subject matter but the playwright's poetry.

THE 1960s: POLITICAL CRISES AND NEW LIBERTIES

Whereas in the 1950s *Streetcar* was frequently played for its political or topical relevance and was firmly set within the context of postwar Germany, in the 1960s it became part of the classical repertoire. In the 1950s, it had been played so frequently all over the Federal Republic, even in the most remote regions, that W. J. of the *Frankfurter Rundschau* maintained that in the 1960s it was running the risk of becoming tedious, especially since its sensationalism and topicality were gone. Although some reviewers argued that with its universal topics of unfulfilled longing, loneliness, and human decline and destruction, *Streetcar* was significant also for the 1960s, most commentators agreed that *Streetcar* was a play of the 1950s with only little relevance for the tremendous problems of the new decade. At most, they granted it enduring worth for the role of Blanche, which provided actresses with an excellent opportunity to prove their talent for subtle nuances of expression.

Times had changed radically since the 1950s, which, in Germany, had been dominated by the establishment of a political system, the economic miracle being its most conspicuous achievement. However, international crises of the 1960s such as the war in Vietnam and the violent end to the "Prague Spring" had finally taught people that human barbarism was not necessarily associated with animalistic primitivism, that the real menace to mankind stemmed from other causes. Consequently, Stanley's brutality was no longer seen as a threat to civilization, but simply as a manifestation of the outrageous manners of an uneducated man. The race riots in U.S. cities and universities demonstrated that the United States, and especially the South, was disrupted by much more serious social problems than those Williams dealt with in *Streetcar*. This made the play look old-fashioned, as did the fact that, perhaps because of the moral and political uncertainties of the 1960s, Germans had become avid readers of Freud so that Williams's psychoanalytic exposure of sexual instincts was no longer a taboo-breaking sensation (Wagner).[6] Given the new sexual freedom of that decade, Williams's treatment of sexuality was regarded as prudish rather than provocative. After the arrival of the Theatre of the Absurd and some more radical experiments with theatrical expression, Williams was considered a traditional and conservative playwright. When they compared this plays with most contemporary experimental dramas, which lacked consistency of dramatic structure and morality, reviewers began to see the coherence of the eleven scenes in *Streetcar* more clearly. They detected the logic and the naturalistic laws behind Blanche's fate and commented on the tragedy of her decline.

THE 1970s: STARS AND SPECTACLE

In the 1970s, only a few reviewers found *Streetcar* a relevant play. Some still thought it topical because, they argued, the gap between dream and reality was wider than ever before (eth.), and the *Badische Neueste Nachrichten* maintained that women like Blanche were still to be found in European society: disconcerted and sticking to values that had long been destroyed by the masses and could be kept only in an asylum (Wa.). The *Wiesbadener Kurier* even considered the play very modern because it treated the drug problem; "liquor could just as well be hashish," the reviewer for this paper warned, reminding his readers that drugs had begun to be a problem in Germany (TPH). But after the experience of the 1960s, a decade of high politicization, reviewers generally agreed with Friedrich Roemer,

who found the play noticeably dated because its "presentation of psycho-
pathy seemed strangely private."

Streetcar may have been old hat with the older generation who had been
offered it for more than two decades and now probably went to see it for
nostalgic reasons. Disappointed, many left before the last curtain (Gliewe).
However, as Ohff suggests, the case might have been very different with
the younger generation who had grown up in postwar Germany and who
acutely experienced the politicization of public life in the 1960s caused by
the international and national problems of that period. The years at the
turn of the decade were marked by riotous demonstrations all over the
Federal Republic and by the formation of underground groups that were
politically motivated and that gave vent to their revolutionary fanaticism
in assassinations of public representatives. Ohff presumes that the success
Streetcar enjoyed in Germany in the 1970s was due to escapist tendencies
of an overpoliticized generation that deliberately preferred plays discussing
private, not public, problems personified by everyday human beings, not by
heroic representatives of ideologies. Similarly, many critics of the 1970s
argued against a sociological approach to *Streetcar* (e.g., Lubbers; Oppel,
"Williams;" and Petersen).

Many directors seemed to agree with the majority of reviewers that *Streetcar* was timeworn, but nonetheless they thought it worth producing provided
they could heighten its attractiveness by casting star actors, exploiting spectacular effects, or experimenting with new approaches. For instance, Charles
Regnier's production for the Schweizer Tournee Theater, which toured the
Federal Republic for several years (1972–1974), relied on the appeal of star
actors known from their movie and TV roles (Sonja Ziemann as Blanche,
Götz George as Stanley). Furthermore, it exaggerated Stanley's machismo
and exploited the spectacular elements, obviously with the purpose of grand-
standing.

The Bochum theatre tried to heighten the attractiveness of its production
(1974) by casting an ex-convict as Stanley. Burkhard Driest, an actor, script-
writer, and novelist, had been known from television in his roles as a criminal
to which he had added authenticity because of his well-publicized experience
in the penitentiary. This casting insinuated that Stanley was a felon. Reviewers agreed that Driest's Neanderthal appearance conformed with their
ideas of Stanley (Tamms), but that he failed completely in his acting.

An interesting experiment was performed in Trier in 1973. As part of its
long-standing cooperation with French theatres, the Stadttheater Trier tried
to open new levels of meaning in *Streetcar* by casting two reputed French-
speaking ballet dancers, Irene Skorik and Germinal Casado, as the leads.
Consequently, choreography assumed greater importance than dialogue,
particularly so because they spoke German with a heavy French accent. The
change of priorities and the decisively unrealistic scenery gave the production
a stylized quality of artificiality, of unreality within a closed world of art.

Irene Skorik's restless walks through the narrow two-room apartment became "a ballet of entrapment," emphasizing "the artistic quality over the
social criticism," as Hermana Hofer regretted.

In an even more radical attempt to reinterpret the play, Charles Lang, at
the Freie Volksbühne Berlin, cast the German black actor Günther Kaufmann as Stanley and changed the text considerably: he cut the initial as
well as all the outside scenes—this meant the dropping of the roles of the
Mexican Woman and the Negro Woman—eliminated the role of Eunice,
and changed the end of scene 10 so that a consenting Blanche enjoyed
Stanley's sexual advances. After five private performances, limited to the
members of the Freie Volksbühne theatre club, the public premiere was
prevented by court action because of a complaint filed by Williams's German
and American agents. Finally, a compromise was reached, and Kaufmann's
black features were eliminated by makeup. The court procedures delayed
the premiere by two months so that the compromise version could be played
only four times before the summer break. Lang professed that he saw Stanley
as the "progressive force of democratism" (sic, Kersten) and that his casting
emphasized this idea and gave the play greater topicality, since a Pole was
no longer sufficiently controversial and provocative (Müller). Although Lang
denied the charge of racism and reversed the accusation, arguing that Williams and his agents were reactionary because they would not consent to a
black Stanley,[7] the cover of the playbill shows a photo from the movie *King
Kong* with the giant gorilla holding the fragile white woman in his paw.
The racist allusions are obvious, belying Lang's denials. The experiment
was scoffed at by most reviewers and members of the audience not only
because of the casting but also because Lang's Blanche was a hysterical
bitch exciting derisive laughter from the audience rather than sympathy.
Gabriele Fäth recommended that her readers go and see the movie version
starring Marlon Brando and Vivien Leigh, which was shown in Berlin at
the same time.

THE 1980s: REINTERPRETATIONS AND EXPERIMENTS

After the political, ideological, and philosophical uncertainties of the
1960s and 1970s, to which the theatre reacted with a number of experiments, directors in the 1980s frequently returned to classic drama with its
universal themes of human passions and dreams and with its famous roles
for great actors (not necessarily star actors). In contrast to those of previous
decades, many productions of *Streetcar* in the 1980s consequently emphasized its general human interest. They explicitly did not intend to catch a
southern atmosphere or the milieu of the French Quarter.[8] In the 1960s
and 1970s, *Streetcar* had frequently been denigrated as antiquated because
it had been regarded as an irrelevant treatment of an individual's psycho-

pathy or of the specific problems of the American South in the 1940s, using the psychological symbolism of the early twentieth century. In the 1980s, many saw it again as a comment on contemporary, if not universal, themes, such as the "distortion of reality and escapism" (Münder), the lack of "kindness, humaneness and understanding" in the modern world (Troppenz), "the search for love, the concealing of desperation, the feeling of being destroyed by your fellow humans" (Mudrich), the "inability of man to communicate." (Bastian), "the unwillingness of an elbow society to accept its outsiders" (Krause), or the conflict between culture and primitivism (Rappl). Mani Wintsch, director of the Essen production (1983), even compared the two worlds that clash in the play with the social contrast between the north and the south of Essen (Ch.M.). Dieter Westecker concluded that *Streetcar* had never been so topical as in the 1980s.

To emphasize its universal, and hence contemporary, significance, a number of directors downplayed or even eliminated the New Orleans locality of *Streetcar* and experimented with the stage setting. Some exploited Brechtian devices of alienation (e.g., projections of stage directions in Hamburg or a medium high transparency as a semifourth wall in Frankfurt); others de-historicized and/or de-Americanized the setting by reducing the usually detailed environment to the bare essentials or by replacing the naturalistic setting altogether by an abstract and stylized steel or wood construction that was to capture the psychological situation of entrapment, not the working-class milieu of New Orleans. The Giessen production (1980), for instance, employed "fantastic colored light effects" and used a gauze on a white wooden framework and, after scene 10, a revolving stage to change the two connecting rooms into a transparent showcase and cage expressing the idea that there was "no way out of a closed society" ("Einen Käfig für alle"). Otto Pautz of the *Kieler Nachrichten* described the stage setting of the Schleswig production (1982) as "a completely abstract decor made of glass, steel scaffolding, a staircase and linen cloths."

An interesting experiment was performed in Saarbrücken (1982): On a kind of arena stage, the walls were invisible and the doors only suggested so that an effect of Brechtian alienation was achieved (Mudrich). On the large open stage in Düsseldorf (1988), a square playing area was marked off resembling a boxing ring (Frese).

Some productions underlined the topicality of the play by introducing popular songs as background music, for example, songs by Frank Sinatra, Louis Armstrong, and George Gerschwin in Bremerhaven (1983), John Coltrane and Yusef Lateef in Esslingen (1983). The Kiel production (1985) even used a "New Wave" decor and disco tunes of the 1980s (Munk). A few reviewers, however, disliked the de-emphasis of southern topicality and would have agreed with Hartmut Krug, who castigated the Berlin production (1982) with its gauze curtains and glaring neon lights for its cool setting "in a no-man's-land of clinical sterility."

The tendency of the 1980s to change the original version for a modern interpretation most frequently resulted in more or less significant cuts or a rewriting of the conclusion. For instance, the English-speaking "Caféthea-ter" in Frankfurt (1983) replaced the last episode in which Blanche is taken away to an asylum with her symbolic burial; the actors emptied buckets of earth against the door behind which Blanche was taking her last bath (Scheidges). In Hof (1987), moral conservatism probably prohibited adultery going unpunished: Blanche was not led away by the Doctor and the Matron, but committed suicide in the bath by cutting her wrists; and at the very end, there was no *"luxurious sobbing"* and *"sensual murmur"* but only Stella pointing a gun at Stanley (Sziegoleit).

The most radical German reinterpretation, however, was done by American choreographer John Neumeier in the Schauspielhaus Stuttgart. His ballet version, which used Prokoffief's "Visions Fugitives" and Alfred Schnittke's "First Symphony," commenced with Blanche sitting on her bed in the asylum and remembering decisive episodes of her dubious career. In a series of nightmarish flashbacks, she relives her wedding on Belle Reve, her discovery of Allan's homosexuality and his suicide, her nymphomaniac love affairs, her flight to her sister, her rape by Stanley, and her commitment to the asylum.

Another significant change in the productions of the 1980s was a reinterpretation of Stanley and Blanche. In the previous decades, reviewers had seen Stanley primarily as the incarnation of harsh and brutal reality that crushes a fragile Blanche—although some had sympathized with his healthy "matter-of-factness" (Karsch) and admired his unerring instinct for the truths of life (Thiem). In the 1980s, the relationship between the antagonists was frequently seen in a completely different light: Stanley was much less exclusively a ruffian; sometimes he was even an almost Babbitt Everyman. More often than not, he was interpreted as a victim of either his emotions or Blanche's scheming; his unscrupulous behavior was regarded as the understandable overreaction of a helpless man who feels constantly humiliated by Blanche's air of superiority and entrapped by her intrigues; he instantaneously recognizes that Blanche is an imminent danger to his happiness because her plans to conspire with Stella against him and to split up his team by seducing Mitch would leave him isolated and lonesome. So, because of a reversal of sympathies in the 1980s, for many reviewers Stanley became "the key figure of the play" (Ueding). In the Hamburg (1982) and Kiel (1985) productions, he was cast as a vulnerable young man who tried to repel Blanche's attempts to destroy his life rhythm (Neubauer, Munk), in Saarbrücken (1982) as "a man with whom you sympathize" (Mudrich), and in Bremerhaven (1983) as "a highly sensitive man" whose brutality was simply a particular form of justifiable "self-defense" (Bastian).

For some reviewers, Blanche and Stanley were no longer extreme opposites but were quite comparable in their psychological dispositions: Günther

214 • Confronting Tennessee Williams's A Streetcar Named Desire

Schloz regarded Stanley and Blanche as "two neurotics" who go for each other, Munk saw them equally driven by a craze for tenderness and affection, and Klaus Lamza described them as both "lost in the madhouse of psychic wrecks." This change toward a more positive interpretation of Stanley as a victim was severely criticized by reviewers who thought in feminist terms. To them the change implied condoning male brutality as amiable and normal behavior (Krug).

The disparagement of Blanche[9] in some productions seems to have been intensified in Hamburg, where a theatre in the Reeperbahn, the most notorious red light district of Germany, was deliberately chosen in order to place Blanche in her proper environment (Rehder). At the same time, this change from the entertainment district of New Orleans to that of Hamburg emphasized the modernity and universality of the play. Probably with the same purpose of denigrating Blanche, Adolf Dresen in the Frankfurt production eliminated the end of scene 6 in which Blanche tells Mitch of Allan's homosexuality and suicide; the result was that Blanche's moral decline now lacked its essential link of causality and that her nymphomania and prostitution assumed a very different quality (Iden).

STREETCAR IN THE GDR: THE MARXIST APPROACH

So far my survey of the German reception of Streetcar has been limited to the Federal Republic. However, the fact that context determines the categories of reception is just as clearly demonstrated by the play's history in the (former) Communist German Democratic Republic.

Although Streetcar had its first GDR premiere as late as March 1974 (in Leipzig), Marxist reviewers in the East had noticed, and dutifully deprecated, productions of this "late bourgeois" play in the West since the 1950s. In general, they attacked Williams for not understanding the laws of social progress, for not emphasizing the class struggle, and for subscribing to antiprogressive politics (Schröder, Brüning 253). Reviews of Viertel's West Berlin production (May 1950) faulted Streetcar for dealing with the idea of the inevitable destruction of humanity (e.g., Eylau), an attitude that they classified as representative of American drama and as typical of late capitalism and that they contrasted with the optimistic future a socialist country offered its citizens. Gerhard Kaiser of the BZ am Abend thought Streetcar dated because it demonstrated the "putrefaction of capitalism," the "hangover" of a class that was about to step down, and drew characters who were still objects of their environment and never knew that they could think rationally and act purposefully. For Hans Ulrich Eylau of the Berliner Zeitung, Streetcar was just another of the cultural imports from the West, borne on a "pseudorealistic flood of pathological studies." He argued that their pessimism was inappropriate for a world that was about to find a more solid and safer basis in socialism.

This negative attitude of the 1950s was still monotonously repeated in the 1960s. The pattern of the Marxist criticism was summarized by Jutta Friedrich in 1963. She concluded that Williams could have no place on the stages of the progressive socialist GDR because in his plays he proved himself influenced by "American capitalist society and its lack of freedom of thought as well as by the Cold War, the American psychosis over nuclear weapons, and the corrupting power of money" (159). She criticized Williams for his attitude of "resignation," "fatalism," and "escapism" (173) and for not seeing that "a change in American society was necessary" (175) and that such a change could be achieved only by the "solidarity of the working class" (177). His characters, who accepted society as it is and consequently escaped into subjectivism, were typical representatives of capitalism because their uncompromising individualism alienated them completely from their fellow men and reflected the gap between the interests of the individual and those of society; only Stanley lived "in harmony with society" (160).

Following her Marxist premises, Friedrich analyzed *Streetcar* as a critique of the social structure of America with Blanche representing tyrannical aristocracy and holding the Anglo-American prejudice that the Slavic races were inferior (101). Whereas Blanche was reactionary, impeding the progress of mankind, Stanley represented "the ruling class of the future" (102); his victory at the end justified his healthy primitivism. Although she praised *Streetcar* for its rudimentary criticism of American capitalism, for its incidental description of social problems in the United States (immigrants and racism), and for its message that "private property is the root of all evil" (167), she condemned it because it did not draw the right conclusions, that is, did not agitate for a change in American society.

When *Streetcar*, despite these ideological attacks, was finally allowed to premiere in Leipzig in March 1975, it was primarily praised for its dramatic effectiveness. Although the production stressed the social background by giving "a very detailed description of the symptoms of a diseased society" (Stephan), Marxist reviewers still found it difficult to accept Williams's psychologizing that, they argued, might cover the fact that Blanche's catastrophe was caused by the socioeconomic conditions of late bourgeois American society. For Georg Antosch, it was a play from another world, since the GDR had found a way of life that aimed at harmony between the individual and society.

Thus, curiously enough, *Streetcar's* history in the German Democratic Republic started just as it had in the Federal Republic of Germany twenty-five years before: It was introduced to propagandize for, or against, the United States, and it was received by reviewers as a play from another world, which, for most audiences in the West, was attractive for its capitalist success, or, for most reviewers in the East, repulsive for its capitalist blights. That *Streetcar* has withstood these attempts of exploitation and misuse testifies to its universality and enduring worth.

It can be expected that after the reunification of Germany, which has, finally, ended the 40-year period of cultural isolation and intellectual starvation in the East, audiences there will now be offered a wider selection of drama from the Western hemisphere. *Streetcar* will certainly remain (or, in the East, become) a standard fare on the stages of the united Germany, not only because of the now classical role of Blanche, which is a challenge for all aspiring star actresses, but also because of its theatrical qualities of conflict and suspense. However, a completely new translation is more than overdue; many complaints about the datedness of the play were probably caused by Viertel's antiquated language and awkward phrases.

That *Streetcar's* popularity in Germany extends beyond the theatregoing public is demonstrated by the fact that two annotated (English language) editions of the play (edited by Herbert Geisen and Helmut Wolf, respectively) are available for use in German high schools and that students flock to classes that discuss the play. This, of course, cannot be explained by *Streetcar's* theatrical qualities but must be attributed to its suggestiveness and the complexity of the themes and problems it treats. Thus, potential theatregoers are constantly recruited in German schools and universities, who will probably ensure *Streetcar's* presence on the German stage for a long time.

In the German system of state-subsidized theatres, serious drama takes precedence over light entertainment. This attitude reflects the preference German theatregoers have given to thought-provoking plays, as contrasted to light comedy. Hence, it should not be surprising that German reviewers have always searched for the message of *Streetcar* and, as my survey of critical responses demonstrated, found it to treat universal problems of mankind, but also to relate to the concerns of the times. This dualism of the play's significance and the fact that it invites varying, if not contradictory, interpretations has ensured its popularity in Germany for more than forty years and will do so for a considerable time. It has been essential for such a success in a non-American culture that its thematic richness and diversity counterbalances its southern topicality of setting. The play's German reception underlines Philip Kolin's statement that "*Streetcar* can never remain the exclusive right of any specific cultural repertoire" ("Williams in Ebony" 179). It has spoken to audiences in West Germany for forty years and will continue to speak to the people in the united Germany with their extremely different backgrounds, histories, and concerns.

NOTES

1. As Lange (741) points out, there are no reliable statistics about the number of American plays that were translated into German. Sources vary between forty-four and eighty.
2. All English quotations from a German text are, of course, my translations.

3. There was a second, unpublished translation by Paul G. Buchloh and his students at the University of Kiel, entitled *Triebwagen Sehnsucht*. Unfortunately, it is no longer extant. Buchloh states that this version was produced at the theatres in Kiel and Bochum, but there are no traces of such a production in the archives of these theatres.

4. Joachim Redetzki even thought the play was set in the residential area of New York immigrants!

5. Only very few German reviewers noticed that there are humorous scenes in *Streetcar*; almost without exception, they reproached members of the audiences for every giggle.

6. That psychological positions created sensations in the 1950s was probably due to the fact that Freud's works had been forbidden by the Nazis because they were written by a Jew.

7. Similarly, Günther Kaufmann accused Williams of racism (Müller). Obviously, he and Lang did not know that Williams had agreed to quite a number of black or multiracial productions, as Philip Kolin ("Williams in Ebony") demonstrated.

8. If directors attempted to give the play a specific setting, it was that of the 1950s, that is, they took up the decade when *Streetcar* premiered in numerous German theatres.

9. The tendency to make Blanche responsible for her moral decline had, however, begun much earlier. For example, in her 1961 dissertation, Maria Felsenreich had argued that Blanche handed herself over to Stanley without resistance and Blanke (1969) thought that Blanche was to be blamed for the rape because she too easily gave way to her repressed desires.

WORKS CITED

Anders, Ferdinand. "Ein seelisches Schlammbad." *National-Zeitung* [Berlin] 12 May 1950.

Antosch, Georg. "Theatralisch faszinierend." *Neue Zeit* [Berlin] 18 Mar. 1975: 4.

A.S.V. "Blumen für die toten Welten!" *Der Mittag* [Düsseldorf] 24 Sept. 1951.

Bastian, Günter. "Blick zurück auf frühes Williams-Stück." *Nordsee-Zeitung* [Bremerhaven] 12 Feb. 1983.

Be. "Endstation Sehnsucht." *Kölner Stadt-Anzeiger* 20 Feb. 1953.

Blanke, Gustav. "Das Bild des Menschen im modernen amerikanischen Drama." *Die Neueren Sprachen* 18 (März 1969): 117–29.

Brüning, Eberhard. "Amerikanische Dramen an den Bühnen der Deutschen Demokratischen Republik und Berlins von 1945 bis 1955." *Zeitschrift für Anglistik und Amerikanistik* 7 no. 3 (1959): 249–69.

Buchloh, Paul G. "Umsetzung und Dramenanalyse." *Literatur in Wissenschaft und Unterricht* 11. Beiheft "Moderne englischsprachige Dramatik in Hochschule und Schule" (1978): 54–62.

Ch.M. "Zwei Welten auf Endstation." *NRZ Neue Ruhr Zeitung* [Essen] 26 Mar. 1983. N. pag.

CRS. "Eine Seele stirbt." *Basler Nachrichten* 27 Sept. 1951.

"Diskussionen um 'Endstation Sehnsucht'...endlos." *Weser-Kurier* [Bremen] 15 Nov. 1950. N. pag.

Dobson, Eugene, Jr. "The Reception of the Plays of Tennessee Williams in Germany." Diss. U Arkansas, 1967.

Dr. K. "Sehnsucht ohne Hoffnung." *Rheinische Post* [Düsseldorf] 22 Jan. 1954. N. pag.

Drösemeyer, H. "Jugend und 'Endstation Sehnsucht.' " *Weser-Kurier* [Bremen] 7 Nov. 1950. N. pag.

"Einen Käfig für alle, die sich in der Welt nicht zurechtfinden." *Wetzlarer Neue Zeitung* 15 Apr. 1980: 4.

"Endstation Sehnsucht." *Der Bund* [Bern] 28 Feb. 1951: 3.

eth. "Sonja Ziemann als brave Blanche." *National-Zeitungn* [Basel] 24 Oct. 1973.

Eylau, Hans Ulrich. "Wie der Mensch zerstört wird." *Berliner Zeitung* 12 May 1950. N. pag.

Fäth, Gabriele. "Als Endstation falsche Töne." *Volksblatt* [Berlin] 13 July 1974: 6.

Felsenreich, Maria. "Der Einbruch der nordamerikanischen Dramatik in die deutschsprachigen Spielpläne." Diss. U Wien, 1961.

Fiedler, Werner. "Die Irre von New-Orleans." *Der Tag* [Berlin] 12 May 1950.

Frenz, Horst. "Amerikanische Dramatiker auf den Bühnen und vor der Theaterkritik der Bundesrepublik." *Nordamerikanische Literatur im deutschen Sprachraum seit 1945.* Ed. Horst Frenz and Hans-Joachim Lang. München: Winkler, 1973. 79–102.

———, and Mary Gaither. "German Criticism of American Drama." *American Quarterly* 7, no. 2 (1955): 111–22.

———, and Ulrich Weisstein. "Tennessee Williams and His German Critics." *Symposium* 14 (Winter 1960): 258–75.

Frese, Hans Martin. "Mit offenen Karten." *Rheinische Post* [Düsseldorf] 18 Jan. 1988. N. pag.

Friedrich, Jutta. "Individuum und Gesellschaft in den Dramen von Tennessee Williams." Diss. U Jena, 1963. [summary reprinted as "Individuum und Gesellschaft in den Dramen von Tennessee Williams." *Zeitschrift für Anglistik und Amerikanistik* 13 (1965): 45–60.]

G. " 'Endstation Sehnsucht.' " *Badische Neueste Nachrichten* [Karlsruhe] 4 Apr. 1956: 8.

Gehring, Hansjörg. *Amerikanische Literaturpolitik in Deutschland 1945–1953. Ein Aspekt des Re-Education-Programms.* Stuttgart: Deutsche Verlagsanstalt, 1976.

Gliewe, Gert. "Äußerlich gut gewachsen..." *tz* [München] 14 Nov. 1973: 8.

h. "Begierden—ausgelacht." *Der Mittag* [Düsseldorf] 28 Nov. 1950.

H.G.P. " 'Endstation Sehnsucht.' " *Lippische Landes-Zeitung* [Detmold] 26 Nov. 1951. N. pag.

Hofer, Hermana. "Artistische Talfahrt ins Dunkel." *Trierische Landeszeitung* 1 June 1973.

Iden, Peter. "...und Dresens 'Endstation Sehnsucht.' " *Frankfurter Rundschau* 2 July 1984: 12.

Jauslin, Christian. *Tennessee Williams.* Velber: Friedrich, 1969. Rev. ed. Munich: DTV, 1978.

Kaiser, Gerhard. "Sensation ohne Aktualität." *BZ am Abend* [Berlin] 12 May 1950.

Karsch, Walther. "Tennessee Williams: 'Endstation Sehnsucht.' " *Der Tagesspiegel* [Berlin] 12 May 1950.

Kersten, Hans Ulrich. "Stanley ist entfärbt." *Nürnberger Zeitung am Wochenende* 13 July 1974: 2.

Koepsel, Jürgen. *Der amerikanische Süden und seine Funktionen im dramatischen Werk von Tennessee Williams*. Bern: Lang, 1974.

Kolin, Philip. "Why Stanley and His Friends Drink Jax Beer in Tennessee Williams's *A Streetcar Named Desire*." *Notes on Contemporary Literature* 20 (Sept. 1990): 2–3.

———. "Williams in Ebony: Black and Multi-Racial Productions of *A Streetcar Named Desire*." *Black American Literature Forum* 25, no. 1 (1991): 147–81.

Kracht, Fritz André. "Rise and Decline of U.S. Theater on German Stages." *American German Review* 33 (June–July 1966): 13–15.

Krause, Manfred. "Flucht in Scheinwelt endet im Irrenhaus." *Westdeutsche Allgemeine WAZ* [Essen] 12 Mar. 1983. N. pag.

Krug, Hartmut. "Endstation Zeitlosigkeit." *Allgemeine Zeitung* [Mainz] 4 Nov. 1982.

Lamza, Klaus. "Ein realistisches Endspiel." *Recklinghäuser Zeitung* 8 Dec. 1988: [8].

Lange, Wigand. *Theater in Deutschland nach 1945. Zur Theaterpolitik der amerikanischen Besatzungsbehörden*. Frankfurt: Lang, 1980.

Lasky, Melvin J. "Berliner Tagebuch." *Der Monat* 7 (Feb. 1955): 475–76.

Lubbers, Klaus. "Tennessee Williams." *Amerikanische Literatur der Gegenwart*. Ed. Martin Christadler. Stuttgart: Kröner, 1973. 425–49.

Missenharter, Hermann. "Im Dschungel der Liebe." *Stuttgarter Nachrichten* 29 June 1953: 2.

Montijo, Edwin. "Das entblößte Herz." *Der Kurier* [Berlin] 11 May 1950.

Müller, Liselotte. "Doch nicht Endstation für 'Endstation Sehnsucht.' " *Hannoversche Allgemeine* 11 July 1974: 13.

Münder, Peter. "Endstation Sehnsucht." *Szene* [Hamburg] 9 (März 1982): 68.

Mudrich, Heinz, "Wie Blanche kaputtgeht." *Saarbrücker Zeitung* 18 Oct. 1982: 24.

Munk, Christoph. " 'Endstation Sehnsucht' im Studio: Ein Stück aus heutigen Tagen?" *Kieler Nachrichten* 4 Mar. 1985: 13.

Neubauer, Simon. "Der Untergang einer Haltlosen." *Weser-Kurier* [Bremen] 23 Feb. 1982. 8.

Ohff, Heinz. "Die Straßenbahn ist abgefahren." *Der Tagesspiegel* [Berlin] 21 Dec. 1972: 4.

Omansen, Willibald. " 'Endstation Sehnsucht' auf der Bochumer Bühne." *Bochumer Anzeiger* 17 May 1952.

Oppel, Horst. " 'Every Man is a King!'—Zur Funktion der lokalhistorischen Elemente in *A Streetcar Named Desire*." *Studien zur englischen und amerikanischen Sprache und Literatur: Festschrift für Helmut Papajewski*. Ed. Paul G. Buchloh et al. Neumünster: Wacholtz, 1974. 507–22.

———. "Tennessee Williams: *A Streetcar Named Desire*." *Das amerkanische Drama*. Ed. Paul Goetsch. Düsseldorf: Bagel, 1974. 183–207.

Pautz, Otto. "Wirkungsvoll pointiert." *Kieler Nachrichten* 30 Mar. 1982: 21.

Petersen, Carol. *Tennessee Williams*. Berlin: Colloquium Verlag, 1975.

Pfäfflin, Friedrich. *Berthold Viertel (1885–1953): Eine Dokumentation.* München: Kösel, 1969.

Quadflieg, Eberhard. "Ein gereinigter Viertel-Williams." *Aachener Nachrichten* 14 Mar. 1955.

Rappl, Erich. "Die Tragödie hinter dem Reißer." *Nordbayerischer Kurier* [Bayreuth] 19 Feb. 1987: 10.

Redetzki, Joachim. "Immer noch kraftvoll." *Kieler Nachrichten* 23 Feb. 1982: 10.

Rehder, Mathes. "Endstation Reeperbahn." *Hamburger Abendblatt* 18 Feb. 1982: 10.

Roemer, Friedrich. "Wehmütiges Wiedersehen mit einem Bühnenhit." *Die Welt* [Berlin edition] 21 Dec. 1972: 18.

Sanden, Gerhard. "Amerikanische Bühnensensation." *Die Welt* [Hamburg] 15 Apr. 1950: 3.

Schaefer, Hans Joachim. "Zum Verständnis amerikanischer Dramatik." *Begegnung* 18 (Nov. 1963): 318–22.

Scheidges, Rüdiger. "Rabiat verkürzt." *Frankfurter Rundschau* 7 June 1983: 8.

Schloz, Günther. "Alles durcheinander." *Stuttgarter Zeitung* 5 July 1984: 26.

Schröder, Max. "Bornierte Analyse." *Sonntag* [Berlin] 21 May 1950: 10.

Schueddekopf, Jürgen. "Weltsprache der menschlichen Bedrängnisse." *Die Neue Zeitung* [München] 17 Apr. 1950.

Stephan, Erika. "Endstation Sehnsucht." *Sonntag* [Berlin] 25 May 1975: 5.

Stobbe, Rudolf. " 'Medizinmann' Tennessee Williams." *Hamburger Echo* 14 Apr. 1950.

Sziegoleit, Ralf. "Am 'Eigentlichen' weit vorbei." *Frankenpost* [Hof] 6 Feb. 1987: 12.

Tamms, Werner. "Vorliebe für Aktion deckt Zwischentöne zu." *Westdeutsche Allgemeine WAZ* [Essen] 2 Dec. 1974. N. pag.

Thiem, Willy H. *Tennessee Williams.* Düsseldorf: Schauspielhaus, [1956].

TPH. " 'Endstation Sehnsucht'—von heute aus gesehen." *Wiesbadener Kurier* 18 Dec. 1973: 7.

Troppenz, Uwe-M. "Die Flucht in den rosaroten Papierlampion." *Flensburger Tageblatt* 30 Mar. 1982: 6.

Ueding, Cornelie. "Von Zufall und Lüge." *Süddeutsche Zeitung* [Munich] 26 Feb. 1982: 16.

Viertel, Berthold. "Tragödie aus dem Geist des Jazz." *Die Neue Zeitung* [München, Berlin edition] 10 May 1950.

———. "Bornierte Analyse." *Sonntag* [Berlin] 28 May 1950: 14. Rpt. in Berthold Viertel. *Schriften zum Theater.* Ed. Gerd Heidenreich. München: Kösel, 1970: 127–30.

Wa. "Endstation: die Effekte bei T. Williams." *Badische Neueste Nachrichten* [Karlsruhe] 26 Oct. 1973: 11.

Wagner, Klaus. "Was ist geblieben?" *Theater heute* (Feb. 1967): 26.

Wentworth, Harold, and Stuart B. Flexner. *Dictionary of American Slang.* New York: Crowell, 1960.

Westecker, Dieter. "Phantasie bleibt auf der Strecke." *Westdeutsche Zeitung* [Düsseldorf] 18 Jan. 1988.

Wicke, R. "Der Ausweg in die Illusion." *Coburger Tageblatt* 3 Oct. 1951.

Williams, Tennessee. *Endstation Sehnsucht*. Transl. Berthold Viertel. Frankfurt: Fischer 1954.

———. *A Streetcar Named Desire*. *The Theatre of Tennessee Williams*. 7 vols. to date. New York: New Directions, 1971. Vol. 1: 239–419.

———. *A Streetcar Named Desire*. Ed. Herbert Geisen. Stuttgart: Reclam, 1988.

———. *A Streetcar Named Desire*. Ed. Helmut Wolf. Frankfurt: Diesterweg, 1975.

W. J. "Morbides Theater." *Frankfurter Rundschau* 27 Dec. 1966: 12.

Zuber, Ortrun. "Problems of Propriety and Authenticity in Translating Modern Drama." *The Languages of Theatre: Problems in Translation and Transposition of Drama*. Oxford: Pergamon, 1980. 92–103.

———. "The Translation of Non-Verbal Signs in Drama." *Translation: Agent of Communication*. Ed. M. G. Rose. Hamilton, N. Z.: Outrigger Publishers, 1980. 61-74. (a special issue of *Pacific Moana Quarterly* 5 no. 1 [Jan. 1980]).

15

A Streetcar Named Desire: Play and Film

Gene D. Phillips, S.J.

Concerning the movies of my plays, let me say that there is no unmixed
blessing or affliction that I know of.
———Tennessee Williams[1]

It has been said that both the stage and the screen have chewed at the same
breast. This observation is a rather picturesque way of noting how often
film studios have turned to the stage for material—despite the difference in
techniques, since film appeals primarily to the eye, and the stage play primarily to the ear.

Tennessee Williams plays, like *A Streetcar Named Desire*, have been
successful in both media, for example. Indeed, film scholar Foster Hirsch
has written that the plays of Tennessee Williams are deeply theatrical "because of their lush and literary imagery, cascading set speeches, concentrated
time spans, limited settings, and confined action." And yet, he continues,
these unmistakably stage-bound works, such as *Streetcar*, have been translated into "eminently successful movies that challenge rigid conceptions of
'theatrical' and 'cinematic' formats" (Hirsch 2). The Williams films retain
the spirit of the original play, especially, as in the case of *Streetcar*, when
Williams himself worked on the screenplay. His personality still dominates
the film version. In sum, "a movie based on a Tennessee Williams play is
a Tennessee Williams film," Hirsch concludes, "because its chief nourish-
ment comes from the playwright himself" (2).

In harmony with Hirsch's observations, I would add that, for me, a
Williams play like *Streetcar* proves easily adaptable to the movies for several
reasons: His loosely constructed plays are easily modified for the screen;
his central characters are boldly drawn figures experiencing an emotional

crisis with which film audiences can easily identify; and his plots are mel-odramatic enough to grip a movie audience's attention.

In essence, there is no better example of a Williams play inspiring a superior film than *A Streetcar Named Desire* (1951). As a matter of fact, Williams managed to capture the public's imagination in his play with one of the most legendary figures of twentieth-century popular culture: Blanche DuBois. Blanche, battered suitcase in hand, walked straight into theatrical history with her very first line in the play: "They told me to take a street-car named Desire, and then transfer to one called Cemeteries, and ride six blocks and get off at—Elysian Fields!" (246).

As the play opens, Blanche has come to seek refuge with her sister Stella, who is married to Stanley Kowalski, since (as we later learn) she has been driven out of the town of Laurel, Mississippi, where she had taught high school English, because of her scandalous private life. She has become a slave of desire, "the name of that rattle-trap streetcar that bangs through the Quarter, up one old narrow street and down another," as she says later in the play to Stella. "It brought me here" (321). Desire did indeed bring her to her sister's flat, that is, in the sense that her sordid past has closed every other door to her, and she is aware from the moment of her arrival that this is her last stop, for she has no place else to go.

In the end, Blanche finds her "Elysian Fields" in a paradise that exists totally in her fevered imagination, a paradise where she will always be the youthful and beautiful southern belle with a gentleman caller ready to love and protect her. We watch Blanche systematically withdraw into her own insulated, private world as the play unfolds. She decorates her little cubicle in the Kowalski flat with whatever scraps of finery she still has left. Even though only a wispy curtain separates her little domain from the rest of the slovenly flat and the harsh world of reality that lies beyond it, she is proud that she has managed to make it look "almost dainty." Within the narrow borders of her little realm, Blanche creates a soft, exotic atmosphere that veils the unpleasant realities of life that she does not care to confront, one of which is the ravages that time and her past indulgences have left upon her once-beautiful face. To this end, she covers the naked light bulb in her cubicle with a colored paper lantern that subdues the light. Her efforts to cover up her past are reflected in this attempt to keep anyone from getting a really good look at her.

Blanche convinces herself for a time that Mitch, Stanley's sidekick, will fill the role of the gentlemanly suitor she longs for. Blanche's expectations of Mitch are smashed, however, when Stanley informs him of Blanche's past, and these revelations crush Mitch's illusions about Blanche's moral character.

With the defection of Mitch, Blanche goes on hoping that some gentleman caller will yet propose to her. It is for this gentleman caller that she is waiting at the end of the play, when she is taken away to the asylum—still clutching the paper lampshade as a last relic of her romantic dream world. Blanche takes the proffered arm of the Doctor from the state asylum who has come for her, saying, "Whoever you are, I have always depended on the kindness of strangers" (418)—which only goes to show, Williams wryly observes in his autobiography, what sometimes happens to ladies who depend on the kindness of strangers. In short, Blanche's last gentleman caller has finally arrived, only to escort her to a mental institution.

Although *Streetcar* was a great success on the stage, some critics and theatergoers complained that the play was sensational and sordid, dealing as it does with the moral disintegration of its central character. Consequently, Williams was aware that care would have to be exercised if a film version of the play were to steer successfully through the narrow straits of the film industry's production code and reach the screen with its artistic integrity intact. As it happened, Williams was engaged to do the screenplay, with the help of Oscar Saul, and the film script kept very close to the original text of the play. Elia Kazan was signed to direct the film after he had directed the play on Broadway. Vivien Leigh, the star of the London production, was set to play Blanche (and eventually won an Oscar for her performance in the film), and most of the principal members of the Broadway cast, including Marlon Brando (Stanley), Karl Malden (Mitch), and Kim Hunter (Stella), were brought out to Hollywood to repeat their roles in the film. This combination of talents, all of whom had been associated with *Streetcar* on the stage, was assembled to ensure that the movie version would be as close to the genuine article as possible, and so, for the most part, did it turn out.

Elia Kazan told me in an interview that he always treated a screenplay with the same respect that he would give to a work for the stage, and this remark is certainly borne out in his direction of the film version of *Streetcar*. The only significant alterations made in the original play were dictated by censorship demands, as we shall shortly see. But if one places the movie script next to the text of the play and compares the two, page by page, it is immediately apparent that the screenplay follows the stage play scene for scene, and almost line for line.[2] Kazan has said:

I filmed the play as it was because there was nothing to change. I have no general theory about opening out a play for the screen; it depends on the subject matter. *Streetcar* is a perfect play. I did consider opening out the play for the screen initially, but I ultimately decided to go back to the original play script. It was a polished script that had played in the theater for a year and a half.[3]

With the exception of a few excisions and transpositions, most of the play's dialogue was preserved in the screenplay as it was finally filmed. Given Williams's propensity for writing long speeches of highly charged poetic language, already mentioned, his stage idiom transfers to the screen with surprising ease. Even the lines of dialogue added to the original text take on the same poetic flavor. For example, when Mitch berates Blanche for hiding her past from him, he says accusingly, "I thought you were straight." Blanche replies, "What's straight? A line can be straight or a street. But the heart of a human being?"

This adherence to Williams's original play did not mean, however, that the film of *Streetcar* was at any time in danger of becoming a mere photographed stage play. For a start, the play does not have the customary structure of two or three acts. Instead, as suggested above, the play is divided into a series of scenes—eleven slabs of action, as one critic put it. Since the pattern of the drama is not the conventional act structure, but something closer to the sequence of a film, it is not surprising that *Streetcar* translated easily to the screen. To put it another way, in striving for a continuous flow of action in plays like *Streetcar*, Williams tried to bring the techniques of the screen into play on the stage; and in doing so, made his plays more easily adaptable for the screen.

Kazan, we recall, scrapped his initial notion of opening out the play for the screen, when he found that it would serve no useful purpose. He had thought, for instance, of beginning the film in Blanche's home town and dramatizing the events that precipitated her leaving home and moving on to other places and then finally arriving in New Orleans like a refugee at her sister's front door. After such a version of the film script was worked out, he put it away for a while and then reread it a week or so later and found it "a total loss. I realized that the compression of *Streetcar* is its strength. And so I decided to photograph the play almost as Williams had composed it for the stage."

Nevertheless, the screenplay does open out the play for the screen in a few carefully selected scenes by taking the action to places that are only referred to in the play. Thus, the opening scene of the film is a short location sequence, showing Blanche arriving at the New Orleans train depot. An engine emits a blast of steam, from which Blanche emerges like an apparition materializing from a cloud of mist.

Blanche then boards the streetcar named Desire and arrives at Elysian Fields. Told that Stella is with Stanley at the neighborhood bowling alley, she sets out to meet her sister there—instead of waiting for her at the tenement, as she does in the play. Amid the noise and sweat of the bowling alley, Blanche still seems like a vaporous apparition from another planet, as she stands next to a garish juke box in her frilly white frock. By contrast, Stanley and Stella are clearly in their element, and Blanche already senses that she is going to be painfully out of place in their alien world.

In another instance of opening out the play for the screen, Blanche tells Mitch about the suicide of her husband Allan Grey while they talk on the pier fronting a dance casino, rather than after he takes her home, as in the play. This new setting for the scene is appropriate because Allan Grey killed himself at a dance casino very much like the one where Blanche recalls the suicide. Furthermore, the fog swirls around the pier as she talks, providing a spectral atmosphere for Blanche's tale of regret and death.

Another brief location sequence dramatizes a scene not portrayed in the play, in which we see Mitch express shock and disbelief at Stanley's revelations about Blanche's shady past, as they take time out from their factory jobs. The grating crash of the machinery in the background expresses the jolt that Mitch has just received.

The only addition to the original play that I find superfluous is the material added to the end of the play's scene 9, just after Blanche becomes hysterical when Mitch walks out on her. A crowd collects around the porch of the tenement, drawn by Blanche's screams from inside, and a policeman knocks on the door of the Kowalski flat to investigate. Blanche assures him from inside that everything is fine, and he disperses the crowd. This interlude serves only to slow down the tempo of the action temporarily and adds nothing to the audience's understanding of Blanche or her situation, since her increasing withdrawal from the threatening, inquisitive outside world has been thoroughly documented by this point in the film. The other extensions of the play's action, however, from the train depot to the bowling alley to the dance casino and the factory, are in keeping with the spirit of the film's literary sources, for they represent the acting out of events that are referred to in the original play but not presented on the stage.

Any further attempts to have the camera roam beyond the principal setting of the squalid tenement would have been extremely ill-advised because the atmosphere of the story is one of confinement, of people locked together in conflict at close quarters. Indeed, Kazan employed tight close-ups and deep shadows to create this sense of constriction, which betokens Blanche's imprisonment of both body and soul. The cluttered Kowalski apartment thus has a claustrophobic air that seems to imply that the very walls are closing in on the trapped Blanche. In fact, the walls really were closing in as the film was being shot. "What I actually did," Kazan explains, "was to make the set smaller; as the story progressed, I took out little flats, and the set got smaller and smaller."

Foster Hirsch praises the brooding texture of the film, which set the tone for later Williams movies such as *Baby Doll* and *The Rose Tattoo*. All of them have what Hirsch terms a look of "steamy Southern Gothic." These densely atmospheric settings take on a life of their own, he contends, and moving the action away from these inherently pictorial settings any more than is necessary would only dilute the total impact of the film. Plays like *Streetcar* "don't need much rearranging for the movies," says Hirsch. "Those that stay closest to the original structure, to Williams's original visual design [as the film of *Streetcar* does] are usually the most successful" (4).

Although Kazan's camera is confined for the most part to the tenement setting, he adroitly keeps moving it round the set so that the film does not become static or stagey. In effect, he was using the same method of making *Streetcar* into a *moving* picture that William Wyler employed while directing the screen version of another play, *Detective Story*, made the same year as *Streetcar*. "My approach to filming a play," Wyler told me, "has been to retain the basic construction of the original, while at the same time lending the story the illusion of more movement than took place on the stage." Wyler extended the action of *Detective Story*, which on the stage took place in a couple of rooms in a police station, by playing it throughout the entire two-story building, from roof to basement. "The constant movement back and forth among the various playing areas kept the film from becoming static while retaining the tight construction of the play," Wyler concluded (Phillips 24).

Kazan used the same technique in filming *Streetcar* and with equal success. He moved the action fluidly throughout the whole tenement building without, at the same time, sacrificing the stifling feeling of restriction that is so endemic to the play, since Blanche sees the entire tenement, not just the Kowalski flat, as a jungle in which she has become trapped. Kazan's use of different areas of the tenement is exemplified in the poker scene, in which the director cuts back and forth between the occupants of the flat above Stanley's apartment, and Stanley's apartment itself, where the game is being held. The woman upstairs prepares to pour scalding water through the floor boards on the poker players as an incentive for them to break up their raucous game (an episode suggested by an incident that took place when Williams was a young writer living in a New Orleans tenement). In a hilarious bit of comic relief, the players move their table away from the target area just before the irate lady can flood them, and continue playing.

In the movie, as in the play, Blanche's curtained-off cubicle is established as her preserve, the territory where she feels untainted by the vulgar slum in which she has been forced to live. She likes to think of it as her citadel of enchantment, but the barred shadows that fall across her face at times, when she shuts herself into her room, imply that she is locked into a suffocating world of illusion.

A fine example of Kazan's skilled use of lighting occurs in the scene in which Mitch ruthlessly tears the fancy paper lantern off the light bulb in her cubicle to see her as she really is. He holds the now naked bulb next to her cheek, and its merciless glare exposes a face marred with lines of age and dissipation that even heavy cosmetics can no longer conceal. The cinema audience was able to see Blanche's tortured face at this moment in a way that was impossible for any theater audience, and this is one reason why Vivien Leigh, who played Blanche on both stage and screen, felt the movie was superior to any of the stage productions. "The camera, in bringing the characters so close to the audience, was able to highlight nuances in expressions on the actors' faces and to reveal subtleties of feeling that were lost in their passage over the footlights" ("Blanche DuBois on Stage and Screen" 311).

Kazan had a mockup of the apartment set built in a corner of the sound stage, and while the technicians were setting up a shot, he would rehearse his players for the following day's shooting. Since the actors brought with them the experience of playing their parts on the stage, the shooting went along very smoothly. "The only person who had any difficulty in re-thinking the play for the screen was myself," Kazan remembers. "It was difficult to get involved in it again, to generate the kind of excitement which I had had for it the first time around. The actors were fine—but for me it was marrying the same woman twice; you know that there won't be any surprises this time."

"Vivien Leigh had one *Streetcar* in London under Laurence Olivier's direction," Kazan continued. "I never saw that production, so I don't know how his approach to the play may have differed from mine; I just did my own. After the first week of shooting Vivien seemed quite agreeable to going down a somewhat different path." When, during the first week, Leigh would begin a rehearsal with "When Larry and I did it in London..." Kazan would politely intervene and say, "But you're not doing it with Larry now; you're doing it with me." After this happened a few times, she began to follow Kazan's lead.[4]

According to Leigh, Olivier (who was her husband at the time) wanted to emphasize that Blanche was "a soft and gentle creature," yearning for love, while Kazan concentrated more on Blanche's stronger qualities, delineating her as a person "whose tongue was the weapon of a frustrated woman" ("Blanche DuBois on Stage and Screen" 310). All of these elements are in Blanche, as Kazan indicates in his notes on directing the play, and he was able to help Leigh bring out both sides of Blanche's personality in her performance in the film. Underneath her surface toughness, Blanche comes across in the film as a fragile creature longing for love and security and finding neither; and Kazan made sure that Leigh's portrayal of Blanche did not allow the latter facet of Blanche's character to overshadow the former.

Despite *Streetcar*'s reputation as a distinguished, prize-winning play in more sophisticated circles, the industry censor, Joseph Breen, the official administrator of the code of the Motion Picture Association of America (MPAA), was worried that the play would not be appropriate material for a mass medium like the movies. What Breen was saying, in essence, was that movies are a family medium, and hence only pictures suitable for the whole family should be produced. It followed, in his mind, that *Streetcar* was not a family play, and it could not be retooled into a family film without refining, to some degree, its mature content. Accordingly, Kazan began the delicate task of satisfying the Breen office, while making as few concessions as possible in altering the play for the screen, in order to preserve its serious intent and artistic integrity.

Breen's demands were essentially twofold: Reference to the homosexuality of Blanche's late husband, Allan Grey, must be obscured if not obliterated, and Stanley's drunken rape of Blanche must be entirely eliminated from the screenplay. Williams agreed to rewrite Blanche's monologue about her husband's suicide—with no little regret that "we couldn't mention homosexuality as a human problem." Kazan himself felt that the nature of Allan's problems came through on the screen in Williams's revised treatment of this scene as well as it came through on the stage. Essentially, Williams reworked the speech, by substituting for Blanche's recollection of discovering Allan in bed with another man the implication that Allan was impotent with his new bride: "At night I pretended to sleep, and I heard him crying," Blanche says in the film at this point. Finally, when she guesses the reason for his failure in the marital bed, she tells him, just as she does in the play, that he is weak and that she has "lost all respect for him."

These hints, along with Blanche's description of Allan as unusually sensitive and tender, are enough to telegraph to a mature moviegoer that Allan is homosexual, even without the play's explicit reference to his having a male lover. Therefore, Vivien Leigh believed, as did Kazan, that Williams rewrote the speech so cleverly that the suggestion of Allan's homosexuality was left intact.

Although the studio was willing to go along with the film censor's demand to eliminate the rape scene entirely from the movie, Williams absolutely refused to yield to Breen on this point. He accordingly wrote Breen a strong letter in which he maintained that "*Streetcar* is an extremely and peculiarly moral play, in the deepest and truest sense of the term.... The rape of Blanche by Stanley is a pivotal, integral truth in the play, without which the play loses its meaning, which is the ravishment of the tender, the sensitive, the delicate, by the savage and brutal forces of modern society" (Schumach 75). He reminded Breen that he had come out to Hollywood in the midst of preparations for his new play, *The Rose Tattoo*, to deal with the demands of the censor's office and that everyone associated with the film had shown similar cooperation, even deference to the Code Commission. "But now we are fighting for what we think is the heart of the play, and when we have our backs against the wall—if we are forced into that position—none of us is going to throw in the towel! We will use every legitimate means that any of us has at his or her disposal to protect the things in this film which we think cannot be sacrificed, since we feel that it contains some very important truths about the world we live in" (Schumach 75). Two years before *Streetcar* went into production in the summer of 1950, *Johnny Belinda*, a film for which Jane Wyman won an Oscar as a deaf mute who becomes the victim of a rapist, had established that this previously taboo topic could be treated tastefully in a Hollywood movie.

So Breen finally consented to allow the rape to remain in the movie of *Streetcar*, provided that Stanley was appropriately punished for his transgression.

In directing the film, Kazan was able to deal with a psychological dimension of the rape that did not come out as clearly on the stage: To what extent does Blanche share some of the guilt for her rape? Because the camera brings the audience closer to the action than was possible in the theater, moviegoers sense that, to some extent at least, Blanche subtly encourages Stanley's sexual interest in her throughout the film. Her coquettish glances and gestures in his direction bring out the fact that Blanche is drawn to Stanley's animal charm as much as she is revolted by his brutish vulgarity. Moreover, all along Blanche has envied Stella's sexual fulfillment, and now that Blanche is left alone with her drunken brother-in-law while her sister is in the maternity ward having his baby, Blanche, likewise drunk, seems subconsciously to be toying with Stanley. In addition, when one recalls Blanche furtively peeking at Stanley's biceps when he changes his shirt the first time she meets him, it is difficult to see her delicate request in this later scene that he not change his clothes in her presence as genuinely sincere.

When Stanley, like a teased animal, finally grasps Blanche, Kazan depicts the ensuing rape subtly, but without diluting its dramatic power. Blanche aims a whiskey bottle at Stanley to fend him off, but the bottle misses its mark and smashes an ornately framed mirror instead. Then she passes out. We see her limp form lying in Stanley's arms, as it is reflected in the cracked glass, which symbolizes how Stanley is finally shattering Blanche's illusions about her own refinement and moral character.

Kazan then cuts from the image of Stanley holding Blanche's body, framed in the smashed mirror, to a street cleaner's hose in the gutter outside, just as a blast of water gushes forth and then dwindles to a trickle. "Some of the symbolic cutting in the film such as cutting from the rape to the street cleaner's hose, seems, in retrospect, to be a little too obvious," Kazan commented, "though I thought it was good at the time. In any event, it was certainly a forceful cut, and enabled me to underline the rape implicitly by using the phallic symbolism of the hose, because in those days we had to be very indirect in depicting material of that kind." Furthermore, the director had prepared the audience for this symbolic suggestion of Stanley's violation of Blanche by the use of similar phallic imagery earlier in the rape scene: Stanley uncaps a bottle of beer and sends foam squirting up to the ceiling, in a spectacular symbol of his potent virility. The visual impact of this phallic image prior to the rape itself, then, combines with the street cleaner's hose immediately following the rape to suggest with artistic indirection the climactic rape itself, which is, in fact, never actually seen on the screen at all.

But Breen was still not satisfied. Stanley had to be condignly punished for his lust; and so the ending of the film was revised at his behest, in order to give the impression that Stella was going to leave Stanley, by having her say to her newborn infant, "We're not going back in there. Not this time. We're never going back." This was a shrewdly ambiguous way to end the movie, since the unsophisticated viewer could believe that Stella would make good her resolution. The more mature moviegoer, however, would realize that Stella had left Stanley earlier in the film, in the wake of a domestic quarrel, and then returned to him when he begged her forgiveness; and hence there is ample reason to believe that she will do so again.

Still, Williams was never satisfied with this compromise ending: "*A Streetcar Named Desire* was a brilliant film until the very end, when the distortion of the censorial influences made it appear that Stella would no longer live with Stanley because of what had happened to Blanche at his hands. I am sure that Kazan was as reluctant as I was to accede to this moralistic demand" (Letter from Tennessee Williams to the author, quoted in *The Films of Tennessee Williams*, page 85).

Kazan believes that the film suffered somewhat from censorship, though it was not marred in any substantial way. "Every little bit is important to the integrity of the work as a whole. For example, the censorship took away some of the ambivalence from the character of Stella: the fact that she could be both angry at Stanley and attracted to him at the same time." This latter eventuality was the result not just of the changes made in the script while the film was in production, but of some minor cuts made in the finished film by the studio before its release, in order to get a favorable rating from the Catholic Legion of Decency.

Once the movie had been granted the seal of the Code Commission, Kazan and Williams assumed that there would be no further negotiations over the picture's moral content; and both went on to other projects while awaiting the release of the film in the fall of 1951. Kazan began to hear rumors that the film's editor, David Weisbart, had been summoned to the executive offices of Warner Brothers in New York for further editing of the film. Since Kazan could get no straight answers from the studio in Hollywood as to the nature of these cuts, he flew to New York to investigate. He learned that the Legion of Decency, which rated the moral suitability of films for their Catholic subscribers, had advised Warners that *Streetcar* was going to receive a "C" (condemned) rating, meaning that Catholics would be discouraged from seeing the film.

Since the MPAA did not develop a rating system of its own as a guide for viewers until 1968, many non-Catholics followed the Legion's ratings; and, hence, Warner Brothers feared heavy losses at the box office if the Legion condemned the picture. "I was told that the 'C' rating was an invitation for every local censor board in the country to snip at a picture," Kazan said. Consequently, although the Legion had not requested cuts in the film, but simply pronounced its verdict on their rating of it, Warners invited a prominent Catholic layman to suggest to the studio how the film might be altered in order to gain a more favorable rating from the Legion.

In all, twelve cuts were made in the movie at his behest, amounting to about four minutes of screen time. Although none of these cuts were fatal to the film, Kazan nonetheless believes that they left their mark on the movie's artistic merits. The material that was excised represented for him "small but necessary bits that built mood or motivation as I needed them," he explained. "Their rough excision leaves small holes or unprepared climaxes that make my work appear cruder than it was. I see it as lost fragments of a subtly told story, whose omission leaves the characters less fully explained than the author intended and than the actors, before, had conveyed" (Kazan, *New York Times*).

The cuts range from the excision of the last three words of Blanche's remark to a handsome newsboy, "I would like to kiss you softly and sweetly on the mouth," to the re-editing of the scene in which Stella slowly descends a flight of stairs to accept the embrace of her weeping and repentant husband after their violent quarrel early in the film. In the latter instance, a long shot was substituted for a series of close and medium shots that were judged by the Catholic adviser to be "too carnal." In reality, they simply conveyed Stella's anger melting gradually into forgiveness, and her succession of emotions is not apparent to the filmgoer when viewed from the distance imposed by a long shot. This explains Kazan's feeling that these alterations robbed Stella's character of some of its ambivalence.

Some of the complex motivational forces at work in the rape scene, which I discussed above, were also obscured by yet another cut: Stanley's line, "You know, you might not be bad to interfere with," uttered shortly before his attack of Blanche, indicates that he is acting impulsively and has not considered raping Blanche until her coquettish behavior stimulates him to consider the possibility. The removal of this line makes his action seem premeditated and therefore more coarse and brutal than it actually was. "How it serves the cause of morality is obscure to me," Kazan commented, "though I have given it much thought" (*New York Times*).

One of the overall elements of the film that bothered both the Breen office and the Legion of Decency was the fact that it was difficult to determine who were the "good guys" and who were the "bad guys" in the movie. Making Stanley seem more cruel in the rape scene and Stella "less carnal" in the reconciliation scene presumably were adjustments geared to stress the meanness of Stanley and the goodness of Stella, in order that a clearer distinction between the villainous and the admirable characters could be established in the Hollywood tradition of family films. But this approach to the movie involves precisely the kind of oversimplification of character that Williams had avoided in his design of both the play and the film. "You're not in there rooting for someone," said Kazan. "There is no hero, no heroine;

the people are people, some dross, some gold," possessing the kind of complex personalities that are not easily assessed and understood.

Looking back on the censor's objections to *Streetcar*, Kazan said that the studio wanted the MPAA seal of approval to ensure that the movie was a family film that would keep no one away from the box office. At the same time, it wanted it to have a notorious reputation that would pull still more people than ever in to see it. "The whole business," Kazan concluded, "was rather an outrage" (*New York Times*).

But no tampering with the film could make *Streetcar* family fare in the old Hollywood sense of the term. It was an adult film in the very best sense of that term. Moreover, its box office success proved to the industry as a whole the films designed with mature audiences in mind could be just as profitable as movies aimed at the whole family. Indeed, *Streetcar* marked the first time that the censor's office was confronted with a Hollywood film that was definitely not family fare. In essence, Williams's screenplay and Kazan's skillful direction proved that adult subject matter could be proper material for the screen, if treated with the kind of discretion and artistry that the movie version of *Streetcar* exhibited.

NOTES

1. Letter from Tennessee Williams to the author, October 23, 1975, quoted in Gene D. Phillips, *The Films of Tennessee Williams*. The author also talked with Williams at the Cannes International Film Festival in the spring of 1976, the year that Williams was president of the international jury. Unless otherwise indicated, all of Williams's remarks cited in this essay are from this interview.

2. Concerning Kazan's reputation for making faithful film adaptations of literary works, see Louis Giannetti. *Masters of the American Cinema*. 339, 344.

3. The author interviewed Elia Kazan about *Streetcar* in Hollywood in January 1976. Unless otherwise indicated, all of Kazan's remarks cited in this essay are from this interview.

4. For further information on the London Stage production of *Streetcar*, see Philip Kolin.

WORKS CITED

"Blanche DuBois on Stage and Screen: An Interview with Vivien Leigh." *Drama on the Stage*. Ed. Rudolph Goodman. New York: Rinehart and Winston, 1961. 307–11.

Garrett, George P., O. B. Hardison, Jr., and Jane Gelfman, eds. *Film Scripts One*. New York: Appleton-Century-Crofts, 1971. [Includes the screenplay for *A Streetcar Named Desire* by Tennessee Williams and Oscar Saul.]

Giannetti, Louis. *Masters of the American Cinema*. Englewood Cliffs, N.J.: Prentice-Hall, 1981.

Hirsch, Foster. "Tennessee Williams." *Cinema* 8 (Spring 1973): 2–8.

Kazan, Elia. "The Director's Notebook." *Drama on the Stage*. Ed. Rudolph Goodman. New York: Rinehart and Winston, 1961. 307–11.

———. "*A Streetcar Named Desire*." *New York Times* 21 Oct. 1951. sec. 2:1.

Kolin, Philip. "A Letter from Sir Laurence Olivier to Tennessee Williams." *Missouri Review* 13 (1991): 141–57.

Phillips, Gene D., S. J. "William Wyler." *Focus on Film* Spring 1970: 5–10.

———. *The Films of Tennessee Williams*. Philadelphia: Art Alliance P, 1980.

Schumach, Murray. *The Face on the Cutting Room Floor: The Story of Movie and Television Censorship*. New York: Morrow, 1964.

Williams, Tennessee. *Memoirs*. Garden City: Doubleday, 1975.

———. *The Theater of Tennessee Williams*. 6 vols. New York: New Directions, 1971–76.

A Bibliography of Scholarship
on Tennessee Williams's
A Streetcar Named Desire

Adler, Thomas P. *A Streetcar Named Desire: The Moth and the Lantern*. Twayne Masterwork Studies No. 47. Boston: Twayne, 1990.

Barranger, Milly S. "New Orleans as Theatrical Image in Plays by Tennessee Williams." *Southern Quarterly* 23 (Winter 1985): 38–54.

Berkman, Leonard. "The Tragic Downfall of Blanche Dubois." *Modern Drama* 10 (Dec. 1967): 249–57.

Bernard, Kenneth. "The Mercantile Mr. Kowalski." *Discourse* 7 (Summer 1964): 337–40.

Bigsby, C.W.E. *A Critical Introduction to Twentieth-Century American Drama 2: Williams/Miller/Albee*. Cambridge: Cambridge UP, 1984.

Bloom, Harold. *Tennessee Williams's A Streetcar Named Desire*. New York: Chelsea House, 1988.

Bock, Hedwig. "Tennessee Williams: Southern Playwright." *Essays on Contemporary American Drama*. Ed. Hedwig Bock and Albert Wertheim. Munich: Max Hueber Verlag, 1981. 5–18.

Burks, Deborah G. " 'Treatment Is Everything': The Creation and Casting of Blanche and Stanley in Tennessee Williams's 'Streetcar.' " *The Library Chronicle of the University of Texas at Austin* 41 (1987): 16–39.

Callahan, Edward F. "Tennessee Williams's Two Worlds." *North Dakota Quarterly* 25 (Summer 1957): 61–67.

Chesler, S. Alan. "*A Streetcar Named Desire*: Twenty-Five Years of Criticism." *Notes on Mississippi Writers* 7 (1974): 44–53.

Clurman, Harold. "Tennessee Williams." *The Divine Pastime: Theatre Essays*. New York: Macmillan, 1974. 11–18.

Corrigan, Mary Ann. "Realism and Theatricalism in *A Streetcar Named Desire*." *Modern Drama* 19 (Dec. 1976): 385–96.

Debusscher, Gilbert. "Trois images de la modernité chez Tennessee Williams: *Un micro-analyse d'Un tramway nommé Desir*." *Journal of Dramatic Theory & Criticism* 3 (Fall 1988): 143–56.

Dowling, Ellen. "The Derailment of *A Streetcar Named Desire*." *Literature/Film Quarterly* 9 (1981): 233–40.

Downing, Robert. "Streetcar Conductor: Some Notes from Backstage." *Theatre Annual* 8 (1950): 25–33.

Fedder, Norman J. *The Influence of D. H. Lawrence on Tennessee Williams*. The Hague: Mouton, 1966.

Hanks, Pamela Anne. "Must We Acknowledge What We Mean? The Viewer's Role in Filmed Versions of *A Streetcar Named Desire*." *Journal of Popular Film & Television* 14 (Fall 1986): 114–22.

Hurrell, John D., ed. *Two Modern American Tragedies: Reviews and Criticism of "Death of a Salesman" and "A Streetcar Named Desire"*. New York: Charles Scribner's Sons, 1961.

Jackson, Esther Merle. *The Broken World of Tennessee Williams*. Madison: U of Wisconsin P, 1966.

Kazan, Elia. "Notebook for *A Streetcar Named Desire*." *Directors on Directing: A Source Book of the Modern Theatre*. Ed. Toby Cole and Helen Krich Chinoy. Indianapolis: Bobbs-Merrill, 1976. 364–79.

Kolin, Philip C. " 'Affectionate and Mighty Regards from Vivien and Me': Sir Laurence Olivier and the London Premiere of *A Streetcar Named Desire*." *Missouri Review* 13, no. 3 (1991): 143–57.

———. "*A Streetcar Named Desire*: A Playwrights' Forum." *Michigan Quarterly Review* 29 (Spring 1990): 173–203.

———. "*A Streetcar Named Desire*, Scene 8." *The Explicator* 49 (Summer 1991): 241–44. With Jürgen Wolter.

———. "The First Critical Assessments of *A Streetcar Named Desire*: The *Streetcar* Tryouts and the Reviewers." *Journal of Dramatic Theory & Criticism* 6 (Fall 1991): 45–68.

———. "The First *Streetcar Named Desire* in Mainland China." *Tennessee Williams Literary Journal* 2 (Winter 1990–91): 19–32. With Sherry Shao.

———. "Our Lady of the Quarter: Blanche DuBois and the Feast of the Mater Dolorosa." *ANQ: A Quarterly Journal of Short Articles, Notes and Reviews* 4 (Apr. 1991): 81–87.

———. "The First Polish Productions of *A Streetcar Named Desire*." *Theatre History Studies* 12 (1992): 67–88.

———. " 'Red Hot!' in *A Streetcar Named Desire*." *Notes on Contemporary Literature* 19 (Sept. 1989): 6–8.

———. "Rutting in *A Streetcar Named Desire*." *Notes on Contemporary Literature* 22 (Jan. 1992): 2–3.

———. "Why Stanley and His Friends Drink Jax Beer in Tennessee Williams's *A Streetcar Named Desire*." *Notes on Contemporary Literature* 20 (Sept. 1990): 2–3.

———. "Williams in Ebony: Black and Multi-Racial Productions of *A Streetcar Named Desire*." *Black American Literature Forum* 25 (Spring 1991): 147–81.

Miller, Jordan Y., ed. *Twentieth Century Interpretations of "A Streetcar Named Desire": A Collection of Critical Essays*. Englewood Cliffs, N.J.: Prentice-Hall, 1971.

Mood, John J. "The Structure of *A Streetcar Named Desire*." *Ball State University Forum* 14 (Summer 1973).

Murphy, Brenda. *Tennessee Williams & Elia Kazan: A Collaboration in the Theatre.* Cambridge: Cambridge UP, 1992.

Nelson, Benjamin. *Tennessee Williams: The Man and His Work.* New York: Obolensky, 1961.

Phillips, Gene D. *The Films of Tennessee Williams.* Philadelphia: Art Alliance P, 1980.

Porter, Thomas E. *Myth and Modern American Drama.* Detroit: Wayne State UP, 1969.

Schlueter, June. "Imitating an Icon: John Erman's Remake of Tennessee Williams's *A Streetcar Named Desire*." *Modern Drama* 28 (1985): 139–47.

Spector, Susan. "Alternative Visions of Blanche DuBois: Uta Hagen and Jessica Tandy in *A Streetcar Named Desire*." *Modern Drama* 32 (1989): 545–61.

Tharpe, Jac, ed. *Tennessee Williams: A Tribute.* Jackson: UP of Mississippi, 1977.

Thompson, Judith J. *Tennessee Williams's Plays: Memory, Myth, and Symbol.* University of Kansas Humanistic Studies 54. New York: Peter Lang, 1987.

Tischler, Nancy M. *Tennessee Williams: Rebellious Puritan.* New York: Citadel Press, 1961.

Vlasopolos, Anca. "Authorizing History: Victimization in *A Streetcar Named Desire*." *Theatre Journal* 38 (Oct. 1986): 322–38.

Index

About the Contributors

CALVIN BEDIENT is a Professor in the Department of English at UCLA. Among his books are *Eight Contemporary Poets*, which was nominated for a National Book Award; *In the Heart's Last Kingdom: Robert Penn Warren's Major Poetry*; and *He Do the Police in Different Voices: The Waste Land and Its Protagonist*. He has published numerous essays and reviews in *Salmagundi*, *Parnassus*, *Partisan Review*, *Sewanee Review*, *The New Republic*, and other journals.

HERBERT BLAU is a Distinguished Professor of English and Comparative Literature at the University of Wisconsin, Milwaukee. He has extensive experience in the theatre and has authored *Take Up the Bodies*, *Blooded Thought*, *The Eye of Prey: Subversions of the Postmodern*, and the seminal study *The Audience*.

ROBERT BRAY, Associate Professor of English at East Tennessee State University, was born in the Mississippi Delta and has lived in New Orleans, the two key locales in Williams's drama. He teaches graduate seminars on Williams's drama and fiction and has published a number of articles on Williams in journals such as *The Many Forms of Drama* and *The Tennessee Williams Literary Journal*. Bray has been on the Scholar's Panel at the Tennessee Williams Literary Festival and served as technical adviser for a major production of *The Rose Tattoo* while on a Fulbright in Rio de Janeiro.

BERT CARDULLO teaches in the theatre department at the University of Michigan, Ann Arbor, and has published widely on drama and film. He is the editor, most recently, of *The Film Criticism of Vernon Young* as well as the translator of *German-Language Comedy: A Critical Anthology*, and he has been the film critic of *The Hudson Review* since 1987. Cardullo's first published essay was on *Streetcar* in *Tennessee Williams: A Tribute*.

LAURILYN J. HARRIS is Associate Professor of Theatre Arts and Drama at Washington State University. More than fifty of her articles, essays, and reviews have appeared in scholarly journals, encyclopedias, and anthologies such as *Theatre Research International, Theatre History Studies, The Journal of Creative Behavior, Theatre Journal, Notable Women in the American Theatre, Theatre Annual, Theatre Southwest, American Theatre Companies,* and *Nineteenth Century Theatre Research.* In addition, she serves on the editorial board of *Theatre Annual.*

W. KENNETH HOLDITCH is founding Publisher and Editor of *The Tennessee Williams Literary Journal* and was a founder of the annual Tennessee Williams Literary Festival in New Orleans. His publications include *In Old New Orleans,* a collection of essays that he edited and to which he contributed; the introduction to John Kennedy Toole's novel *The Neon Bible,* which has now been translated into a dozen languages; numerous essays on Faulkner, Williams, Hellman, Dos Passos, and others; short stories; and poems. He is Research Professor of English at the University of New Orleans.

LIONEL KELLY is Director of American Studies at the University of Reading, Reading, England, where he has taught for many years. His most recent publications include essays on Ezra Pound, T.S. Eliot, Wallace Stevens, F. Scott Fitzgerald, and Ernest Hemingway. He is American literature editor of *The Year's Work in English Studies,* and reviews editor of *The Modern Language Review.* He is editing a special issue of *The Yearbook of English Studies,* for 1994, on "Ethnicity and Representation" in American literature.

WILLIAM KLEB is Associate Professor of Dramatic Art at the University of California, Davis, where he teaches courses in theatre history, theory, criticism, and playwriting. He has published articles and reviews in *Theatre Survey, Theatre History Studies, Performing Arts Journal,* and *Theatre* (for which he serves as contributing editor). His essay on Sam Shepard appears in *American Playwrights Since 1945: A Guide to Scholarship, Criticism, and Performance.*

PHILIP C. KOLIN is the Charles W. Moorman Distinguished Professor in the Humanities at the University of Southern Mississippi and the founding co-editor of *Studies in American Drama, 1945–Present,* published by The Ohio State University Press. He has written or edited fifteen books, including *American Playwrights Since 1945; Conversations with Edward Albee; David Rabe: A Stage History and A Primary and Secondary Bibliography; Shakespeare and Feminist Criticism: An Annotated Bibliography and Commentary; Shakespeare in the South: Essays on Performance;* and *Successful Writing at Work* (now in its fourth edition). He has written extensively about *Streetcar Named Desire* on the world stage for such journals as the *Tennessee Williams Literary Journal, Missouri Review, Theatre History Studies, Journal of Dramatic Theory and Criticism,* and *Black American*

Literature Forum. His playwrights forum on *Streetcar* appeared in the Spring 1990 issue of the *Michigan Quarterly Review.*

EDWARD MORROW is currently pursuing his Ph.D. in computer science at the University of Missouri at Kansas City. He is also the author of *The Grim Reaper's Book of Days* (Carol Press, 1992).

LAURA MORROW has written more than a dozen articles on the drama and is co-editor of *Contemporary Literary Theory.* She is the recipient of grants from the National Endowment for the Humanities, the Louisiana Endowment for the Humanities, the Folger Library, and UCLA's William Andrews Clark Memorial Library. She has won numerous awards for both scholarship and teaching and serves as a panelist/reviewer for the National Endowment for the Humanities. She also co-edits the *Quarterly Journal of Ideology* and is editor of Peter Lang's series on British Restoration and Eighteenth-Century Drama.

GENE D. PHILLIPS, S.J. is a Professor of English at Loyola University in Chicago. He has been a contributing editor to *Literature/Film Quarterly* since 1977 and a member of the editorial board of the *Tennessee Williams Literary Journal* since its inception in 1989. He is the author of *Graham Greene: The Films of His Fiction*; *Fiction, Film, and F. Scott Fitzgerald*; *Fiction, Film, and Faulkner*; and other volumes on literature and the film.

JUNE SCHLUETER, Professor of English at Lafayette College and co-editor of *Shakespeare Bulletin*, is author of *Metafictional Characters in Modern Drama*; *The Plays and Novels of Peter Handke*; with James K. Flanagan, *Arthur Miller*; and, with James P. Lusardi, *Reading Shakespeare in Performance: "King Lear."* With Paul Schlueter, she has edited *The English Novel: Twentieth Century Criticism, Vol. 2: Twentieth Century Novelists, Modern American Literature, Supplement II*, and *An Encyclopedia of British Women Writers.* In addition, she has edited *Feminist Rereadings of Modern American Drama*; *Modern American Drama: The Female Canon*, and, with Enoch Brater, *Approaches to Teaching Beckett's "Waiting for Godot."*

MARK ROYDEN WINCHELL is Professor of English at Clemson University and managing editor of the *South Carolina Review.* In addition to ten books on such writers as Joan Didion, William F. Buckley, and Leslie Fiedler, he has published numerous critical essays and reviews in the *Sewanee Review, Southern Review*, and other leading journals. He is currently writing a critical biography of Cleanth Brooks.

JÜRGEN C. WOLTER is a professor of English at Wuppertal University, Germany, where he teaches American Literature. He has published numerous articles, predominantly on American drama, and books on Thomas Deloney and the American drama before the Civil War. His special fields of interest are American drama and southern literature.

Recent Titles in
Contributions in Drama and Theatre Studies